PT 17

BALLPLAYER

Center Point
Large Print

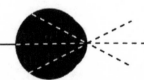

**This Large Print Book carries the
Seal of Approval of N.A.V.H.**

BALLPLAYER

CHIPPER JONES
with Carroll Rogers Walton

CENTER POINT LARGE PRINT
THORNDIKE, MAINE

This Center Point Large Print edition
is published in the year 2017 by arrangement with
Dutton, an imprint of Penguin Publishing Group,
a division of Penguin Random House LLC.

The text of this Large Print edition is unabridged.
In other aspects, this book may vary
from the original edition.
Printed in the United States of America
on permanent paper.
Set in 16-point Times New Roman type.

ISBN: 978-1-68324-505-6

Library of Congress Cataloging-in-Publication Data

Names: Jones, Chipper, 1972– author. | Walton, Carroll R., collaborator.
Title: Ballplayer / Chipper Jones, with Carroll Rogers Walton.
Description: Center Point Large Print edition. | Thorndike, Maine :
    Center Point Large Print, 2017.
Identifiers: LCCN 2017024630 | ISBN 9781683245056
    (large print : hardcover : alk. paper)
Subjects: LCSH: Jones, Chipper, 1972- | Baseball players—United
States—Biography. | Large type books.
Classification: LCC GV865.J633 J66 2017b | DDC 796.357092 [B] —
dc23
LC record available at https://lccn.loc.gov/2017024630

To the people who make up my team every single day, Larry and Lynne Jones, B. B. Abbott, and the queen of my castle, Taylor Jones

CONTENTS

FOREWORD

The first time I saw Chipper Jones play, he was in high school at the Bolles School in Jacksonville, Florida. As general manager of the Braves, I had gone to watch him with Paul Snyder, our scouting director, leading up to the 1990 draft. I told Paul, "Don't show me which one he is." I wanted to try to pick him out.

They were doing exercises with their T-shirts on, not in uniform, and I picked him out immediately. It had to be him, he just stood out. He was six foot four, and you could see right away what an athlete he was. He was a smart kid, too. He had a great family upbringing. He had everything going for him—everything. He's just one of those guys who comes along every once in a while. Jim Beauchamp, our bench coach for a lot of years, used to call guys like Henry Aaron and Willie Mays—and Chipper Jones—chosen. He was chosen.

He's going to be a first-ballot Hall of Famer, one of the greatest switch-hitters that ever played the game. Generally, switch-hitters don't hit the same on both sides, but Chipper hit .300 both ways. Other managers used to turn Chipper around and make him hit right-handed. He hit more often left-handed because there were more right-handed starters, so they probably did the right thing. But it never bothered me one bit because he could really hit right-handed, too.

When Chipper was younger, I loved to watch him run the bases. It reminded me a little bit of Mickey Mantle. Jim Hegan, the great catcher for the Cleveland Indians who caught for Bob Feller, Bob Lemon, and Mike Garcia—all those great pitchers—was our bullpen coach with the Yankees when I got called up in 1968. He told me, "You're going to love watching Mickey Mantle run." It was special, even with a bad knee at the end of Mantle's career. Chipper could run, too. After his knee injury, Chipper picked his spots, but he could steal a base in a heartbeat. And when he took off, you knew he was going to be safe.

Chipper was a tremendous student of the game. He had tunnel vision every night. You'd watch Chipper on the bench and he was zoned in on the game, the pitcher. His wheels were spinning from the first inning to the ninth inning. Nothing ever got away from him, ever. His concentration level was so much higher than most players'.

The chosen ones, so to speak, could hit at any time, and Chipper was always ready to hit. He could walk up there with tennis shoes on and still hit a home run. The great thing about Chip, he could hit the ball to the opposite field out of the ballpark, both ways. He's a big kid with a fairly long swing, but he could get out in front of the ball with anybody. His ball just kept carrying. You would think there would be a weakness in there; there wasn't. Chipper would get jammed maybe once every fifty games. It was amazing. If they tried to pitch him inside, he killed them. The Mets were one of the teams that did and he got them good in 1999.

You know how great he was? He led the league in hitting at age thirty-six. He was second in the league when he was thirty-five. Leading the league that late in his career is something only the greats do. Stan Musial did it. Ted Williams did it.

Chipper was the face of our organization for all those years we were winning division titles, with his ability, his good looks. The name Chipper Jones rings a bell with everybody. We were on TV all across the country with TBS during those days, and I think his name was almost as big in Seattle, Washington, as it was in Atlanta. But Chipper had the personality to go along with the name. He was a superstar player but he always took the time to sign autographs and take pictures, interact with kids.

Chipper Jones was one of the greatest ball-players in the league, and we had him. It made my managing job easier. He was a gamer. He had bad knees forever and he played through everything. And he was as clutch a hitter as they come.

Chipper had a ton of great moments in a Braves uniform. His career was something special. I'm glad he decided to share his story, not just with Braves fans but baseball fans across the country.

—Bobby Cox,
Hall of Fame Manager

PROLOGUE
The Last Big Play

The ball came at me like a freaking bullet, and all I could think was *Try not to wear it.*

The batter, Matt Holliday, hit it just enough to my right, up the line at third base, that I knew I could backhand it. As long as I stayed down and came up, I'd pick it.

It was a play I'd made hundreds of times over the course of my nineteen seasons in the major leagues. When I was new to third base as a rookie with the Braves, I was scared to death of balls like this. I came off pretty brash and cocky in those days, but most of my confidence came with a bat in my hands. On defense, I had my fears.

But at forty, even when the game was starting to speed up on me again, I could make this backhand pick and throw on instinct. I was ready for a ball like this, even in the biggest do-or-die game of my life: If we lost to the Cardinals in a one-game wild card playoff, my career was over.

I'd always prided myself on being pretty good at endings. From the time I was a kid, I'd say to myself, *Two outs, bottom of the ninth, what are you going to do?* I'd like to think coming through for my team in big situations defined me as a ballplayer as much as being a switch-hitter, a National League MVP, or an Atlanta Brave for my entire career.

Leading up to the night of October 5, 2012, I'd had six months to mentally prepare for what that end might look like, long before Holliday ever picked up a bat and walked to the plate in the fourth inning in front of a packed house at Turner Field.

In April of that year, toward the end of spring training, I'd announced I would retire at the end of the season. I got a little misty-eyed telling my teammates, "I hope we go out with a bang here in 2012."

Seven knee operations had taken their toll, and my body was telling me it was time to hang it up. Percocet and Red Bull were part of my daily routine my last season. Some days I could hardly get out of bed. But by October, I felt like a kid again. I was riding the adrenaline high, and I was determined to make what I still consider the best year of my career last as long as I could.

We won ninety-four games during the regular season but had finished second to the Washington Nationals in the National League East and settled for the wild card.

Bud Selig had added another wild card team from each league to the playoff format in 2012. So instead of playing the Nationals in a best-of-five Division Series, we had to play St. Louis—a team that finished six games behind us in the standings—in the first-ever one-game wild card playoff for the right to play the Nationals.

It was an instant Game 7, great for TV ratings, corporate dollars, and Bud Selig. For me? It meant I'd played twenty-six hundred games in my major league career to have it come down to one. And that one game against the Cardinals came down to a ground ball.

Up until that point, we'd been in complete control. We were up 2–0, but it felt like 6–0 to me and to the fifty thousand Braves fans at Turner Field. The crowd was as electric as any I've ever played in front of in Atlanta. We had eighteen outs to go and Kris Medlen, the hottest pitcher in baseball, on the mound.

But in the playoffs, a runner at first base constitutes a rally, and that's what Holliday had when he hit the rocket toward me.

And I reacted the right way. I mean, I stuck it in the pocket of my glove. I picked it perfectly. But when I grabbed the ball, I had a two-seam grip.

I had time to change to a four-seam grip—Carlos Beltran wasn't halfway to second base—and make an easy throw. We turn a tailor-made double play and we're all but out of the inning. But instead of taking an extra crow hop and getting a four-seam grip, something in the back of my mind said, *Throw it anyway*.

And the ball sailed.

For a second, I thought Uggs, our second baseman Dan Uggla, had a chance to catch it. But it hit off his glove. Jason Heyward charged the ball in right field, and Beltran and Holliday were both safe. The Cardinals had runners on first and third with nobody out, and Allen Craig, their cleanup hitter and one of the best hitters in the league that year, was coming up. You could feel the momentum shift.

I was standing there at third base thinking, *You've got to be kidding me. There's no way that this is how a storybook season ends.*

The fates had lined up for me in 2012. I mean, baseball had written me a six-month-long Hollywood script.

There was a laundry list of cool moments. Not just the tributes and ovations—those go without saying—but things that happened between the lines: A home run my first game back from knee surgery with my parents in the stands. Two walk-off homers, when you're lucky if you get one in a year. A five-hit game the day I made my last All-Star team, with my new girlfriend, Taylor, in the stands, waiting to go on our first real date.

It just seemed that I punctuated a lot of key games with big nights at the plate, kind of the way Cal Ripken did on his way to breaking Lou Gehrig's record for consecutive games played in 1995. Cal homered the night he became baseball's new Iron Man, with the president of the

United States in the stands and who knows how many millions watching on TV.

I grew up playing shortstop, idolizing Cal, and now here I was in my final season, tipping my cap to the fans. Kids were calling me by my first name, watching to see how I would go out. And now, in front of God and everybody, my career was going to end in the first game of the playoffs because I rushed a routine throw?

I knew better. Just double-clutch, even if it meant getting only one out: *Get the one out.* We're still out of the inning with a lead. But my error opened the floodgates. The Cardinals scored three runs that inning. They beat us 6–3.

As ready as I was for that play, as much as I wanted the ball, and despite all my experience playing in big games, in the end—my end—it didn't matter. I had the game in my hands, and I threw it away. On the last night of my career, when I thought I had this game pretty well mastered, baseball was going to force me to fail one last time.

CHAPTER 1
Chip off the Old Block

The first wood bat I ever held was as big as I was. It was a Louisville Slugger with Mickey Mantle's signature etched on it. Dad kept it in the den closet, and that thing was like gold.

He'd had it since he was a shortstop at Stetson University, but Dad never hit with it. He used one of the Jackie Robinson models Stetson got from Louisville, or a Carl Yastrzemski, maybe a Nellie Fox or an Al Kaline. But the only time he put his hands on that M110—a skinny-handled, thick-barreled model like Mantle used to swing—was to admire it.

I was three when we moved to Pierson, Florida, after Dad took a job teaching math and coaching baseball at Taylor High School. He let me take the Mantle bat out and hold it under his supervision, but it never left the den. It wasn't as if I was going to take it out in the backyard and play with it anyway. Hell, the thing swung me.

"This was Mickey's signature bat," Dad told me the first time I tried to hoist it onto my shoulder. It was so heavy I almost lost it over my back. I thought, *How do you hit a baseball with this?* Then my dad picked it up and put it on his shoulder. *Oh, OK, that's how.*

Mickey Mantle was the reason my dad fell in love with the game of baseball and the reason he hoped I would, too. It didn't take long.

Whenever those closet doors swung open and that bat was out, Dad started telling Mantle stories.

"The whole reason I want you to hit left-handed is because of this guy," he'd say. "He was my favorite player. He was the best switch-hitter in history."

As a kid, Dad saw Mantle hook a line drive for a home run over his head in the right field bleachers at Memorial Stadium. My dad grew up in Baltimore, before his family moved to Vero Beach, Florida, and his uncle took him on the bus to see the Yankees play the Orioles. On those days, Dad was a Yankees fan. He said Mick's homer was still on the rise when it sailed over his head.

"God-awful swing of the bat," he'd say. "From a guy who was only five foot ten, but as strong as an ox."

Storytelling was as much a part of my baseball upbringing as taking swings in the backyard, especially where Mantle was concerned.

When I got older, people actually told me I looked like Mickey Mantle—even my manager, Bobby Cox, who played with Mantle in 1968 with the Yankees. But as a kid, I didn't even know what Mantle looked like. I didn't see many pictures of him. I only heard my dad talk about him. I just thought he had to be the coolest guy ever because he had the coolest name ever: Mickey Mantle.

Mickey was one of those baseball players people knew by their first names, like Whitey, Reggie, Yogi, Babe, Hank, Cal. I wanted to be like that, too, and knowing Dad, that's probably why he and Mom settled on "Chipper."

I was born Larry Wayne Jones Junior. My dad is Larry Wayne Jones Senior. A couple of days after they brought me home from the hospital, my dad's aunt Dolly came to visit and said I looked so much like Dad that I was a chip off the old block. Mom started calling me Chip, which became Chipper, and it stuck.

On the first day of kindergarten, my teacher, Mrs. Taylor, called me Larry when she took roll. I didn't answer. I'm not even sure I knew that was my name. Dad always said the name Larry wouldn't be remembered, but Chipper would be. There are now a few Mets and Yankees fans who might disagree with him, but to everybody else, I was always just Chipper.

My parents nailed the name. Trying to switch-hit like Mantle wasn't going to be nearly as simple. But before I could think about swinging left-handed, I had to learn how to hit the fastball.

• • •

We lived on a ten-acre farm, and like pretty much everybody else in Pierson, we grew fern. Our backyard pitcher's mound was basically a sand pit, with a root for a rubber. Dad stood in it, with his back to the hay barn, as he went into his windup. Forty feet away, I took my stance in front of a chalk strike zone we drew into wood paneling on the back wall of our garage. Dad was pushing thirty years old. I was seven. But that was how we did it: father against son.

Dad would throw a tennis ball, and I swung a piece of PVC. I used to wear the rubber handles off aluminum bats, and PVC pipe was more durable, not to mention more abundant because we used PVC to irrigate the fernery.

"Put the bat on your shoulder, pick it up, push it back," Dad preached. "Keep it level through the strike zone."

We played simulated games all the time, my whole childhood. But one particular afternoon, we were working on something specific. Dad was trying to teach me not to step in the bucket.

Stepping in the bucket is what you do when you're scared to death of the ball. You bail out. So when I swung—and this was right-handed, my natural side—I was stepping toward shortstop instead of the pitcher. If your upper body goes toward shortstop as well, the only way you can generate any power is by pulling the ball. My dad always wanted me to use the whole field.

"Step at me," Dad said as he threw, again and again. "Step at me."

But with every swing, I stepped toward short, bailing out. Finally, Dad tried logic.

"I'm not going to hit you," he said. "I will never hit you."

No sooner had the words come out of his mouth than he drilled me right in mine. A tooth went flying, blood everywhere. I started squalling.

I glared at him, with my hand to my mouth and my tongue rooting around where that bottom tooth used to be. "You just said you weren't going to hit me!"

Mom was on her horse on the other side of the house. I chased her down, wailing the whole time. "Dad hurt me! He said he wouldn't hurt me, and he hit me in the face. He knocked my tooth out!"

When you get older, you learn that getting hit by pitches is just part of the game; I got hit eighteen times in my career at the big league level. The degree of pain it caused didn't matter to me as much as where the pitcher hit me. That told you what his intentions were.

Paul Quantrill hit me on purpose in Toronto in 1999, but he did it the right way. We had hit Carlos Delgado earlier in the game in retaliation for showboating. The night before, Delgado hit a bomb off the hotel in right field at SkyDome and flipped his bat within two feet of our dugout. So everybody knew something was coming. Delgado took his base, and it was over. But then our reliever John Hudek hit Craig Grebeck in the back of the neck. Hudek didn't mean to do it, but it looked bad, and I was coming up second in the next inning.

Quantrill threw the first pitch six inches outside, which made me think nothing was going to happen. So I dug in on the next one, and he hit me right between the numbers. It pissed me off, but I was young and stupid. I was too hot-headed to realize that's exactly the way it should be done: Hit a guy in the back, the butt, or the leg. Don't throw at his head.

My dad's intent was pure, of course, not that my mom was buying it. She didn't bother getting off her horse when I came crying to her. She rode over to Dad and met him with one of her patented stares.

"What the hell is wrong with you?" she said.

Dad didn't have much to say. He was counting his blessings it was just a tennis ball. I found out years later he told Mom that night he was afraid he had just ruined baseball for me. He was worried I might never want to get back in the box.

It was going to take a lot more than losing a baby tooth to keep me away. Yeah, it was a baby tooth, and it was already loose, not that I was going to tell Dad. I was too busy milking it.

All Dad did that day was pretty much cure me of stepping into a pitch for the rest of my life. I stepped in the bucket my whole career. It's one reason I added a toe tap, to help me keep my weight on my back side. I took a little step toward the pull side so I could clear my hips, and my hips and hands could explode through the swing at the same time. "Hips and hands!" was another of my dad's sayings.

Actually, my little step in the bucket probably helped me avoid getting hit throughout my career because I could jackknife out of the way. But as a kid, fear of the ball was never my biggest motivator. Wanting to beat my dad was.

Even when I was seven and eight years old, Dad could throw a tennis ball as hard as the good Lord would let him, and I could put it in play. Switch-hitting is what he used to give me a new challenge. He dangled it out there one day when I was talking a lot of smack, and I bit—hook, line, and sinker.

"All right, buddy boy, turn around to the other side," he said. "See what you can do."

I'd seen Dad bat left-handed. He didn't switch-hit in college, but I knew he could do it.

"All right," I said.

At first, hitting left-handed felt really weird, like a reverse swing. To make it feel more normal, I tried hitting cross-handed, with my left hand as my bottom hand. But whenever Dad saw that, he said, "Boy, fix them hands."

Growing up an only child in rural Volusia County, Florida, I could entertain myself for hours by throwing up rocks and swinging at them. I tried to hit an oak tree, first from the right side, then from the left.

I'd tell myself, "OK, hit a ground ball." *Voom.* "Hit a line drive." *Voom.* "All right, go deep." *Voom.* Then I'd turn and do it from the other side. It was both ways, all the time.

Goofing around, I'd brush my teeth left-handed. I tried to write left-handed. To this day, my handwriting is only a hair messier left-handed, but you can tell it's my signature.

Switch-hitting took a more serious turn on Saturday afternoons. Every week, I looked forward to four o'clock, after the Major League Baseball *Game of the Week* was over, when I got to strut my stuff in front of Pops in the backyard.

Dad and I would watch the game on NBC, then go out back and imitate the two lineups. More often than not, one of the teams on TV was the Dodgers. They were my dad's favorite growing up in Vero Beach, where the Dodgers trained for sixty years. I was a huge Dodgers fan, too.

Dad usually let me be the Dodgers, and he'd take the other team, and we'd emulate the hitters in their lineups. Hitting like Steve Garvey, I kept my hands in tight, rode them low. For Dusty Baker, I held my bat high, straight up. As Mike Scioscia, I kept the bat flat and started it on my shoulder.

I wanted to hit left-handed as much as possible, so I put my own twist on the lineup. The Dodgers used to bat Davey Lopes, who was right-handed, leadoff, but I wanted another lefty in there, so I put center fielder Kenny Landreaux in the number two spot.

Reggie Smith, a switch-hitter and a utility guy, was going to play somewhere for me, maybe left field. If he was in left, I put Franklin Stubbs, another left-hander, at first base. Scioscia, a lefty, always caught for me over Steve Yeager, a righty.

Playing those imaginary games in the backyard helped me learn to switch-hit. I learned how to play the game when I took the field with my buddies.

A baseball uniform was the holy grail for me. I got my first real one at age nine when I moved up to Little League with the Pierson Lions Club. You could not rip that thing off me. It had a royal-blue shirt with "Pierson" in diagonal cursive across the chest and a big swoosh underneath, white pants, and stirrups. I thought it was the prettiest shirt I'd ever seen. I'd wear the whole uniform to bed. It was like jammies.

I had to wait until I was ten to get the number

10, the number my dad had worn since he was a kid. He wanted to wear 7, Mantle's number, in Little League, but the coach's son had it, so Dad took 10. My friend Leonard Butts had it my first year in Little League, but I got it my second year. I had to wait a year for it when I got to the big leagues, too.

Dad was still wearing number 10 as the varsity baseball coach at Taylor when I was in elementary school. Every day after school, I'd stop at the Handy Way, grab a Coke and a candy bar, and head across the street to the high school field for their practices.

If they were hitting, I'd shag flies. If they were taking infield, I'd flip balls back to the hitter. If they finished early enough, Dad would throw BP to me.

Dad idolized Mantle. I idolized Dad.

I used to go through his scrapbooks all the time and read about his Stetson teams. I would sit Indian style in front of the closet where the scrapbooks, photo albums, and Mantle bat were, and read about Dad and Mom. It was a full day's worth of entertainment for me.

My dad was everybody's all-American in high school in Vero Beach—quarterback of the football team, shortstop on the baseball team, point guard on the basketball team.

I loved to look at his Stetson box scores in

the *DeLand Sun-News*, but I had no clue how to read them. So I'd just scan the articles for Dad's name. "Larry Jones chipped in with a single and a double to pace the 10-hit attack by the Hatters."

Dad got a tryout with the Cubs after college. They wanted him to sign, but I was on the way, and quite honestly, the Cubs weren't offering a lot of money. He decided to get a job and start preparing for life as a father.

He'll tell you he lived vicariously through me and my baseball career, but when I was a kid, it was the other way around. I wanted my name in the newspaper, too. As it turns out, that's not too hard playing Little League in a small town.

The first time I saw my name in the paper, it was in a Little League box score in the *DeLand Sun-News*. It said, "Jones, 2B [for second base], 2 1 0."

"Wow," I said. "I'm hitting .210!"

"First of all, .210 is not good," Dad said. "And secondly, that's not your batting average." I learned how to read the box score that day: two at-bats, one run, no hits.

Mom—a professional horse rider—was a pretty big deal in our neck of the woods, too. Our den was full of her trophies. I learned mental toughness from watching her ride in horse shows. Her discipline was dressage. The best way I can explain it is that it's ballet for horses. She waltzed into that ring. She was always poised, always in control, always confident. She had that little strut about her, that little look in her eye.

I walked up to Mom after one of her rides one day and asked her, "Why does everybody stop to watch you whenever you ride into the ring?"

She got this little shit-eating grin on her face and said, "Because I'm the best."

That was the mentality she had. She wanted me to have it, too, so she turned the tables that day and started talking to me about baseball.

"Chipper, you are really good," she said. "Don't let anybody ever tell you otherwise. When you walk out on that field, act like you're the best player out there. Don't do it with words. Do it with your presence. Walk up to that plate like 'I'm going to hit this ball nine hundred feet.' Sometimes you're not going to be the best player on the field, but don't let anybody else know that."

That is where I learned what Mom, Dad, and I call necessary arrogance, and I took that mentality to the plate from the time I was a kid to my last at-bat as a Brave.

As much as I learned from my mom about the mental side of the game, I had more interests in common with Dad. On weekends, he couldn't do anything without me, whether it was baseball or basketball, hunting or fishing. Sometimes he sneaked out of the house at dawn to go hunting by himself, but I would hear the stairs creak as he tried to tiptoe out the door, or one of our Walker hounds would bark as he loaded them onto his truck. I learned to sleep in my Levi's so I could catch up to him in a matter of minutes.

I was ten when I shot my first buck.

Dad and I were up by County Road 305—we called it the hard road—when we saw a four-point buck cross into our property. It was a fairly young but decent-sized deer for Florida.

We dropped the dogs on his trail, and Dad drove me up to a gate where a dirt road intersected the hard road. He told me to run up to the first curve in the dirt road, about three hundred yards inside the fence line, and wait there. He drove back to an opening where he'd be able to see the deer cross into the woods.

I was halfway up the dirt road when I heard my dad yell. "He's coming right to you, Chipper!"

I started shaking like a leaf. I was scared to death to be in the woods by myself. But I didn't want to be a wimp in front of my dad and all our friends. I tried to hide behind a six-foot-high trash pile of brush and pine scraps. I raised my 12-gauge shotgun and waited.

I could hear the dogs coming, barking every breath. They got closer and closer until that deer busted out of the woods twenty yards in front of me. He stopped and looked right at me. I clicked off my safety, still shaking. Just as he started to take off again, I squeezed the trigger. *Boom!*

I was supposed to aim behind the front shoulder. I had no idea where I hit, but it knocked the deer down.

"Daddy!" I screamed.

The deer tried to get up, so I fired again. *Boom!*

"Daddy!" I screamed.

And I shot again. Every time the deer twitched, I shot again. Needless to say, I killed the deer. I was shooting double-aught buckshot shells, which have a dozen pellets in each round. I was probably putting five or six pellets in that deer every time I shot the gun.

Dad drove up in the truck and said, "Why were you yelling?"

"Because I wanted you to come get this deer," I said.

"Well, did you kill him?" he said.

"I think so," I said.

Dad started laughing.

"That deer came out of the woods weighing one hundred and ten pounds," he said. "When he died, he weighed one hundred and twenty he was full of so much lead."

I've heard Dad tell that story a hundred times. There are a lot more *Boom! Daddy!*'s when he tells it. It's funny listening to him tell it. It wasn't funny then.

• • •

Dad and I competed in everything. It wasn't just baseball. It was H-O-R-S-E in the driveway, backgammon, Monopoly, Scrabble. If we were in a boat together fishing, we'd bet five dollars on who could catch the most or the biggest fish. Before I was old enough to bet money, we used chores. Loser feeds the dogs or washes down the dog pen.

When it came to backyard baseball, Dad never let me win. It wasn't his style. So I was that much more determined to beat him and all the more excited the first time I did.

I was on the mound, and I had the lead. Dad was batting lefty. (If I had to switch-hit, so did he.) If he put a ball in play, he won, so I had to strike him out. Dad had a little hole in his lefty swing down and in, so I knew that if I got to two strikes, I could throw my slider and he couldn't hit it.

He fouled my first pitch off, a fastball, for strike one. I snuck another fastball by him. Strike two. Then I worked that slider down and in, and he swung over the top of it.

"Yeah, uh-huh," I said. "Ball game."

Dad walked inside the house with his tail tucked.

"Lynne, I can't beat him anymore," he told Mom when he got to the kitchen.

I think I was eleven.

CHAPTER 2

"I Got This"

Pierson is a blue-collar town. Everybody works in the fern business. We had a garden full of leatherleaf fern behind our house, two and a half acres, to supplement my parents' income. Mom didn't make much with the horse business, nor did Dad as a public school teacher.

My parents also used the fernery as punishment. If I made a C or a D on a report card, out into that fernery I went. I was weeding. I was fertilizing. I was cutting. I was packing. All it took was one day of working in that fernery before I said to myself, *No way am I doing this my whole life.*

I hated that fernery. I absolutely despised it. The only time I ever enjoyed walking into that place was when I hit home run balls up on the saran, the screen that shielded the fern from the sun.

Weeding was the worst. It was backbreaking. Fern is thick and you can't see to the bottom, so you've got to get on all fours. And the beds of fern were three feet wide and seventy-five yards long. There were snakes and hornets down in there. Your next reach could be your last. I'd have much rather my dad whupped my ass than have me weed that damn fernery.

The only thing fern was good for was pocket change. My first paying job was in a fern-packing shed. Richard Hagstrom, who was also my Little League coach, and Ronald Jones were the two big fern dealers in town, and Mr. Hagstrom's packing plant was five hundred yards from my house.

During the summers, starting at age fourteen, I'd work four or five hours in the morning packing boxes, twenty-five bunches a box, lined in plastic, stapled shut. We stacked hundreds of boxes into coolers, and on Thursdays and Fridays, container trucks showed up. We'd pack boxes onto the back of those semitrucks, and they shipped out all over the world. Seventy-five percent of all decorative greens you see in flowerpots, vases, and arrangements come from my hometown.

Growing up, I played baseball with guys who had a ton of talent. I saw them graduate high school and get the opportunity to go to college and further their education and their careers, and they gave it up to come home and work in their daddy's fernery or packing shed.

That was not going to be me. I didn't want to live in Pierson for the rest of my life. I was going to play shortstop in the major leagues. I had that fire in my belly.

Neither of my parents passed out a whole lot of pats on the butt or more than an occasional "Great job, son." I went 6-for-6 in a Little League game once, and during the ride home, all Mom and Dad could talk about was me cutting the grass when we got back.

As the high school coach in a small town, Dad didn't want people to think he was coddling me. Most of the time if he said nothing, that was a good thing. But if I loafed down to first base on a pop-up or didn't run out a ground ball or made an error or struck out twice, he had a lot to say.

Mom was a perfectionist in pretty much everything she did, so her standards were high for me, too. She thought I was a good player for the town of Pierson, but she expected that from me.

So when praise came, it really resonated with me. That's why I'll never forget Dad's reaction the night I hit three home runs in a Little League game against Altamonte Springs. I was only twelve, but I got confirmation on the car ride home I might really have a future in baseball.

The Lions Club Twins from little ol' Pierson, Florida, were playing against big bad Altamonte Springs, a suburb of Orlando, for the district championships. Altamonte had some really good players, including Jason Varitek, who went on to catch for the Boston Red Sox.

Varitek was playing third base that game. The coach's son, Jerrey Thurston, was catching. He wasn't as good as Varitek ended up being, obviously, but he got drafted by the Padres the same year as me.

We played them twenty miles south of Pierson in DeLand, which is home to Stetson University. It's a town of about thirty thousand people, a booming metropolis compared to Pierson.

Across the street from Bill Page Field was an old folks' home. All the studs in Little League could fly not only the chain-link fence but Amelia Avenue and send balls into the front yard of that old folks' home. Kids would dodge traffic to chase them down and, if they brought them back to the concession stand, could trade them for a cup full of bubble gum. I had kids scurrying that night.

I had hits in my first two at-bats before I really got it going in the sixth inning. Altamonte was up a run, and I tied it with a homer. They scored two more in the eighth, and I hit a two-run homer to even it up. Down one in the eleventh, I hit another solo homer to tie the game again.

Usually when you hit a home run in Little League, even the guys on the other team stick out a hand and say "good job" as you round the bases. After my first home run that night, I got nothing from the kids from Altamonte. The second one I hit, you could see them looking at each other like "Are you serious?" After the third home run, some of them finally stuck out their hands as I circled the bases. One of the guys who did was Varitek. That's when he and I forged our friendship.

From that day forward, I think Jason respected me as a ballplayer. I know I respected him. As a big leaguer, he was the best catcher I ever faced at calling a game, setting hitters up. He and some of those Red Sox pitchers worked me over.

That night against Altamonte, I just ran out of at-bats. They scored again, and I didn't come up the next inning. We lost 8–7.

That was the first game where I completely immersed myself in the competition. I wasn't worried about batting average or home runs. I was only focused on doing what I had to do to win the ball game.

Taking the loss was tough. I'd lost two or three Little League games in my life up until that point. We had some good players in Pierson, with my best friend, B. B. Abbott, at catcher and my buddies Leon and Leonard Butts, one at shortstop, the other at pitcher. We won everything. But that game sent Altamonte Springs to the Little League World Series in Williamsport, and our season was over.

I sat quietly in the backseat of our Nissan Maxima on the way home to Pierson with Mom and Dad. I kept thinking, *No way did I just hit three homers and get five hits in a game and we lost.*

Between trying to process the loss and being exhausted from the game, I started to drift off. Then my dad said something that jolted me awake.

"I think Chipper is one of the top ten players in the country at his age group," he told my mom.

I think I sat straight up. *Did he just say what I think he said?*

"Oh, stop being such a Little League dad," Mom said. Typical Mom. But I was fixated on what Dad had just said. *Top ten players in the country?*

I thought I was a pretty good player. I figured maybe top five in my area, but in the country?

Dad's favorite saying was "Speak when spoken to; otherwise shut up," and he wasn't talking to me, so I didn't say a word. But all of a sudden the loss wasn't so daunting. I knew then I could walk away from a loss with pride.

The first time I was largely the one responsible for my team losing, it made just as big an impression on me. I was thirteen and playing in the finals of the Babe Ruth All-Stars tournament in Sarasota, Florida. I came up with the bases loaded and two outs in the bottom of the last inning. I was facing Jules Van Landuyt, a lefty. Good pitcher.

He ended up playing at the University of Central Florida and signing with the Cubs.

Everybody in the stands knew we were two of the best thirteen-year-olds in the country squaring up. Everybody on my team expected me to come through. I had lived this situation in the backyard hundreds of times. Now it was time to actually do it.

I battled him for twelve pitches. He threw me seven or eight fastballs in a row, and I kept fouling them off. That made me think, *Is he going to keep pumping me heaters?* For some reason, I got in my mind that he was going to throw something else. Stupid.

He threw me what big leaguers like to call a cock shot—a belt-high, hittable fastball—and I completely froze. I took it. Strikeout. Game over.

My dad, who was one of our coaches that day, met me beside the dugout. "Was the ball outside?" he said.

"Nope," I said. "Right down the middle."

I put my head on Dad's shoulder and fell apart. I broke down crying right there in front of everybody.

Later on, back at the hotel, when I had calmed down, Dad told me, "Man, that's nothing. You play this game enough? You're going to do it again"—which to a thirteen-year-old was hard to take. I mean, my world had just ended.

Little did I know it then, but I would use the

memory of that strikeout for the rest of my career. It gave me fuel never to let hittable fastballs go by.

Not only did I have the advantage of being the son of a baseball coach, but I also spent my childhood playing with kids who were two, three, four years older. B. B. Abbott, my best friend, was two years older and a lot better than me. His friends were a lot better than me, too. I had to play at a higher level if I wanted to compete with the big boys.

I also played with older kids just hanging around Dad's practices at Taylor. When I was in elementary school, I got to play "500" with high school guys. That's the same game big leaguers play during batting practice to break up the monotony. (John Smoltz, Greg Maddux, and Tom Glavine used to power shag in the outfield with the Braves playing 500.) If you caught a fly ball in the air, you got 100 points. If you caught a line drive on one hop, it was 50. And if you dropped a fly ball, it was minus 100. As an only child, I just loved being around the guys. And I'd be lying if I said I didn't win a time or two.

By the eighth grade, I was playing varsity at Taylor. Dad knew it was coming and quit as coach. His philosophy was that fathers are either too hard on their sons or not hard enough, and he didn't want all the questions from other parents about "Chipper this, Chipper that." Dad still taught at the high school but he took a volunteer coaching job at Stetson, where his old college roommate and my godfather, Pete Dunn, was the head baseball coach.

I was overmatched as an eighth grader from time to time, but I didn't embarrass myself. Taylor was a smaller 2A school, and we were beating some of the larger 5A schools in central Florida with me contributing. I wasn't switch-hitting on a regular basis yet—just in batting practice, the backyard, or an occasional Little League or Babe Ruth game. But I was holding my own as a right-handed hitter.

I hit my first home run toward the end of the year, and I got it against Steven Williams, a lefty, who was drafted by the Orioles the following year. You have a little success with something, then you start thinking to yourself, *I got this.*

My first year on varsity opened up more doors for me than I ever imagined. During my eighth-grade season, scouts came to see some of my older teammates and got a glimpse of me in the process. That spring George Zuraw, a scout for the Cincinnati Reds, gave me my first taste of the big time. He invited me to a workout for the top fourteen- to sixteen-year-olds in the area.

The Reds were the team B.B. grew up cheering for; my imaginary Dodgers had played his "Big

Red Machine" in the backyard for years. This was huge. I didn't know much about how the scouting system worked, but I knew it was one of those "you're on our radar" workouts. If you did well, they'd keep following you. Mom drove me an hour south to Sanford, Florida, outside of Orlando.

I was nervous. There were probably twenty other kids there—from Orlando, from Altamonte Springs, from that Babe Ruth tournament in Sarasota. Seeing familiar faces must have put my mind at ease, because I had a good day.

I hit from both sides of the plate and I hit well. I had one of the best defensive workouts I would ever have. They hit me slow rollers at shortstop, and I made a bare-handed play where I threw from down under—gloved it and got rid of it in the same step—a play I became known for as a major leaguer. I could feel everybody there go, *Damn*.

It wasn't until I became a third baseman my rookie year in Atlanta that I made the bare-handed play very often. As a shortstop coming up through the minors, you're taught to glove slow rollers and transfer the ball to your throwing hand, not barehand them. At third base, though, on do-or-die bunt plays like that, you have to come in, barehand on the run, and throw accurately.

Out of the three or four plays I got at third

base during a game, one or two were those slow rollers, especially with the pitching staff we had with the Braves. I can't tell you how many swinging bunts Maddux got or how many guys tried to pull that Smoltzie slider off the outside corner and only got enough of it to hit me a weak ground ball.

I took great pride in not letting guys bunt on me. *If you're going to get on base, you're going to have to hit it by me.* I'd bet 60 to 70 percent of the highlight plays I made on defense were on that bare-handed play. I guess I'd had it in my back pocket all along.

I was already feeling pretty good at the end of that workout for the Reds. Then, when I got to the parking lot, Mr. Zuraw called Mom and me over to his car.

He opened up the trunk, where he had several boxes of wooden bats. "I'm going to give you two of these bats to start hitting with," he said. "And I'm going to give your mother contact information so you can order more. You need to start getting used to these because after you graduate high school, that'll be the last aluminum bat you ever use."

Whoa, wood bats? He actually thinks I can play professional baseball.

When Mom and I pulled out of that parking lot, my head was huge. Even my mom, who'd been skeptical of Dad's compliment after the

Altamonte game, told me she was about to pop her buttons listening to Mr. Zuraw. We didn't see him open his trunk for any other player.

Until that day, I'd swung nothing but aluminum bats and PVC pipe, unless you count dry swings in front of the den closet with Dad's old Mickey Mantle bat.

It was time for a new challenge. I was excited. I didn't know enough yet to be scared.

CHAPTER 3

The White Elephant

Bolles was the enemy, the big-city private school in Jacksonville. We played them almost every year in the regionals, and Bolles was usually the team knocking us out. Heading into my tenth-grade year at Taylor, my parents wanted me to transfer there. I'd be more challenged academically and face stiffer baseball competition against bigger schools. But the idea of leaving home—leaving my parents, friends, and teammates—was the last thing I wanted to do. And I knew people from Pierson were going to hate me for it.

When you're fourteen years old, your parents have the last say. Mom and Dad played it cool, though, and suggested we just take a trip to Bolles to see what it was about.

I knew a kid from Little League named Kirk Robinson, who transferred from DeLand High School to Bolles and boarded there. Robinson ran a 4.4 40 and bench-pressed over five hundred pounds. He still holds most of the Florida high school weight-lifting records. He went on to play running back at the University of Florida, where he backed up Willie McClendon.

He was a junior when I went to visit Bolles. Great dude. He showed me around, and I got to see how impressive everything was, from the state-of-the-art football stadium to the immaculate baseball field to Bolles Hall and the dormitories. It felt like a college.

Kirk made Bolles sound like the coolest place. He told me how great the athletics programs were in baseball, football, basketball, swimming, diving—pretty much everything. He warned me it was going to be tough academically but said if I applied myself, I'd make it.

I went from being dead set against Bolles to feeling that it was an opportunity I couldn't pass up. I was excited, and a little scared, but I was ready to do it, or at least I thought I was.

I drove a white 1983 Ford Escort in a parking lot full of BMWs, Honda Preludes, Camaro Z/28s, and even Porsches. My car stuck out so much, people starting calling it the White Elephant. I didn't fit in that well either. I was from a different place than most Bolles students. They came from affluent families. My mom and dad lived from paycheck to paycheck. I went to Bolles on a work program and got financial aid.

The first time I went under center as quarterback at football practice and yelled out the cadence, the offensive line fell out laughing because they thought I sounded like a hick. The coaches had put the new country bumpkin at starting quarterback as a sophomore over an incumbent junior. I knew I wasn't the best quarterback and told the coaches I'd rather play wide receiver. Justin Sherrod and I alternated starts for a while before they took my suggestion and moved me.

At Bolles, we had to dress up every day. Dress shoes, socks, belt, slacks, collared shirt, tie. Once I graduated high school, I thought, *I ain't doing that anymore.* Bobby Cox's rule on the road in the big leagues was always that we had to wear a sport coat or suit on the chartered flights. Fine, but I never wore a tie. The only way I am wearing a tie is for court or a funeral, and funeral is a toss-up.

The hardest adjustment for me at Bolles was academics. I went there thinking I could take four advanced placement classes since I'd been making As and Bs at Taylor. They had me in AP English, Algebra III, AP Spanish, and AP Chemistry. I was absolutely overmatched.

The workload left me feeling mentally fried, and when I was overwhelmed, I called my parents, crying, begging them to let me come home. I was scared to death I wouldn't be eligible to play baseball in the spring. On my first progress report I had an F, two Ds, and three Cs.

Mom was probably more upset than Dad that I was away at school. That's the only time I remember Dad being the tough-love guy and

Mom falling apart a little bit. Usually it was the other way around. But Dad wasn't having any of it. He said coming home was not an option.

"I can't handle all this work," I said, bawling.

"You better get on it and do what you've got to do," he said. "Because if you're ineligible, you ain't playing, and if you're ineligible, you ain't coming home either. And if that happens, we're all going to be miserable."

I called home every day. This was before cell phones, so I had to use a pay phone at the end of the hall in our dormitory. Crying on the phone to your mom didn't exactly go over well with guys in line behind you. Luckily, I had a dorm adviser, Charles Edwards, who let me call home during evening study hall.

Coach Edwards would peek his head in at seven thirty and say, "El Jahy"—that was his Southern drawl for LJ, as in Larry Jones—"don't you need to make a phone call?"

"Yessir."

"Better get on it, then," he said. "And when you get done, you better get your tail back in here."

I got really close to Coach Edwards and not just because he lived thirty feet from my door. I think it started with the conversation he and Dad had the first time they met. My dad looked Coach Edwards dead in the eye and said, "If he steps out of line, you jerk a knot in his tail."

That's Southern-speak for whupping. My dad had given him a say-so in how his son was brought up. It was a sign of respect.

I gave Coach Edwards grief every once in a while because I was a rebellious, cocky punk at sixteen years old, but Coach Edwards knew I was raised right and could be reined in easily, and he didn't hesitate to call my dad a time or two. He trusted me to babysit his little girl, Terah, so he and his wife could go out for dinner and a movie. My roommate and I would make five or ten bucks apiece and splurge on two Domino's pizzas.

Coach Edwards talked to me like someone from Pierson. Color didn't matter—Coach Edwards is African-American—background didn't matter. We hit it off. It didn't hurt that he was a great athlete. He played wide receiver at Vanderbilt and coached our wide receivers and defensive backs on the Bolles football team. He was good at everything. He could shoot hoops. He could run a pass pattern. He talked my kind of smack, and I loved it. And when we were joking around, he let me call him Chuck.

He had keys to the gym. Every night after study hall, my roommate, Bailey Luetgert, and I were knocking on his door, begging him to come shoot hoops or play dodgeball with us.

We used to play a game called 'Nam ball, as in Vietnam. It's no-holds-barred dodgeball. Instead of one ball, there are ten, and you better have your head on a swivel because you're going to have volleyballs rolling everywhere. One night my junior year, I stepped on one and blew out my ankle.

I was in a cast for four weeks with torn ligaments. I missed ten games that baseball season, and I hit only .270. Not until the playoffs started did I really get healthy. Coach Edwards had to answer to Don Suriano—our baseball coach—for that one, but I certainly wasn't going to hold it against him. I could have hurt myself any number of ways.

I was lucky enough to have a long list of influential coaches and mentors in my life, especially after I got drafted, but Coach Edwards was one of the first. He was like a second dad to me and was instrumental at a time when I needed it the most.

Pretty early in my sophomore year, Coach Suriano and my parents decided I should drop the AP classes and go at a slower pace. I became the king of extra help. If school started at nine o'clock, I was in a classroom at eight o'clock, getting individual help from my Spanish teacher, going over the previous day's Algebra III homework, comparing notes with my Western Civilization teacher.

I started sitting in the front row. I quit socializing during class. I started to figure out how to budget my day between practices and study hall and make it all mesh. By the end of the first semester, I had one D+ but everything else was Bs and Cs.

I had never worked so hard in my life. I wondered how long I could keep it up. But it's like everything else, the more you do it, the easier it gets.

It didn't hurt that during my last two years, I roomed with Ron Patrick, the quarterback on our football team and one of the smartest people I know. I shared notes with a guy who scored 1400 on his SAT and eventually went to Princeton.

I was settling in socially, too. I had a new girlfriend at school, and I quit going home to Pierson on weekends. My best friend was a basketball player named B. J. Thompson. He wasn't the stereotypical Bolles student either, so we hit it off right away. B.J. and I played two-on-two pickup basketball games on the outdoor courts at the beach on weekends. We'd sneak into the Ponte Vedra Beach Club, where all the rich kids and their families had memberships, and hang out by the pool.

I still had plenty of Pierson in me, though. Some of the rich kids used to look at me funny when they saw my fishing shoes, a nasty old pair of tennis shoes with no shoelaces that I kept in my closet.

Fishing has always been therapeutic for me,

just like hunting. On weekends when I got bored, I'd wade out into the St. Johns River on Bolles's campus or walk the docks, catching bass left and right. By the time I graduated, I had four or five guys out there fishing with me.

Bolles got to feel more like home. Going home, though, never felt quite the same again.

I felt like a traitor the first time I went back to Pierson to play Taylor the spring of my sophomore year. It was probably the most scared I've ever been on a baseball field. I didn't know how I would be received by the crowd. I didn't know how I would be looked at by my friends. I feared getting beat. I also feared ten-run ruling them.

It was hard to look my buddies across the diamond in the eye. I was trying to beat people I loved, that I went to school with and played Little League ball with. And the success of their whole season was in my hands. The winner went to the sectionals. The loser went home.

I've never seen the stands so packed. There were six or seven hundred people in the entire town of Pierson; I bet you five hundred of them showed up. The bleachers were full. People were four or five deep down each baseline and sitting on the back of their pickup trucks out beyond the outfield wall. The press box was packed.

My parents were in lawn chairs down the left

field line. They always kept to themselves so Dad didn't have to listen to second-guessing and bad-mouthing from parents.

I wasn't pitching, which made it a little easier, but I was so nervous when I came to the plate. After every strike called on me that day, there was a loud cheer. I heard some sneers and jeers from the stands. "Hey, traitor, what's up?" But I knew everybody in Pierson. All I had to do was turn around, look at them, and say, "Hey, what's up? Scoreboard."

I used to do the same thing when I was in the big leagues to disarm hecklers. Most people don't think you're going to turn around, so they keep gabbing. But once you let it be known you've identified them and you start interacting with them, it defuses the situation.

I think a lot of guys from Pierson would have done the same thing I did if given the opportunity to go to Bolles. The mothers and the fathers were a different story. And some of the rednecks we hunted with didn't understand it. I think they were probably jealous.

My close friends didn't blame me. I'd just finished the ninth grade. I was under my parents' control and while I was a part of making the decision, it was my parents who wanted me to go. B.B. almost came to Bolles, too. I tried as hard as I could to convince him, but he didn't want to leave Taylor his senior year.

My first game back in Pierson was B.B.'s last high school baseball game. I played a role in handing him his final defeat. Not that I did much in the game—I got a base hit or two—but we broke it open late and beat them handily. His coach pinch ran for him to give the crowd a chance to acknowledge him, and as he ran right past me from second base, I gave him a little nod.

Off the field, I had a hard time looking people in the eye. When I walked into Carters Kitchen, the little restaurant in Pierson, you could see the contempt on people's faces. They might say all the right things to your face, but I knew they were pissed.

I had no reason to feel ashamed, but I did. We knocked Taylor out of the playoffs every year I was at Bolles, and I hated that I was on the team that did it. I don't think it ever got any easier.

I think, subconsciously, that feeling is a big reason why I never went to free agency in the big leagues. I never even got close. Whenever we got to the end of a season, I had a new contract in hand or a multi-year deal already in place. I never wanted to be in any uniform other than the Braves'.

We played Taylor in football almost every year, too, and my junior year, Dad raised the stakes right before our teams met.

He was still the offensive coordinator for

Taylor, and they had a really good squad that year. I already had a bad feeling about the game.

Then I showed up for practice on Monday, four days before the game, and all my Bolles teammates were wearing T-shirts under their pads that said, " 'Bolles can be had'—Larry Jones." Apparently my dad had popped off in the DeLand paper.

I called Dad that night. "Are you trying to make my life miserable?" I said.

"Chip, I just spoke my mind," he said. "You guys are coming off a five and five year. You got your brains beat in week one. I think we're going to pummel you guys, to be honest with you."

I can't say anything now because I went on to be just as outspoken as my dad during my big league career. The year after I retired as a player, during an appearance on a morning radio show in Atlanta, I was asked for my prediction on the Division Series between the Braves and Dodgers. I said the Dodgers would probably win it in four. My loyalties were with the Braves, of course, but power pitching wins in the postseason, and there were no two hotter power pitchers in the game than Clayton Kershaw and Zack Greinke. They'd be pitching three or four times in the series.

It just so happened that the Braves had asked me to throw out the ceremonial first pitch before Game 1 that night at Turner Field. The Braves brass and some of the players got wind of my prediction and boycotted catching my first pitch. They sent Homer, the mascot, to do it, which had never happened in my twenty-three years with the Braves. It was total disrespect and I was pissed. I wasn't being malicious with that prediction. I had the stats to back it up. And oh, by the way, I was right. The Braves lost that series in four.

I found out later that Tim Hudson, a guy I'd been teammates with for years, was behind the boycott. I called Huddy that offseason and told him I didn't appreciate what they'd done. He said, "Yeah, it wasn't the right thing to do. It turned out to be pretty embarrassing for everybody involved." He kept saying, "Man, you were right. They were a better team than we were."

Dad was right, too. Taylor whipped us in that game, 27–6. My Bolles teammates wouldn't like it, but all I felt afterward was pride.

My hometown buddies finally beat Bolles in football. We'd beaten Bolles in baseball, but we'd never beaten them in football. I had an excuse to walk over to their team huddle after the game—I went and hugged my dad. After their coach spoke to the team, he asked if anybody had anything to say. I walked into the middle of Taylor's huddle still wearing my Bolles jersey.

"I'm so fucking proud of you guys," I said. "I am so proud to be from Pierson, Florida."

• • •

One consolation when I went to Bolles was that I still got to play American Legion with guys from my hometown, including B.B., in the summertime. We all played for DeLand Post 6, which had all the small-town boys from central Florida. It was all-star-caliber games for the entire summer, and we loved it.

Usually you didn't start American Legion until you turned sixteen. But unbeknownst to me, the coach for Post 6, Dennis McComb, got special permission for me to play in the state tournament at age fourteen in place of some injured guys.

Mom, Dad, and I were on our way home from a Babe Ruth tournament in Gainesville, when McComb contacted my dad. It felt like I had just been called up to the big leagues. We drove home, staying long enough for me to repack, and then met the team in Haines City. Boardwalk and Baseball was our baseball mecca, a theme park where all of Florida's big amateur tournaments were held and where the Kansas City Royals used to train.

I thought I'd be coming off the bench, maybe pinch hitting, but Coach McComb started me in right field in my first American Legion game. That's where I was when Kenny Felder reached second base in the second inning.

Everybody in the tournament knew who Kenny Felder was. Niceville's right fielder was a freak of an athlete, a two-sport guy. He went on to play quarterback at Florida State and got drafted in the first round by the Brewers.

Playing right field was culture shock for me. I had always played shortstop and pitched, but Coach McComb gave me a great piece of advice before the game: "If it's hit to you, catch it. And whenever you're throwing to a base, make sure you throw it through the cutoff man; don't try to fly the ball all the way there."

That came in handy when Felder took off from second on a line drive to right field because the adrenaline was flowing. The ball one-hopped me, and I caught it on the move, with my momentum going toward the plate. I fired it through the cutoff man, aiming at his cap bill. That not only held the batter at first base, given the chance we might cut it off, but it kept my throw under control and on line to one-hop home plate.

Playing the outfield never really felt natural to me, not even after I played there for two and a half seasons in the big leagues. But I still used what McComb taught me that day in Haines City to gun down my share of runners at the plate for the Braves.

I threw out Bobby Abreu one time in Philly, and Jeromy Burnitz in New York. Against the Expos, I nailed Vlad Guerrero at second trying to stretch a double in a game in San Juan, Puerto Rico. But the one that caught everybody by surprise—including our broadcaster Skip Caray—was Opening Day in 2003 against the Montreal Expos. I threw out Jose Vidro at the plate from pretty deep left field to get Maddux out of a jam. Apparently, Skip thought they had gone to commercial and told Pete Van Wieren on the air that he didn't know I had that throw in me. Quite honestly, I didn't either.

Whether I was in the big leagues or playing Legion ball, I had plenty of see-what-you're-made-of moments. That day at Boardwalk and Baseball was one for both me and B.B., who'd been behind the plate. He caught my one-hopper, held on through the collision, and tagged Felder out. The next day the DeLand paper had a picture of B.B. standing over Kenny Felder, holding up the ball to the umpire.

It was the first under-fire throw I'd ever made from the outfield to home plate against one of the best athletes in the state, from a position I'd never played in, during my first Legion game.

It was one of those times when I thought to myself, *All right, I belong here. I can play here.* That throw probably put me on the radars of some scouts there to watch Felder.

Playing American Legion ball is also where I got serious about switch-hitting. Playing in big games and state tournaments in high school, I hit from the side I was most comfortable with—the right. But American Legion wasn't all about wins and losses. It was about honing your skills. So for those sixty to sixty-five games a summer, if we were facing a right-handed pitcher, I hit left-handed.

There was one time I made the mistake of batting righty vs. righty in a key spot, and it taught me a valuable lesson. I was sixteen and we were playing in a tournament against Jacksonville Post 88. This was one of the games where winning actually mattered a lot.

If we won, we got to go to the state tournament. If we lost, our summer was over.

We had some pretty good players on our club, but we were the hicks from the sticks. Jacksonville was the big-city team with a bunch of guys who were either going in the first two or three rounds of the major league draft or to big-time Division I schools like Ole Miss, University of Georgia, and the Naval Academy. We had one Division I player, Brett Barker, and he was going to Central Florida. It was David vs. Goliath.

We were down seven runs in the ninth inning, and I led off against their closer. He was a submarine guy, which meant he threw from a low angle, almost underhanded. Submariners are rare at any level in baseball, much less American Legion, and I made the mistake of thinking I needed to face him right-handed.

I knew his sinker—a sinking fastball—would

tail into me right-handed. I thought if I scooted up in the box, I could catch one before it sunk and golf the ball over the short porch to left field and win the game for us. What I didn't account for was him throwing me the Frisbee slider that was 8 to 10 mph slower and started at my hip and broke off the plate away. He struck me out on back-to-back sliders.

You're an absolute idiot, I thought. *You want him to throw the sinker, not the slider, and you're going to see more sinkers left-handed than you would right-handed. And left-handed, not only are you a low-ball hitter, you like that ball out away from you. He's going to stay middle of the plate away against you left-handed.*

It was a dumb decision. But I got lucky. We rallied. We batted around, and I got a chance to face him again. This time, with the tying runs on base, I went up left-handed.

I didn't have to worry about looking bad on the slider anymore. He wasn't about to make a mistake with that pitch breaking into me and have me bomb one over the three-hundred-foot right field fence. Sure enough, I got what I was expecting, and what I wanted: a sinker out away from me. I smoked it off the center field wall for a double to tie the game. As I got to second base, I could only shake my head.

One of my buddies, Albert Groholski, came up behind me and hit a two-run homer to win the game and send little ol' Post 6 to the state tournament. My mom and dad filmed the game, and I can still hear the audio of B.B.'s dad, Bernon, going nuts. Nobody could believe we pulled it off. All I could think about was how lucky I'd been to get a second chance to bat left-handed.

The whole premise behind becoming a switch-hitter is so you don't have to see that slider breaking away from you. If I was ever going to see the fruits of years of practicing two swings, learning two sets of mechanics, and basically doing twice the work, I had to go up there and hit left-handed with conviction.

By my senior year at Bolles, I felt like I was ready to take the next step to professional baseball. But I still had to prove it to my dad, who was a tougher critic than any major league scout.

One night while I was playing shortstop, with a bunch of scouts in the stands, a guy hit a pop-up to no-man's-land out behind third base. You're taught: *Don't take your eyes off the ball.* So I was looking up at the ball, not at who was where. As the shortstop, I had priority over Steve Carver, our third baseman, so I called him off. But the left fielder, Alan Verlander, had priority over me. Verlander called for the ball; I pulled up. He never got there, and the ball dropped.

We won the game handily anyway. We boat-raced them. But after the game, my dad was furious. He could not wait to get me out in the parking lot.

"Do you know how many people were here watching you play?" he said through gritted teeth. "And you lollygagged?"

"Whoa, whoa, whoa," I said. "Lollygag?"

"Why on earth did you not catch that ball down the left field line?" he said.

"My fucking left fielder called me off," I said.

Somehow I managed not to flinch. I had never cursed to my dad's face in my life. Apparently, it never dawned on him the left fielder might have called me off.

I turned and headed for my dormitory. I left my parents standing in the parking lot.

Usually after games it was hugs and "love you," "see you at the next game," or "I'll be home this weekend." Those few minutes in the parking lot were our only chance to really connect. But I was furious. Dad had watched me my whole life. He knew that pop-up behind third base was one of my favorite plays to make as a shortstop. He'd seen me go diving into too many fences down that line to think I pulled up. Yet instead of asking what happened, he jumped to the conclusion that I pulled up.

I'd spent that whole year dealing with draft stuff and college recruiting on my own up at Bolles. I was under a lot of pressure. The stress was probably getting to me a little bit, to all of us.

My mom called me after they got home that night and said, "Your dad was wrong," which made me feel good. "But you really shouldn't have cussed at him," she said.

Dad called me a day or two later, and we worked it out. I'd been disrespectful reacting that way. Dad was just thinking bigger picture. He didn't want anyone to walk away from the field thinking something negative that might prevent me from being a high pick in the draft.

I was focused more on each game. I wasn't dwelling on where I was going to go in the draft.

My mom and dad were used to having their finger on the pulse of everything that was going on with me, but they couldn't anymore.

I was growing up. After that, Dad loosened up a little.

CHAPTER 4
Draft Day

The first major league ballpark I ever went to was Atlanta–Fulton County Stadium. I was fifteen. My American Legion team was playing a tournament in Gainesville, Georgia, an hour north of Atlanta, and we went to see the Braves play the Reds in June 1987. We had tickets in the upper deck, on the third base side. I walked out through the tunnel, looked down and thought, *My goodness, how green is that grass?*

I thought it was the most beautiful place I'd ever seen on earth. Turns out, Fulton County Stadium wasn't even one of the nicer baseball stadiums in the country, but in my mind, it was a cathedral.

Growing up in central Florida, spring training sites were everywhere, but they weren't the same as big league ballparks. I saw the Tigers play the Reds in a spring training game in Lakeland once, and it looked like one of our American Legion fields. When we walked into Fulton County Stadium and saw how orange that clay was, how bright the uniforms were, it was like we were the Bad News Bears walking into the Astrodome for the first time.

I vowed, *I'm going to play on that field one day.*

I had no idea Atlanta–Fulton County Stadium would be my home park one day or that I would win a World Series there. I just knew I wanted to play on that field.

I wasn't necessarily a Braves fan. I'd have pulled for the Dodgers if they were playing Atlanta. But on that day, I was pulling for the Braves like my Legion teammates were. And what I saw unfold on the field was unbelievable. I was sold.

The first two Reds batters, Kal Daniels and Tracy Jones, hit homers. Doyle Alexander, who was pitching for the Braves, threw at the next Reds guy. He didn't hit him, but tensions were running hot. A couple of innings later, Dale Murphy homered to put the Braves up 6–4, and Bill Gullickson, the Reds pitcher, decided to retaliate.

The next batter was Ken Griffey Sr. Gullickson tried to hit him and missed. On the next pitch, Griffey homered. The writing was on the wall that Gullickson wasn't going to be in the game much longer anyway, so he went after the next guy, too, Andres Thomas, and he drilled him. Thomas charged the mound, and the brawl was on.

Bodies went flying everywhere; a couple of haymakers were thrown. I think Murph was in the middle of it—trying to pull guys off each other if nothing else—but the Braves had some scrappy players back in the '80s with guys like Murph, Bob Horner, Hubby—Glenn Hubbard—and Griffey.

It was the greatest game I'd ever seen in my life. Balls were flying out of the park; guys were getting plunked and charging the mound. I was hooked.

In the months leading up to the 1990 draft, I had no idea the Braves were going to play such a big part in my future. I knew there were a lot of scouts in the stands at my games—most of them had stopwatches hanging out of their pockets or briefcases, so it wasn't hard to pick them out—but I rarely knew who was with what team. I didn't want to know. The Braves scouting director, Paul Snyder, could have walked up to me, and I wouldn't have known if he was from the Atlanta Braves or the Toledo Mud Hens. I was trying to tune all that out and just play high school baseball, have fun with my friends, beat rival schools, and be a teenage kid. That got harder and harder as the year went on.

My sophomore and junior years, there might have been four or five scouts in the stands. My senior year, there were thirty to fifty. Baseball scouts had even shown up at my football practices that fall. I don't know if they wanted to get a feel for whether I might want to play college football, to see what kind of athlete I was, or just to know if I got hurt.

I led the state of Florida in catches as a wide receiver my senior year. That drew some attention from college coaches, and I had sit-downs with both Bobby Bowden at FSU and Steve Spurrier at Florida. Turtle Thomas, the assistant baseball coach who recruited me for the University of Miami, told me I had permission from Jimmy Johnson to play football there, too.

But I didn't have the desire to work at football like I did baseball. I loved Friday nights, walking through the tunnel to "Lunatic Fringe" by Red Rider, coming out in that big stadium and kicking butt, but I hated practicing Monday through Thursday. I knew where my bread was buttered. I told every college football coach who even asked about me, "Don't even mess with it: I'm playing baseball. My goal is to play baseball at the next level."

Once January 1 came around, when Coach Suriano gave me the key to the batting cage because he wasn't allowed to be there, scouts were watching me hit on my own. Then when baseball practice started, a few dozen scouts came every day.

Playing in front of all those scouts is how I learned to tune out distractions. I knew I needed to show these guys what I could do. There was not a single practice my senior year I wasn't balls to the wall.

By the time I was seventeen, I was pretty prepared for the attention. Usually when I immersed myself in the work of baseball, I forgot about it. So I tried to be in the cage or on the field as much as I could.

Coach Suriano knew I wanted to be sheltered from as much as possible, so he handled 95 percent of my phone calls, and my parents fielded a ton back in Pierson, too.

It helped that there were no cell phones back then and no phone in my dorm room. The pay phone in the hall was in constant use, so calls to me weren't going to get through.

When I did talk to scouts, it was during my free periods, either on the phone or sitting down with them there at the school. Meetings with pro scouts were a lot more detailed than with college coaches. Scouts brought in medical guys to go over my medical history. Their doctors gave me physicals. They gave me eye tests. They gave me personality tests. They wanted to know about my background, about my parents, why I was at Bolles, why I didn't stay home. The process was tedious, but I went through it for teams with the first fifteen or twenty picks in the draft.

I'd known I was going to be drafted since I

was a junior. By my senior year, it looked like I was going to go in the first round—I read my press clippings; I make no bones about it. My stock was rising as a switch-hitting shortstop—which is considered a premium position—who had good speed and some pop. I went 7-3 with a 1.00 ERA as a pitcher that year, but I think scouts knew my future was at the plate. I hit .488 my senior year. I think it helped that I was raised by a coach. Scouts seemed to like my approach and my bat speed.

The only question was where I might go in the first round. A lot of the scouts from teams at the top end of the draft were coming to see me play, and not just for a day or two but for weeks at a time. They were at five, six, seven, eight games in a row. I realized I had a chance to go in the top five or six picks.

I tried to figure out where. Some of the teams with the first three or four picks had a specific need, and I knew I wasn't their guy.

I didn't have a very good workout with the Tigers, who had the number two pick, and I kept hearing how they needed a first baseman and loved Tony Clark. I never really had any contact with the Phillies, who had the number three pick, and they needed a catcher. Mike Lieberthal was the logical choice. The White Sox, who had the fourth pick, were looking for help right away, a big power arm, and there was nobody with a bigger, more powerful arm than Alex Fernandez.

So I figured it would come down to the Pirates and Mariners, who had the fifth and sixth picks. The Mariners told me from day one of my senior year that if I was still there at six, they were taking me. George Zuraw had left the Reds and was the assistant general manager for the Mariners in 1990, and he'd loved me since my workout as an eighth grader. I had that to lean on.

Of the teams picking in the top ten, the Braves gave me the least amount of attention, as far as I could tell, and that didn't surprise me. They had the number one pick. In no way did I think I was the best player out of almost fifteen hundred players from the high school, college, and junior college ranks who were about to be drafted. Todd Van Poppel was the crown jewel. He was the Stephen Strasburg of that draft class. Tim Costo was a college shortstop. I was only in high school. I didn't know much about "upside" or being "projectable" as a young player with potential. I just thought Van Poppel and Costo were better, more developed players than me, so they were going to go first.

The Braves were really good at keeping things close to the vest. They didn't want other teams to know what they were thinking. I saw their area scouts from time to time, Tony DeMacio and Dean Jongewaard. I heard Paul Snyder was around some, and Jimy Williams, one of the Braves minor league coaches then, came once. I never saw Bobby Cox, who was the Braves general manager in 1990. I never saw Hank Aaron, who was a senior vice president to Stan Kasten at that point. I heard after the draft that both had come to see me play.

It's not as if Hank Aaron could just walk around on campus. He's got to take it all in from a distance. I'm sure Bobby did the same thing. They might have been watching from the same car. You get a truer sense of what a kid is all about from a distance anyway. If he can't see you, he's not nervous. And you don't want to listen to influences from other scouts.

I did my best to block out distractions, but I developed this sixth sense for when I was being watched. I could be hitting in the cage by myself and feel eyes on me. So I would start looking around at parked cars, checking behind steering wheels for scouts.

As much as I'd heard the name Todd Van Poppel bandied about, I got the chance to size him up myself. I met Van Poppel the fall of my senior year on my one and only college visit to the University of Miami.

Miami had the best program in the country at the time. They won the College World Series under Ron Fraser in 1982 and 1985. My dad really liked him and respected him a lot. I had a really good relationship with his assistant coach, Turtle Thomas. And Coral Gables was only five hours from Pierson, so my parents could come see me play. If I was going to college, that's where I wanted to play.

Mom and Dad drove me all night to Miami after a Bolles football game in Tallahassee. Miami had a pretty good group of guys coming in that weekend: Jason Varitek, Shane Andrews, Rondell White, a left-handed pitcher out of Tampa named Sal Urso, and of course, Van Poppel.

We all knew who Van Poppel was. We all read press clippings and knew who won national player of the year and who was on the all-USA team. I think we were all resigned to the fact that Van Poppel was going to be the first player taken in the draft.

He didn't say a whole heck of a lot that weekend. He wasn't the most social guy in the world. Nights when we hung out with some of the Miami baseball players, he didn't go.

White and Andrews became good friends of mine. I hung out with them in rookie ball when they were with the Expos, and we all shared a facility down at Pirate City in Bradenton, where the Pirates still hold spring training. The three of us played against each other all the way up through the minors and in the same division in the big leagues.

I committed to Miami that weekend, but out of our group of six guys, nobody ended up playing at the University of Miami. Four of us went in the first round of the draft that year. And Varitek, who went to Georgia Tech, got drafted in the first round a couple of years later.

I never did get to know Van Poppel very well. Being lumped in with a guy everybody pegged as the number one pick in that draft, there was a little personal rivalry there. Even if I didn't dislike the guy, I still wanted to do better than him to validate my draft pick.

I gave scouts only little sneak peeks here and there of switch-hitting my senior year. I was more concerned with hitting .500 and a bunch of homers and leading us back to the state championship game than how my left-handed swing would affect my draft status.

But every once in a while I'd let the cat out of the bag and show the scouts there were skills from the other side of the plate. If we were killing a team and I thought the matchup was right, I'd turn around and hit left-handed.

We were playing West Nassau at home one Saturday. From what my dad told me later, the Braves had a few scouts there that day: Paul Snyder, Harold "Hep" Cronin—the first Braves area scout who saw me play—and Jimy Williams, then their roving minor league coach. I don't know if any of them had ever seen me hit left-handed in a game.

I homered early in the game right-handed. We were up 8–0 late, so I told Coach Suriano I wanted to hit left-handed, "just to show off a little bit." On the first pitch I saw left-handed, I hit a home run to dead center field, 450 feet onto San Jose Boulevard, the road that runs out in front of the school.

Jimy Williams told me years later, when he was my third base coach with the Braves, that my home run left-handed was what put me over the top for the Braves. He went back and told Bobby that if he were drafting first, he'd take me in a heartbeat.

It was just happenstance that he was even there. His son had a swimming event in Jacksonville, and Bobby had told Jimy he could leave camp to see his son swim if he stopped by and looked at this kid named Chipper Jones.

At the time, I think the Braves were still leaning toward Van Poppel, and I don't blame them. If I'm the Atlanta Braves and there's a guy coming out of high school who can throw 100 mph and has an idea where it's going, I'm drafting him. That's not just a top-of-the-rotation guy; that's a guy who helps you win playoff games. That's a power arm you can't pass up.

But the draft is about more than just a player's tools and a team's needs. It's also about money.

And Van Poppel and I had different ideas about how important money was in the grand scheme of things. He was represented by Scott Boras. I walked out of a meeting with Boras.

I was very adamant from the get-go, as were Mom and Dad, that we were not going to have some cheeseball agent representing our family. Whoever represented the Jones family was going to be worthy of it.

Scott Boras was not *Scott Boras* in 1990, but he was still a bigwig in the industry. He had represented the number one overall pick each of the two years prior, Andy Benes and Ben McDonald. And he represented Brien Taylor, who went number one the year after I did. I think Boras came to Florida in the spring of 1990 because he had heard there was a possibility I could be the first pick.

My parents and I met him in a conference room at some highfalutin hotel in Jacksonville. I got the impression right away that Scott was very brash, abrasive, and aggressive. That can be good at times, but he said some things that rubbed me the wrong way about who I was as a ballplayer and about negotiating with whoever drafted me.

Scott disputes this now, but I know what I heard, and my parents know what they heard. He told us that day I was going to hit .270 in the big leagues and win a couple of Gold Gloves. I thought to myself, *Man, has this guy watched me at all? My bat is going to get me to the big leagues. It ain't going to be my glove, I can tell you that right now.*

And he said—and this is verbatim—he would have me with books in hand on the front steps of the University of Miami before I signed a contract with anybody. Well, that's not the way I wanted to do business.

I wanted to play baseball in the big leagues, not hold out the first chance I had to start playing in the professional ranks. And if we had to meet somebody in the middle to make that happen, then I was willing to do it. I was not playing this game for the paycheck. I was playing to be one of the greatest. I was not going to be the greatest playing at the University of Miami. I was not going to be the greatest toiling in the minors because I pissed off somebody in the front office who said, "Screw it, we'll leave him down in the minors for another year."

I wanted what was fair; I wanted to be treated the same as everybody else, and I wanted to earn my keep. But I was not trying to be on the cover of *Fortune*. It's amazing how people thought that dangling the money carrot in front of Mom, Dad, and me was going to impress us when quite honestly it turned us off more times than not.

Boras was a little too much of the stereotypical agent for me. He came off as smug and cocky and acted as if he knew me. He didn't know me. I sat in there and listened to him for about five minutes, then I walked out.

My dad came running after me and said, "Uh, what are you doing?"

"I don't like this dude," I said. "Plain and simple. I don't want this guy representing me, and you've got to be kidding me that you're sitting here listening to this."

"Well, it's polite to sit there and listen to it," he said.

"Dad," I said. "I've got a thousand meetings with teams, agents, and scouts, and I've got homework to do."

I was at a point in the process where I was incapable of dealing with bullshit. Scott Boras could be the nicest guy on the planet, but he rubbed me the wrong way that day, and I was not in the mood for it.

With two weeks to go before the draft, my Bolles teammates were tired of all the attention I was getting. Quite frankly, I was, too. I was ready for the whole thing to be done. Unfortunately, those emotions spilled over at the worst possible time.

The day before we were going to play Westminster Christian School of Miami in the state championship game, we were practicing at Lakeland High School, right down the road from

Boardwalk and Baseball. It was hotter than blue blazes, and we'd been out there for two hours.

I was hitting in the last group of batting practice, and before I took my turn in the cage Coach Suriano said, "Hey, take your regular swings right-handed and then after everybody else is done, jump back in there and take ten or fifteen swings left-handed just to show the scouts you can do it."

Everybody on the team thought the last group was it, then I had to go back into the cage to take more swings. When I finished hitting and walked into the outfield, my old roommate Bailey and one of our infielders, Steve Carver, told me that John Olson, our backup catcher, was popping off about me.

John was an underclassman, a junior. He was a tough kid and played some on the football team. But he didn't play much in baseball. I walked over to him, and he was still mouthing off about how sick he was of the way I was being treated.

"What is your problem?" I said.

"You're a prima donna," he said.

"Because I took an extra round?" I said, facing him up.

"Go ahead," he said. "Hit me."

I still had my glove on, so I pointed it down to expose my knuckles, and I jabbed him in the face with my left hand.

The jab was more like a "get off me" push,

as if to say, "You don't want any part of this."
But it had the opposite effect. Olson took a step
back, as though I had startled him—I guess he
didn't think I would really hit him—and I could
see the red in his eyes. He was coming after me.
He threw a big roundhouse and I ducked. Then I
came from down under with my right hand and
got him flush across the temple. He went down to
both knees.

He wasn't out cold, but you could tell all his
faculties weren't there, and he was bleeding
down the side of his face from a cut over his left
eye. I knew he was hurt pretty good, but I had so
much adrenaline going I didn't realize anything
was wrong with me.

The whole team surrounded us and pulled us
away from each other pretty quickly. There were
twenty or thirty people in the stands, and I don't
know how many scouts. Coach Suriano took us
off the field and into the dugout, then sent Olson
to the hospital to get stitches. Then he asked if I
was all right.

"I don't know," I said. "My hand is starting to
throb."

Not only had I hit Olson with my pitching
hand, but I had led with the bottom of my fist.
Instead of hitting him square, my knuckle took
the brunt of the blow, and unbeknownst to me, I
had snapped my fifth metacarpal. They call it a
boxer's fracture.

"Well, let's go to the hospital," he said.

"No," I said. "You ain't taking me to the hospital."

"What if it's broke?" he said.

"It'll still be broke in a couple days," I said. "But if I go to the hospital and it's broke, they're going to put a cast on it, and I won't be able to play. I'm going to pitch tomorrow, then we can go to the doctor afterwards."

So that's what we did.

My dad always told me, "You better not start a fight, but you better damn well finish it." That's all I had in mind that whole time. I didn't ask for it. I didn't egg it on. I walked into a situation that was already heated, and I finished it.

Some of my teammates were pretty mad at me. Some of them were mad at Olson. Some were indifferent. I think everybody was a little pissed off at what was going on. There's no doubt I was treated differently than everybody else was, even though I never wanted to be.

To my teammates' credit, when we stepped between the lines, we were a unit and pulling for each other. It was just the extra stuff that everybody was sick of.

I spent the night before the state championship game with my hand in a bucket of ice, but it was still really swollen the next day. Olson knew better than anybody I wasn't right. He caught me warming up before the game.

When I finished, he was waiting down in the dugout.

"You hurting?"

"Yeah," I said.

"Well," he said. "We need you, let's go. What happened yesterday, it's over. Go out there and win."

You could tell he was sorry. I think John proved something to himself, standing up to me. It probably wasn't the best way to handle it, but looking back now, I don't blame him.

Hitting him was stupid on my part. I cost my team a second straight state championship. I pitched with a broken hand, and we lost. Our second baseman, a sophomore named Jeff Doyle, thought the loss was his fault because he booted a ball in the seventh inning that cost us the lead, but the game never should have come down to that.

I was throwing only 82, 83 mph that day when I should have been around 90, 91. We were beating Westminster of Miami 2–1 going into the bottom of the last inning. But I know if I'd been 100 percent healthy, they never would have scored a run off me.

With one out in the seventh, a kid hit a tailor-made double-play ball right to Doyle. He wasn't used to the turf at Boardwalk and Baseball. Doyle came up; the ball didn't. It went right between his legs. The tying run scored, and the next guy got a base hit, game over. We were two outs away from the state title my last high school game, which would have been our second in a row, and we lost.

Doyle was inconsolable in the locker room after the game. I'd never watched a teammate go through something so devastating. I was the one getting drafted and garnering attention. The game should have fallen on my shoulders, win or lose. That was Doyle's last "Game 7." I knew I'd have more.

When I did play my final game against the Cardinals, and I booted my own tailor-made double-play ball, I couldn't help but think of Doyle. I was grateful I didn't have to watch any of my young Braves teammates endure that kind of disappointment. If anybody had to commit a big error in that game, I'm glad it was me.

Mom and Dad were scared the fight might hurt my draft status. I wasn't. I wasn't ashamed of being in a fight. If somebody was going to look down on me because I stood up for myself and duked some kid, then I wasn't the right guy for them. It turns out some baseball people had labeled me a private school GQ. Finding out I had a little bit of fire in my belly might have changed their minds.

And as it turned out, Todd Van Poppel's actions leading up to the draft had a lot bigger impact on my future than anything I did.

From what Bobby Cox told me later, he went to Texas to see Van Poppel and his parents two days before the draft. He wanted to know exactly what they were thinking, to see the look in their eyes, and to hear the conviction in their voices.

Todd's dad looked Bobby dead in the eye and said, "Do not draft Todd. He's not signing. If the Braves draft him, he's going to the University of Texas."

That's all Bobby needed to hear. You cannot whiff on the first pick in the draft. You have to be sure you can sign that guy.

I was in Jacksonville graduating from Bolles that day, and my prom was that night. A bunch of my buddies and I rented a condo on the beach and spent the night. All the girls had to be home, but some of the guys went back out to the beach and had a couple of beers.

At about eleven the next morning I found out that Coach Suriano was frantically looking for me to tell me to call my parents. When I got Dad on the phone, he told me to come home immediately.

"It's prom weekend," I said. "I'm supposed to be out having a good time."

"The Braves want to sign you with the first pick of the draft," he said. "Tony DeMacio is going to be in Daytona Beach at two o'clock today."

"Be right there," I said.

Never in my wildest dreams did I think the

Atlanta Braves were in play. My roommate, Ron Patrick, and I jumped in my Ford Escort and headed down I-95.

I was pretty calm at that point. Ron was freaking out.

"Dude, do you understand that you are fixing to meet with the Atlanta Braves?" he said. "The Atlanta Braves are about to draft you above everybody else who's eligible in the whole country."

"I wasn't nervous until you said that," I said.

Being the number one pick in the draft still seemed a little far-fetched. There had to be a catch.

I told Dad I'd meet them at the Olive Garden in Daytona Beach. It was the first time I talked face-to-face with DeMacio and Jongewaard about my future as an Atlanta Brave. They had come in for the vanilla stuff—the eye test and personality test—but this was different. This was sitting down and hashing out exactly what it would take to sign me.

That's when it really hit home. *Man, these guys are serious. Y'all are talking about making little ol' me from Podunk Pierson, Florida, the number one pick in the draft?*

Over dinner we just exchanged pleasantries. I kept waiting for them to break the ice and talk about money, but they didn't do it there. They waited until we were back in our living room in Pierson before they got down to business.

"We're interested in making you the first player taken in the draft," DeMacio said. "We need to see about your signability."

I didn't have an agent yet, but Dad had talked to a lawyer he met through his coaching friends, and we had numbers in mind of what I might ask for if I was taken in the top ten to fifteen picks.

"Tony, I want to be an Atlanta Brave," I said. "It's the only team in the South. Y'all's minor league teams are here in the South. It's a great fit for me. I don't want to go through this long, drawn-out process of holding out and negotiating for more money. You give me three hundred thousand dollars, and I'll sign on the dotted line right now."

The Orioles had offered the number one pick the year before, Ben McDonald out of LSU, $250,000. (He eventually signed for $350,000 and got a record major league contract, but he had to hold out all season through contentious negotiations between Boras and the Orioles to do it.)

"We need to talk about that," DeMacio said. "We can't give you three hundred thousand. We can give you two hundred and fifty thousand."

Mom, Dad, and I excused ourselves and went upstairs to their bedroom to talk.

"When they say my hand is OK, I want to be playing baseball," I told my parents.

I was getting my cast off in a day or two, but I wasn't going to be able to start playing for about two weeks.

"I don't want to be holding out for signing-bonus money," I said. "What do you always say, Dad? In the grand scheme of things, you're going to make your money at the big league level. The fastest way to make the most money is get to the big leagues as quickly as possible. Let's just go downstairs and meet them in the middle."

"Chip, you know you can get more money than this," Dad said.

"Well," I said. "If they meet us in the middle, I'm getting twenty-five thousand more than the guy would have got last year, which is about right, and we haven't caused any waves. We can be done with this right now, and they haven't even had the draft yet. All we need to know is that the Braves want me, above everybody else. Let's get it done."

We went downstairs and told Tony we'd meet in the middle.

"Great," he said. "I have a contract right here."

I was signed, sealed, and delivered for $275,000 the night before the draft.

Early the next morning, Dad went to the mall in Daytona and bought three Braves caps so he, Mom, and I could wear them to take pictures later in the day.

Our living room was packed. Cars were parked

all over the yard and in the pastures. We had a bunch of family and friends from Pierson and Jacksonville. Coach Suriano and his son drove down. There were some reporters and TV cameras there, too.

I told the reporters I had slept pretty well, but I was nervous. Draft day was one of the biggest days of my life. Signing a piece of paper the night before didn't really bring any finality to it. Until the Braves called on draft day, it wouldn't be official. They told me they'd call at 12:14.

A few minutes after noon, somebody called for Mom. I answered the phone and tried to fake everybody out.

"Yeah," I said. "Mmm. Yep."

Then I said, "Hey, Mom, it's for you!"

Everybody laughed. It was a good tension breaker because 12:14 came and went. Then 12:15. Finally, at 12:16, the phone rang.

I broke into a smile when I heard the words: "It's Paul Snyder, with the Atlanta Braves. We just made you the first pick in the draft."

While I was celebrating with family and friends, Oakland drafted Van Poppel with the fourteenth pick in the first round. Unbeknownst to the Braves and to me, Van Poppel intended to sign with the A's, which he ultimately did for $1.2 million. Van Poppel became the first million-dollar signee, and he got a major league contract.

It didn't bother me in the least. The Braves weren't going to pay me $1.2 million; they balked when I said $300,000. I was where I wanted to be.

Nobody will ever admit to this, but I think secretly the A's and Boras had a deal from well before the draft. We all know now Van Poppel didn't want to play in a losing organization. The A's were the cream of the crop in baseball at the time. They had just won the World Series the year before, and they went back to the World Series in 1990 for a third straight year. The Braves lost ninety-seven games in 1990 and finished dead last in the division.

But I said it all along: If Todd Van Poppel didn't want to be an Atlanta Brave, I was more than happy to take his place.

I saw it as a challenge to help turn the organization around. I had won at every level I played. I knew I was going to help whichever team drafted me win, period. And I think Atlanta and I always suited each other. It's my kind of town— laid-back, where people don't get overly excited about anything. I always felt as though it was home.

You can look back and say that my parents and I were naive and we got taken advantage of, and you might be right. But we're talking about $275,000. Don't get me wrong; that's a nice check in 1990. But you're going to make your money playing in the big leagues, not from your signing bonus. For a while there, the major league draft got out of hand. When you give an eighteen-year-old $10 million with the first pick in the draft, the incentive to work is not there. You've taken care of him and his family forever.

I believe you shouldn't try to manipulate the draft. Baseball is cyclical. The draft is set up so that the weak get stronger and the strong get weaker. I don't think it helps you individually either. Van Poppel was in the big leagues at the end of the following year, at age nineteen. Do you think he was ready?

Boras negotiated the best possible monetary deal for Todd Van Poppel coming out of the 1990 draft, but not necessarily the best deal for Todd Van Poppel the player. Yes, Van Poppel got $1.2 million and he got invited to big league camp, but looking back, most people will probably tell you that wasn't the best scenario for his development.

Where teams can mess up is how they handle their top picks once they're drafted. There's no way an eighteen- or nineteen-year-old kid should be exposed to big league camp, big league life-style, big league hitters that early. A guy has to earn his way to big league camp. If an eighteen-year-old kid feels as if he doesn't belong, that he's in over his head, now you've given him a confidence problem.

To his credit, Van Poppel made it to the big

leagues. Maybe he didn't become the superstar everybody thought he would, but he made it. And he hung around for a long time. Say what you will about him—that he moved around to six different teams, won only forty games in eleven years, and never became the next Roger Clemens—but you can't say Todd Van Poppel wasn't a success.

As for me, I don't have any qualms saying that I was the Braves' plan B. If Todd Van Poppel had told the Atlanta Braves he would sign, I'm fairly confident the Braves would have taken him. I'd venture a guess they're pretty happy he didn't, though.

CHAPTER 5
Carry a Big Stick

Rookie ball had already started when I got my cast off, so I got thrown right in the fire. Pirate City in Bradenton was my first stop. Four of us lived in a room, with two bunk beds. It was like boot camp.

Nothing about Bradenton was fun. Games were at noon in the heat of the day. It was hotter than forty hells. Breakfast was at seven thirty, and nobody slept through it because lunch was just a brown bag with an apple, a baloney sandwich, and Gatorade. There was no nightlife whatsoever. It was the perfect place to stash seventy-five guys to learn about baseball.

That's the minor league process. You've got to eat, drink, and breathe baseball. They want to find out who is soft and weed those guys out. They're going to work you until you throw up. They're going to work you until you're dragging your tongue on the ground, until you can't grip a bat because you've got so many blisters on your hands. And if you keep coming back for more, you are the kind of guy they like.

The whole group consisted of eighteen-, nineteen-, and twenty-year-olds from three different organizations, the Pittsburgh Pirates, Montreal Expos, and Atlanta Braves, staying in one hotel. We ate together, dressed together, and played against each other day in and day out.

I started something like 1-for-11 and there was no escaping it. I would run across a pitcher in the cafeteria who struck me out twice that day. I could feel him looking at me and thinking, "That guy sucks. I could get him out in my sleep." And you know what? At that point, he probably could.

I was already nervous about what people would think of me as the number one pick and because I was using a wood bat in games for the first time in my life. It's one thing to hit with one in batting practice, but this was facing 95-plus mph, and doing it left-handed.

Coming off my broken hand, I knew hitting left-handed was going to be even harder. The hand I broke, my right, was my bottom hand, and it was weak. My bat speed was slow. I couldn't get out in front of anything. I put up the worst numbers in my life. I hit .229 overall with a homer, a triple, and a double. To make matters worse, I made eighteen errors at shortstop in only forty-four games.

When you're the number one pick, you can't strike out. You can't make an error. You can't get thrown out stealing. You're supposed to be the best player in America. You should be a god.

And I wasn't. I heard the cracks guys made. "I can do *that* for two hundred and seventy-five thousand dollars."

I took my share of lumps at the plate, literally. I got hit more during rookie ball than in any other year my entire career in the big leagues. Pitchers drilled me right and left. I know some of them weren't on purpose, but some of them were. You don't get thrown at ten or twelve times by accident.

I was pretty good at getting the hell out of the way, and they were still getting me. There were people sending messages. If it takes drilling the bonus baby to make you feel like a man in front of your teammates, then do what you got to do. But quite frankly, it was stupid. I was an easy out. Hit one of the good players.

You always worry about making friends in a new setting, especially coming in with the stigma of the first pick, but I found guys I hit it off with right away.

I became really good friends with Ralph Garr Jr., Don Robinson, and Mark Chambers. I was the only white guy among them. We would get in the Ford Probe my parents bought me for graduation and go to the Circle K up the street. Chambers was twenty-one, so he would buy all the Boone's Farm Strawberry Hill he could carry, and we'd sit on the hood in the parking lot of the Circle K.

We'd tell war stories until we had to go back for our midnight curfew.

I never had trouble relating to Ralph and those guys. I knew I could walk into the room and they would go, "What's up, CJ?" It was comforting to me. It's nice to see a warm smile and not a sneer.

We used to play tonk, which is an abbreviated gin game you play for money.

"You don't know how to play no tonk," they said the first time I said I wanted to play. "Tonk is a brother game."

"Um, excuse me," I said. "I know exactly what tonk is. I grew up playing tonk."

I played sports—and cards—with guys from all different backgrounds growing up in Pierson. I was a social chameleon, and it helped me fit in during rookie ball when I needed it the most.

The Latin guys used to call me Guasón, which meant "the joker," because they said I had a smile like the Joker in *Batman*. I think a lot of those guys accepted me because I didn't come to camp with a big head. We had a shortstop from Colombia named Cristobal Santoya who was wearing number 10 by the time I got to camp. I didn't ask for it or whine about it. I was late because of my hand, and jerseys had already been given out. There was no sense in ruffling any feathers.

I was the number one pick, but I preferred to keep my head down. Michael Jordan was the man back then, so I took 23.

• • •

The only reason I hit as well as .229 that summer was because for about ten days I quit switch-hitting and hit exclusively right-handed. Right-handed, I wasn't that bad, but left-handed, I was miserable.

I went in to talk to our manager, Jim Procopio, and said, "Just give me a week. Let me hit right-handed and get my numbers up because I'm embarrassed. I'll keep working at the left-handed swing in the cages in the mornings. I'm not going to stop switch-hitting. I just want to quit doing it in the games for a little bit to get some confidence."

"Chip, whatever you want to do, bud," he said.

Two, three, four days went by. I had a couple of really good games. I hit my first professional home run. I had three or four multi-hit games. I raised my average from .200 to .230, .240. Then I woke up one morning and everybody from the front office was in Bradenton. Bobby Cox was there, Bobby Dews, Paul Snyder, Rod Gilbreath. Word had gotten back upstairs to the brass that I wasn't hitting left-handed, and they weren't happy.

They sat me down and said, "You are not stopping switch-hitting."

Even though I told Procopio it was temporary, I learned that's not the way things work. And I didn't see my rookie-ball manager again that year. He got fired for giving me that leeway.

Looking back now, my rookie season wasn't about numbers. It was about starting the process and getting my work in, the numbers be damned. I could have gone down there and hit .300 with fifteen bombs. It still wouldn't have mattered. It was about being committed to switch-hitting.

Switch-hitting is a decision you have to make over and over again. Hitting is hard enough from your natural side. The temptation is always there to give it up when you're scuffling from your off side. And you are hardly ever going good from both sides of the plate at the same time. I went through phases in my career when I didn't want to hit left-handed. But switch-hitting is a skill that separates you. It's a big part of why I was drafted number one.

Dad always said, "It's a lot easier to hit breaking balls, curveballs, and sliders coming into you than going away from you." He was the one who encouraged me to switch-hit, but I was the one who was going to have to hone two different swings, each with its own set of mechanics and challenges. And the only way to get good at it was to do it.

I only hit right-handed against a right-handed pitcher once in nine thousand at-bats in my major league career. We were in Boston facing Tim Wakefield, Mr. Knuckleball anyway. I was feeling really good right-handed, and I was in a funk left-handed. I was having trouble staying back on the knuckleball. I wasn't going to homer off a 68 mph knuckleball anyway. I always relied on the pitchers to provide the power when I hit home runs, so without that 90, 95 mph velocity, I was just going to try to play pepper with the left and center fielders—the old-school game you use to work on hitting the ball on the ground.

TP—Terry Pendleton, who was our hitting coach then and a former switch-hitter—told me he'd always hit right-handed against knuckle-ballers like Wakefield and Tom Candiotti. He thought you were less likely to overswing because it was easier to stay inside the ball from your natural side.

Staying inside the ball means keeping your hands ahead of the bat barrel to create backspin, and backspin makes the ball carry farther. When the barrel leaks out in front of your hands, you come around the ball, and that creates topspin. Those balls duck-hook into the ground and become 6-4-3 double plays.

I told Bobby Cox I wanted to hit right-handed against Wakefield, and he let me try it.

Gary Sheffield led off the ninth with a double, so I had a run-producing opportunity. But I had already made up my mind to go up there right-handed. The whole time I was thinking, *Just go back and get your left-handed helmet and hit a ground ball to second and help the team by moving the runner over with nobody out.* But I was still tempted to try for more. *I can stay inside that knuckleball right-handed, hit a line drive somewhere, and still get the guy over, maybe in.*

But this was not Wakefield's first rodeo. He threw me two sliders—no knuckleballs. I hadn't seen a slider from that angle since that week I hit exclusively right-handed in rookie ball. I hit a line drive to center field, but it was caught for an out.

My saving grace offensively my first year in pro ball was meeting Willie Stargell. I got to know him in instructional league in West Palm Beach after our rookie-ball season ended, and I was in complete awe.

I had been a little bit of an Orioles fan growing up because of my dad. I watched Willie play in the '79 World Series when his Pirates came back from 3–1 down to beat the Orioles. Stargell won the MVP. I liked his style.

My read on him was right. When I met him, I could tell he had one of those magnetic personalities. People loved being around him. He came up to me by the batting cage one day, and the first thing he did was grab my bat.

"Man, I've picked my teeth with bigger pieces of wood than this," he said before getting quickly to business.

"You should swing just as heavy a bat as you can get around on ninety miles an hour."

Then he looked me in the eye and said, "We'll have you hitting thirty homers in no time, son."

I'm just coming off a year where I had one homer, one triple, and one double, and he's got me hitting thirty homers?

"Your body is going to change, and you're going to get bigger and stronger," he said, reading my surprised expression. "You should be using a heavier bat in batting practice. Before you know it, you'll incorporate that heavy bat into game situations."

A lot of people think if a guy is throwing 100 mph, you've got to swing harder. Stargell preached shortening up and just making sure you got that big bat barrel where it needed to be at the right time and letting the pitcher provide all the power.

He gave me this big ol' K44 to use. They called them "44 magnums." It must have been 33 inches long and weighed 34 ounces. Most of the time in rookie ball, I had swung a 32-inch, 30-ounce P72 or M110. I liked the way the ball came off the K44, but I didn't like the feel of it. If I was going to swing a bigger bat, it was going to take some time.

I called Dad that night to see what he thought.

"When Willie Stargell tells you something, you respect him enough to heed that advice," he said.

"I'm not going to tell you differently. I was more of a flat-bat, short-swing, hit-.300 type of hitter. They obviously see a lot more potential in you not only to hit .300 but to hit thirty-plus homers. You've advanced well beyond what I can teach you now."

Dad never let his own ego get in the way of my development as a hitter. And that conversation set the tone for the rest of my career. I would get the best of both worlds—heeding the advice of some incredible hitting coaches like Willie Stargell and Don Baylor while having a vigilant dad who knew my swing better than anybody.

Like Stargell, Frank "Hondo" Howard was one of our roving instructors, coaches who bounced around from one Braves minor league team to another during the season. Frank Howard was an icon, too—not just in the Braves organization but throughout baseball. Everybody loved the guy. He was a behemoth of a man, six foot eight with this big, bellowing voice that commanded respect.

He was probably fifty-five, sixty years old when I first met him, but to me he still seemed like Adonis. He was still out there, pounding fungoes (ground balls that coaches hit to fielders from a long, thin bat) and throwing batting practice. He was just a baseball lifer.

Hondo had this old-school windup. He'd go

over his head, with this big leg kick. I was taking BP off him in the tunnel under the stadium one day and it was 100-plus degrees in there. We were all sweating BBs, and Hondo went over his head and fell out backwards. I dropped my bat and ran over to him.

I said, "Hondo, man, are you OK?" I thought I had just witnessed my first heart attack.

"Of course I'm all right," he said, in that deep gravelly voice. "Now help me up and get your ass back in the batter's box."

At that point I just laughed. I gave him a hand and pulled him up. I think he had a little dizzy spell. He never lost consciousness, but it was a scary moment. He stopped long enough to get a sip of water before he went right back to the L screen and started throwing BP again.

Hondo could walk that fine line. He would bust your ass for three hours, and you'd be walking off the field dripping sweat, but he'd be right there with you. He'd give you a "Nice job today, son," in his deep voice. "Did good. Get ready to do it again tomorrow."

Everybody rolled their eyes, but we knew the guy was cool. We hated him at eight o'clock in the morning when we were walking on the field, but we loved him at four o'clock in the afternoon when we were walking off.

Hondo talked a lot about the mental part of the game. He'd walk up to me and say, "Chip, who

102

you got today?" meaning the opposing pitcher.

I'd tell him a guy's name, and he'd say, "What's he got for ya?"

I'd reel off the pitcher's repertoire.

"He's got a little changeup? Little curveball?" he'd say. "Just wait for the heater and hit it off the cocksucker's forehead."

He said that every day, and we loved it. That was Hondo.

Climbing the minor league ladder, you had to find coaches you clicked with, who made you better without tearing you down. Carlos Rios, my infield instructor in rookie ball, was another one of those guys.

I took a lot of heat from other players, teammates, and even coaches in rookie ball, but Carlos would come up and pat me on the back after a rough day.

"You're good," he'd say. "Do it again tomorrow. You'll get it. Don't worry about it."

I needed that. I had heard so much negativity from so many people. I know there were coaches in our system who didn't think I was worthy. They busted my hump really hard. Carlos busted my hump, but at the end of the day, he always had something positive to say. He was a great coach, very thorough. And he had his work cut out with me. For one thing, the Braves didn't like the way I started the double play.

I used to round the ball off toward my right

foot, catch it, and get rid of it. Once you catch the ball, your hands, your glove, the ball, they're fairly close to the ground, so it seemed like the natural thing and the quickest thing to throw it from down there.

Carlos wanted me to center the ball in the middle of my body, to bring the glove into my belt buckle, and then make the transition from catch to throw. And he wanted me to get a little more over the top with my throws. Second basemen were telling Carlos they couldn't pick up the ball coming from me. They thought my glove was in the way. So I had to learn to tuck my glove and make sure I was showing them the ball.

All that was quite an adjustment because I was more of an instinctual shortstop. I just played the game. Whatever was the quickest way to get the ball to second base, that's what I did.

We went through buckets upon buckets of balls, working on pivots. I became a robot. Bring it in, bring it to the middle, get the glove out of the way, feed it to second. You can't imagine how many balls they can stuff in that bucket. And it's one after the other. You throw it, and you're right back in your ready position, in a squat.

I think it was a mental test, too. The Braves wanted to see if I was mentally tough enough to do buckets, day after day after day in that heat.

Part of me thinks that it gave the coaches

something to ride me about, maybe knock me down a few pegs. Here I was, first pick in the draft, bonus baby, cocky. Honestly, though, it was great for me. I wasn't so bullheaded as to think I knew everything. I needed to show everybody— the coaching staff included—that I was not afraid to work and sweat and bleed and do what it took to get better. I wanted to be great. To get there, I needed a guy like Carlos, and I'm forever thankful to him.

CHAPTER 6
Major Motivation

In spring training of 1991, we had roughly eighty-five to ninety newbies in the Braves organization, between the draft and players signed from Latin America. They herded us like sheep into the middle of a field at the complex in West Palm Beach one day so David Justice could speak to us.

David had just won the National League Rookie of the Year in 1990. He was a good-looking guy, engaged to Halle Berry. Everyone in the organization knew who he was.

"Look around," he said. "Look at all your buddies and everybody. Out of these ninety guys sitting here, one, maybe two of y'all are ever going to don a major league uniform. Who is it going to be? Is it going to be you?"

I don't know if he was trying to discourage us or pump us up, but he got our attention. He said it in a pretty matter-of-fact way, and he was right. Tony Graffanino and I were the only two guys out of that group who ever wore a big league uniform.

It's pretty incredible when you think about the percentage of guys drafted who actually make a major league squad at any point. It's something like 3 percent. That's what the whole minor league process is, a gradual weeding out. You start with three rookie-ball teams, you go to two A-ball teams, and then you've got one Double-A team. The true prospects make it up to Triple-A, where you also have guys coming down who can't hack it at the big league level. Whoever perseveres gets the call.

You find out if you really want to play baseball.

As much as I struggled in the beginning, I'm glad I did because it motivated me. I was embarrassed by the way I played in rookie ball. And the surest way to motivate me? Embarrass me.

I needed to get bigger. I needed to get stronger. I needed to get in the weight room and improve in every facet. Taylor High School had an old double-wide trailer they used as a weight room. During the offseason after rookie ball, I worked out there for two hours before everybody got to school. After school, Dad hit me ground balls.

Even on weekends, when Dad and I woke up at the butt crack of dawn and went hunting, we came back at lunch and worked out all afternoon. When I needed to be spotted on the bench press or squat rack, Dad was there.

When I got to spring training in 1991, I was ten to fifteen pounds heavier. I came in thinking, *Man, they better not send me back to rookie ball.*

I expected to advance one classification each year all the way up to the big leagues. That was the natural progression.

What did I do in rookie ball to deserve to play in Macon, the low-A team, my second season? Not a goddamn thing, but coming into spring training in 1991, I was so confident. I was healthy. I was strong. I was swinging the bat good. I felt good defensively.

The day I got to West Palm, they had the Macon roster posted on the bulletin board. I wasn't on it. The Braves had me going back to Bradenton.

It wasn't even Pulaski, Virginia, or Idaho Falls, the advanced rookie league team, where you're playing 7:05 P.M. games. They wanted me back in Bradenton, going through all those drills again at seven o'clock in the morning. I was dumbfounded, and livid.

Chuck LaMar—the farm director then—came up to me that first morning.

"I know you're pissed at me, but I don't see you on that Macon roster right now," he said. "Where you go at the end of this spring? Completely up to you."

All I could think was *OK, well, we'll see.*

I was all business. I wasn't talking to anybody. I was pissed off. And when it was all said and done, I played maybe ten games in spring training with that rookie-ball team.

"You've done some work this offseason,"

LaMar acknowledged one morning. "It's good to see. You're playing your ass off. We're promoting you to the Macon squad tomorrow."

"Fuck yeah!" I said, looking him in the eye. "That's what I'm talking about."

My work in the offseason paid off; my broken hand was behind me, and I was starting to make good on some of the promise the brass saw when they drafted me.

Since I was late making Macon's roster, I didn't have a roommate. Tyler Houston, the Braves' number one pick the year before me, needed a roommate, too. He had just been sent down from high-A Durham to Macon at the end of spring training.

The Braves drafted Houston as a catcher with the second overall pick in 1989. People were calling him the best high school hitting prospect since Darryl Strawberry, who was the best high school hitter anybody had ever seen. It was a lot to live up to.

When Tyler got sent down to Macon and I got called up, he was not happy. He wanted to hate me. Never in a million years would I have thought he and I would become best buds. But we did.

Tyler had a little bit of a reputation. He was intense. He had a short fuse, and it rubbed some people the wrong way. He was brash and arrogant, and he didn't put up a lot of numbers to back that attitude up.

I don't think the Braves really wanted us rooming together. They worried about the dynamic, but they also probably hoped it might motivate Tyler. I think it motivated both of us. If one of us did something good on the field, the other one was jealous. But it was a good kind of motivation because we pushed each other. We showed up and we played hard every day.

We lived in an apartment on the west side of Macon. Two bedrooms, two-story. Good little place. We had fifteen guys on the team, all about nineteen years old, who had never been to college, living in that apartment complex. We were living the frat life. Our apartment was party central.

Rookie ball had been pure work. In A-ball, it was time to have some fun with the game again. I had never played in front of five thousand people before, so when they packed old Luther Williams Field in Macon for a seven o'clock game against the Augusta Pirates, I thought it was the greatest thing in the world. *Now, this is what professional baseball should be about.*

You got to sleep in, get yourself ready to play for seven o'clock, and go out and experience minor league life afterward.

We dressed more like professional baseball players, too. When you're nineteen and twenty years old in A-ball, you try to dress as much like a big leaguer as you can. Tyler and I were the first two guys in Macon to wear Pony high-tops. Eric Davis started wearing them with the Reds in 1990, and by 1991 they were catching on in the minors.

I started wearing mock-Ts that year, too. A bunch of the Atlanta Braves wore mock turtlenecks in cold weather, the navy-blue ones with a cursive red "Braves" on the collar. I wore the mock-Ts all summer. I was tall and skinny, and the plain T-shirts made my neck look long.

That was the year I was starting to get comfortable in my Braves "uni." I was finally getting comfortable in the left-handed batter's box, too.

Probably the best piece of advice I ever got about how to work at switch-hitting was from Hondo, Frank Howard. He told me to take twice as many swings from my weak side as I did from my strong side. "It's boring," he said. "You're going to take your lumps. It's going to be discouraging at times, but one day it'll click. When you get to the point where you'd much rather walk to the plate left-handed than right-handed, you've arrived as a switch-hitter."

I was hitting only .274 at the All-Star break, and I rarely found the sweet spot left-handed, but I was working at it. For every fifty swings I took right-handed, I took a hundred swings left-handed, whether it was tee work, flips from a coach, or live BP. I taped up each finger on both hands and then wrapped tape around my palms like a boxer. Then I wore two pairs of batting gloves on top of it just to endure the blisters. That's what you've got to do to get both swings on par.

Hondo was right. Hitting left-handed finally clicked for me. We were facing Bobby Jones, the Mets' first-round pick that year out of Fresno State. I always took facing a first-round pick as a challenge: I never wanted anyone to come out of a meeting with me, thinking, "I got him."

Jones was making his first professional start for Columbia. Watching him warm up and face the first couple of batters, I thought, *Man, this guy is not overpowering, but he knows what he's doing.* He had three, four pitches and threw them where he wanted. He was the first pitcher I faced in pro ball where I said to myself, *That guy is going to be in the big leagues.*

He stuck it to me pretty good my first at-bat, and I grounded out. But in my second, I hit a fastball out to right center field at Luther Williams Field. We hit three solo homers and beat him 3–0. After that swing, hitting from the left side started to feel like second nature. I went on a tear.

They didn't get me out the second half of that

112

year. If a pitcher threw it over the plate, I centered it. I raised my average 50 points and by the end of the year, I was hitting .326 with 15 homers, 98 RBIs, more than 100 runs, and 40 stolen bases.

Getting that hot came as a result of a lot of hard work and, quite possibly, as my buddies kidded me, from meeting Karin.

Our third baseman, Geoff Orr, came up to me one day and said, "I've got this girl you need to meet. She said something about you the other night when we were all hanging out." I knew exactly who he was talking about: the blonde from the pool hall.

I'd been out with a couple of the guys and caught her looking at me. Oh, I was looking back, but I didn't act on it. I didn't know if she was with Geoff, and I wasn't going to step on anybody's toes. But after Geoff gave me the green light, I was psyched up to meet her. I saw her again a couple of nights later at one of the guys' apartments after a game.

Her name was Karin Fulford, and she was beautiful. We sat outside and talked for hours. I was completely smitten. She was older. She was smart, funny. I've always been attracted to alpha females—women who give it back to me just as voraciously as I give it to them—and she stood toe-to-toe with me. That was attractive. She seemed to have her own thing going and didn't need me to be successful. She was going to Wesleyan College there in Macon. She was an early childhood education major and very focused. Not only was she a beautiful girl, but she had her head on straight. I fell in love with Karin hard.

I couldn't get enough of her. We went everywhere together. We did everything together. I couldn't wait to get back to Macon from off the road. I couldn't wait until games were over, so I could see her.

That frat life we had been living in Macon the first two months of the season was getting old. Karin was good for me. We would come home and chill out after games. She kept me from staying out in clubs and hanging out with the fellas until the wee hours of the morning.

Any player will tell you that when his off-the-field life is going well, it usually coincides with things going good on the field. I was red-hot at the plate from the day I met her.

Karin would probably say she cleaned me up a little. I was a country kid, a redneck in every sense of the word. I wore my hat backwards and a gold crucifix around my neck. I drove a Corvette with a vanity plate that said CHIP23.

I had asked my parents if they would mind if I traded in the Probe they gave me for a Corvette shortly after I got my bonus money. I wanted to do one fun thing with it and put the rest away for a down payment on my first house. I loved that Corvette. It was black with a removable glass top. I thought it was the coolest thing on the planet. It didn't last long.

Karin was basically living with me the next year in Durham and Greenville, and moving two people from town to town in a Corvette was not easy. So we traded it in for a Ford Explorer, which was a lot more practical.

I was nineteen and already settling down.

I got to know David Justice when he came to Macon on a minor league rehab assignment during our playoff series at the end of that year. Tyler knew him from being in big league camp, and he and DJ got along well, which opened the door for me.

"Aha, so *this* is the Golden Child," Justice said, in that animated voice of his, when I walked up. Everybody around the cage started laughing.

The Eddie Murphy movie *The Golden Child* had come out a few years prior, about a social worker rescuing a young boy with mystical powers.

"What are you hitting?" he said.

".320-something," I said.

"Dahammm," he said, giving *damn* about three syllables. "You might really be the Golden Child, huh?"

We hung out, took BP together. He watched

me and gave me some things to work on. He was hilarious and really cool.

He was there for four or five games. He hit a home run to help us win a game against Columbia, even though we ended up losing the series. When he left, he gave me one of his bats.

"I'll see you in Atlanta in a couple years," he said. "You're going to be there. Don't worry about it. Just keep your head down and do your thing."

I was already feeling pretty good about where I stood. I had done my best to shut out the pressure that comes with the "number one pick" moniker. I probably would have felt more pressure if I actually thought I'd been the best player in that draft. But I didn't have that kind of bravado. I always believed certain teams needed certain players, and going number one to the Braves ultimately came down to luck and good timing.

I did have confidence, though, that I would eventually make the big leagues as long as I worked hard. At the end of the 1991 season, I just wanted the call to hurry up and get here.

The Braves were in the throes of a pennant race with the Dodgers, making their worst-to-first run to win their first of fourteen straight division titles. We were in instructional league in West Palm Beach, watching it unfold every night on TV. On the way back to our hotel, we'd stop and buy a case of beer and watch the last three or four innings of their game. We all felt in some way we were a part of it.

Watching the Braves lose Game 7 of the World Series to the Twins was a heartbreaker, but I think deep down we all wanted to be on the first Braves team that won a championship. I was amazed at the epic series they played against Minnesota in 1991. I was beyond jacked up watching Sid Bream slide home to beat the Pirates in the National League Championship Series the following year. But both times a little part of me said, *I hope I'm there when they win the first one.*

CHAPTER 7

On the Defensive

Playing in the minor leagues was definitely a *Bull Durham* kind of experience. That movie is one of my favorites because a lot of it rings true. The interaction with the guys, the bus rides. The luggage racks up top are enclosed now but they used to be open and guys slept on them because it was the only place you could stretch out. On twelve-hour bus rides, you find out if you want to play baseball for a living.

We stayed at a lot of La Quinta Inns. One day I asked one of the Latin guys, "What does La Quinta mean?"

"Denny's in the lobby," he said.

Every La Quinta we stayed in had a Denny's either in the lobby or right next door, and we loved it. With only eleven dollars for meal money, we had to eat at some pretty cheap places. Denny's and Shoney's—wherever there was a buffet—you could find our team bus.

By the end of the season in Macon, the only thing holding me back was my defense at shortstop. I had 33 errors at the All-Star break but I still made the South Atlantic League All-Star Game.

Guys—namely Tyler—were coming up to me saying, "Really?" when they found out.

All I could say was "I don't vote."

I could make the backhand-in-the-hole-and-jump play—the play Derek Jeter made throughout his career with the Yankees—on instinct. I could make the bare-handed play in my sleep. I could go up the middle, pirouette, throw blind to first, and hit the first baseman right in the chest. But you hit me a routine three-hopper that I could take a crow hop on before throwing to first, and I would throw that son of a bitch out of the park.

Some of the fans in Macon thought it would be funny to wear catcher's gear and sit in the stands over our first base dugout. It was pretty funny, but it also pissed me off. I had a cannon back in the day, but I only had one speed: all out. I couldn't flip it over there. I had to rear back and let it rip to know where it was going. I didn't have that finesse Cal used to have, with that fluid toss from a lower arm slot to just get the runner by a half step every time.

The coaches tinkered with my release point and my transfer from the glove so much in rookie ball that throwing the ball across the infield became more mental than anything else. I got to where I was hoping balls weren't hit to me.

My teammates put a "chip-o-meter" calendar up on the board in the clubhouse. They were going to tear off pages until I got to 50 errors.

"I've got way more than that in me, guys," I said. "Y'all better get some more pieces of paper up there."

I think some of them, in their own twisted way, were trying to encourage me to clean up that part of my game. It wasn't that I wasn't working at it. Heck, I worked harder on my defense than hitting coming up through the minors.

I actually improved over the second half in Macon, but I still finished with 56 errors. In A-ball, that's hard to do. That's one every three games, and it seemed a lot more frequent than that.

I was embarrassed by how terrible I was defensively that year. I was named the number one prospect in the league for my offensive performance, but I knew there was a lot of room for improvement. I believed my bat would get me to the big leagues but I was worried my glove might keep me out.

The Braves brought in a bunch of different coaches to try to straighten me out defensively. But I made my biggest strides in the offseason, working at home with Dad.

Sometimes defense was all we did. My throws weren't getting any better and one day Dad finally said, "Let's get on the mound and try to find your release point. You could dot a gnat's ass from sixty feet six inches in high school. Why can't you now?"

So we got back on the mound, me throwing and him catching, and all of a sudden I found my release point. That was it. The throw from shortstop could be twice as far as any pitch, but I just needed to use that same three-quarters arm slot I'd used on the pitcher's mound.

By the All-Star break in Durham the following year, I had only 12 errors. The biggest obstacle between me and the majors was starting to fade.

I didn't want to go to Durham in 1992. I wanted to go to Greenville and play for our Double-A team. I'd played with all the Double-A guys during spring training: Mike Kelly, Javy Lopez, Tony Tarasco, Ed Giovanola, Eddie Perez, Tim Gillis, Ryan Klesko, Ramon Caraballo. I could play with those guys. I could hit Double-A pitching. But with my defense still suspect, they sent me back down to Durham, our high-A team.

"This is not a demotion," Chuck LaMar told me. "We'd like to take the natural progression with you. You're still on target for a classification a year, which is normal. Trust me. If you prove to us you don't need to be in Durham, you won't be in Durham anymore."

I knew if I played well, I'd get called up. Of course, Melvin Nieves, another top prospect for the Braves, hit ten homers the first two weeks of the season in Durham, and he was gone. I thought, *Great, I'm going to be here all year.*

I didn't get off to a very good start offensively. Our manager, Leon Roberts, hit me leadoff—for the first and only time in my career. I was hitting .270 with 4 homers and 30 RBIs at the break, not exactly tearing it up.

About the only thing I had to say for myself offensively was that I hit the bull. At the old DAP, the Durham Athletic Park, you got a free steak if you hit the bull down the right field line. I homered 310 feet to the opposite field off Alan Embree, a lefty and a future teammate of mine, and hit the bull. I never did see a free steak. They gave me a certificate, but I wasn't around long enough to use it.

Apparently, all the Braves needed to see was that I was playing pretty good defense. I was 0-for-4 the night Leon called me into his office and told me I was going up to Greenville.

As ready as I'd thought I'd been for Double-A before the season started, I was still intimidated when I got there. Greenville's lineup was stacked. Javy Lopez was hitting sixth, and he was on his way to winning MVP of the Southern League. They had guys like Mike Bell, who had been in the big leagues. When I showed up, Jeff Treadway was there on rehab assignment.

Treadway was playing second base my first game. The first ground ball hit to me was a double-play ball. I gave Treadway a bad feed and almost got him annihilated at second base. *This guy's going to think I'm terrible.* I went up to him and apologized. He said, "Hey, man, first game here. I'm sure you're a little nervous. Just try to get that throw to the outside of the bag, all right?"

We were facing Steve Trachsel, the soon-to-be major leaguer who got called up to the big leagues with the Cubs the next year. My first at-bat, I doubled to the right center field gap and finally relaxed. *Whew, I belong here,* I thought. *I can do this.*

I took off from there. I had eight extra-base hits in my first nine games. It's no coincidence that's also when I discovered the perfect bat.

Tony Tarasco, a stud on that Greenville team and one of my good friends, had gotten some bats from Ron Gant. Ron, who was coming off back-to-back 30-homer seasons in center field for the Braves, was a protégé of Willie Stargell, too. He swung a big bat, a 35-inch, 34-ounce Rawlings MS20. I picked one up and immediately fell in love with it.

The first bat I used in rookie ball was a 32-inch, 30-ounce Louisville M110. But since my conversation with Stargell, I had been gradually increasing the size of my bats. One of our coaches, Sonny Jackson, gave me a 36-inch, 36-ounce bat to take home for the offseason after rookie ball. The idea was to get used to a bigger bat by taking BP with something bigger than you'd ever use in a game.

"Tape up the barrel," he said, "and it'll last you the whole offseason."

Not only did it last that offseason but the next. I bet I took five thousand swings with that bat before it broke. And by the time I got Gant's 35, 34 MS20 in my hands, it was nothing.

I was swinging what most people think is a log but putting out less effort to hit the ball farther. Willie was right. The ball started jumping off my bat. It was like magic. There wasn't a fastball I couldn't square up.

I ended up with 17 doubles, 11 triples, and 9 homers in 67 games for Greenville. The 11 triples was a Southern League record, and I was only there for half a season.

I swung that same model bat—a blond ash Rawlings MS20 with a blue stripe—for the next twenty years.

Nobody coaches you in the minor leagues on how to handle women. My mom had tried, but I wasn't listening. Before I left home for rookie ball, she sat me down and warned me.

"Watch your back," she said. "There are going to be people trying to take advantage of you, and the women are going to come fast and easy. Just be careful."

I didn't think that applied to me. I was ready to settle down two years into my professional career. From the time I was a little kid, I always wanted to get married and have kids, and I was head over heels. Karin was good for me from a stability standpoint. And I didn't ever want to be away from her.

When I told my parents I was going to propose to Karin, they didn't like the idea, but what were they going to say? They married young, too. My mom was twenty, Dad was twenty-three. And they've been together for more than forty years now. Bottom line is it works for some people; it doesn't work for others.

I was twenty when Karin and I got married on September 12, 1992. I had to miss a playoff game for the ceremony. We had planned the wedding the year before, and that was the only time we could get the church. I figured I'd be in between the regular season and instructional ball at that point, and I would have been, had I stayed in Durham. But when I got called up to Greenville, I knew we were going to the playoffs. That team was awesome; we ended up winning 100 games that year. I knew we had a chance to win a championship and I realized, *Oh shit. I'm going to have to miss a game.*

The Braves wanted me to cancel the wedding. That was not going to happen. I think my teammates knew it wasn't my fault. I didn't want to miss that game either, trust me.

After the series opener in Greenville, I drove to Atlanta and got married while my teammates played Game 2 and lost. I woke up at five the morning after my wedding and drove to Chattanooga for Game 3, which started at noon.

We had a monster game and beat John Roper, who went on to pitch in the big leagues with the Reds. The series went five games, and we hammered them in the finale, which helped get me off the hook.

Little did I realize then, missing a playoff game was just foreshadowing for how poorly timed my getting married was. That ceremony came about five years too soon. I thought I was ready. I was nowhere close. My mom was right.

I was still waiting on the major league call, but that winter I got my first brush with the big time. I got to live out my dad's biggest childhood dream. I got to meet Mickey Mantle.

I used to do autograph shows during the off-season in and around Atlanta for extra cash. I was geared up for your run-of-the-mill card show in Lawrenceville, a suburb north of Atlanta, one day when the card company rep told me I'd be signing with Mickey Mantle. *Me? And Mickey Mantle?* He could have been Jesus Christ for all I had heard about him in my house growing up.

The card show was being billed as the ol' great switch-hitter and the up-and-comer. The night before, I practiced introducing myself in the mirror.

"Hi, Mr. Mantle, how are you?"

"Hey, Mickey, what's going on?"

When I actually met him, I froze. I walked up, shook his hand, and basically threw up in my mouth.

"How you doin', kid," he said in his slow Oklahoma drawl, all cool and laid-back.

Something like *hemmnnnheiii* came out of my mouth. I eventually mustered up a "Nice to meet you."

"You ready to do this?" he said.

"Sure," I said, in my best attempt to loosen up.

I loosened up as the day went on, but I was just the first of many to get tongue-tied around Mantle that day. People were fawning over him. Guys walked up with tears in their eyes; women couldn't shut up. It was uncomfortable just watching it unfold. Mantle took it with a grain of salt, signed their stuff, and sent them on their way.

From where I sat to Mantle's left, I could see a fifth of Jack Daniel's under the table. Periodically he poured it into a cup he had on the table.

It was eleven o'clock in the morning, but to each his own. I wasn't going to judge Mickey Mantle. I had my own vices. The man was a hell of a ballplayer, and I thought it was pretty cool that I was sitting there signing autographs right next to him.

A lot of people didn't even know I was there;

they were so enamored of Mickey. If anybody knew me, it was by name and not by appearance. Most people bypassed me, and that was fine. I had enough presence of mind to shut up and listen. I wanted to see how Mantle treated people, how he handled himself, and he set a good example that day. He tried to accommodate as many people as he could. He signed for three hours solid. He was cordial throughout.

We ate barbecue together for lunch. At one point, I leaned over and said, "Man, seeing all these people go crazy over you, do you ever get tired of this? It's still new for me. I still think it's pretty cool."

He laughed and told me about a recurring dream he had: He is standing at the pearly gates with this worried look on his face like "Is he going to let me in?" God looks at him and says, "Mick, I'm going to let you in. But can you sign these dozen baseballs first?"

I laughed of course, and then I asked him to sign a couple balls. I wasn't about to pass up the chance to get something for my dad.

Dad still has that signed ball, barbecue smudge and all. He says it's his most prized possession.

By Triple-A in 1993, I couldn't think about anything else: *Get me to the big leagues.* We were one phone call away, and everybody knew it. It was time to grow up. And that Richmond team had a different dynamic than any other minor league team I played on; we hated each other.

We had eight position players who had been told by everybody how great we were, and we believed it. We were a who's who of top prospects: Javy, Ryan Klesko, Ramon Caraballo, me, Jose Oliva, Melvin Nieves, Mike Kelly, and Tony Tarasco. Everybody in our Triple-A lineup ended up making the big leagues at one time or another, and in 1993 we were young, brash, and cocky.

But our pitching staff was inconsistent. They were a bunch of older guys on their way out, and they weren't happy about it. Guys like Shawn Holman, Mike Birkbeck, Mike Loynd, and Randy St. Claire. If we got beat 10–9, our young guys bitched about the pitching.

Our clubhouse was combustible. We had Puerto Ricans, Dominicans, white guys, black guys, guys from the hood—a bunch of different ethnic backgrounds. We were at each other's throats constantly.

I got into it with Melvin Nieves. He drove a Lexus, and he used to park under the stadium in Richmond. Everybody else had to park outside. I got sick of it.

"Who died and made you God?" I said. "Why do you get to park underneath?"

Both of us were standing in the home dugout there at the Diamond in Richmond right before a game.

"Don't worry about it," he said.

Then he jabbed me in the face. He had his glove on, but I went ballistic. I picked him up and body-slammed him. When I did, my feet went out from under me, and I fell face-first into a dugout step. I had a big knot in the middle of my forehead for a week.

The next day I beat Melvin to the ballpark, and I parked in that spot under the stadium. When he got to the clubhouse, I said, "I bet your ass didn't park underneath today, did you?"

"That's fucked up, man," he said.

"Yep," I said. "I'll be here at noontime every day. Tomorrow I'm going to let Tarasco park underneath there."

I let it go after a while, but I'd made my point. Pretty soon the team decided everybody could park under there.

It's not as if I normally had problems with Melvin. Melvin and I were roommates in spring training one year. It was just stress. I think anytime there's a fight in the clubhouse or dugout it's stress. Guys don't hate each other. You can count on three fingers the guys I played with that I actually hated in twenty-three years with the Braves.

Jose Oliva was one of them.

We didn't catch him in the act, but from what I saw and heard, Oliva broke one of the cardinal rules of the clubhouse: He stole some of my bats.

I came in one day after BP, and one of the bat boxes on top of my locker was open. *Somebody's been in there.* I looked over at Oliva's locker, and he had a freshly taped box. It was the end of the season. He was about to go home to the Dominican. I asked our trainer to open the box above Oliva's locker while we were out for BP. Sure enough, he found three of my bats and three of Javy's in there. I don't know if he wanted them to sell at home in the offseason or use a couple himself. One thing guys don't stand for in a locker room is teammates stealing from each other. We leave everything right there: our wallets, our rings, our watches.

When we confronted him, Oliva denied it. He got into it with some of the guys over it, but I didn't fight him. After the Melvin thing, I was done fighting. But some other guys wanted a piece of him. Brian Hunter and Keith Mitchell— those boys wanted to fight every day.

Keith was a crazy man. When he snapped, you didn't want to be anywhere close, even when you were on his side in a brawl.

We got in a brouhaha playing the Indians' Triple-A affiliate one night in Richmond. That Charlotte team had a lot of the same guys we ended up facing two years later in the World Series—Manny Ramirez, Jim Thome, and Chad Ogea.

Our teams didn't like each other. Jim and I

always talked; I loved Manny Ramirez, but it was something about their pitchers and our hitters. They had a bunch of major league guys on the way down, and we were minor league guys on the way up. We hit a lot of homers and stole a lot of bases. We were cocky and talked shit and I'd have wanted to deck some of our guys, too.

Well, this one game, Klesko walked off a homer against Dave Eiland, who's now the pitching coach for the Royals. Klesko whirly-birded the bat, started walking up the first base line and yelled like a fucking idiot.

Later in the game, we were kicking their ass pretty good, and they brought in their closer, Bill Wertz, in the bottom of the eighth, even though they were losing. The kid threw 96, 97 mph, and Klesko was coming up. The writing was on the wall: Something was coming.

The first pitch to Klesko was behind him. The benches cleared, but nothing happened. The next pitch was right down the middle, but Klesko flung his bat directly over the pitcher's head into center field. Here we go. Donnybrook.

I got to the pile and the first person I saw was Keith. He was on top, with somebody just drilling him. So I picked him up—Keith's a little guy but yolked—and slung him off the pile. It was the first brawl I'd ever been in, so all I was doing was grabbing people and chucking guys off.

Next thing I know, Thome had me pinned up against the netting behind the backstop. My face was pressed against it, and he was saying, "Don't fucking move." I was thinking, *I'm done.* I was six three, 185 pounds soaking wet. Jim Thome was six two, 230. He was manhandling me. I looked over and my mom was sitting three seats over, gasping.

After the game, we were all in the showers and Keith walked in and said, "Which one of you motherfuckers grabbed me?"

I didn't say a word. I was scared to death of the guy.

"Don't none of y'all motherfuckers ever grab me again when we're in a fight," he said. "You grab dudes from the other team. You don't grab your own teammates in a brawl. Y'all motherfuckers test me again, I'll kill you."

I knew I had to say something, but I wasn't about to do it naked, in front of God and everybody in the middle of the shower. So I prolonged my shower. Everybody else left, and it was just me and Keith.

"Eh, Mitch," I said. "It was me that grabbed you. I got to the pile and just started grabbing everybody. I apologize. It's my first brawl. I didn't really know how to handle it."

He was cool about it.

"Chip, don't ever grab me because I'm liable to knock you out," he said. "Never grab your own teammates. That's the rule. You always grab someone from the other team."

That's something I never forgot. We were in only two or three brawls my whole career, but I made sure never to pull a teammate off the pile. As for Jim Thome, he and I didn't like each other before that day, but since then, we have been the best of buddies. We still laugh about that game.

I had a lot to learn about the mental side of the game, whether it was handling myself in a brawl or dealing with a bad at-bat.

One night in Charlotte, I struck out with a guy on third and one out—easy scoring opportunity—I went to slam my bat in the bat rack and my hand slipped off the knob. The bat bounced back up and popped me in the mouth. My two front teeth broke off halfway down and were embedded in the knob of the bat.

Pretty much everybody on the team saw me do it. Our manager, Grady Little, followed me down into the tunnel and said, "Are you OK?"

"Yeah, I'm OK," I said. "But I'm on fire. This doesn't feel too good. I need to go get it fixed."

"All right," he said. "I'll take you out of the game.

"Needless to say," he added. "I hope you've learned a valuable lesson."

He said it matter-of-factly, not in a patronizing way. Grady is a great baseball man. He's down-home, with a Southern drawl—my speed—and

I really enjoyed playing for him. I was probably closer with Grady than any manager I ever played for, including Bobby. He had a punch line for everything, but he'd stick his foot in your rear when you needed it, too.

"It'll never happen again," I said.

And it didn't. I struck out fourteen hundred times in my career at the big league level. I can't ever remember going into the tunnel and breaking a bat or throwing my helmet off the wall, none of that. I occasionally threw my helmet or my bat at home plate out of frustration with an umpire, but that was it.

So I had to find a dentist in Charlotte, North Carolina. I used to have a gap between my two front teeth, like my dad. That night I had to get them bonded before the ol' chip off the old block had a little too much chip.

The highlight of my Triple-A season was facing the Rocket. Roger Clemens threw a rehab start for the Red Sox's Triple-A team in Pawtucket that July while he was coming back from a groin injury.

It was a day game in Pawtucket. We had known we were going to face him for a couple of days, so everybody was up bright and early. We got on the bus to head to the ballpark, and nobody said a word. Usually it was jovial; "Fuck you" this and that. We were all just sitting there thinking, *This is my one opportunity against Roger Clemens.*

Tarasco got up in front of the bus and broke the silence.

"What are y'all, a bunch of scared motherfuckers this morning?" he said. "Damn, we are always hyped up on the bus and having fun, and y'all got your heads up your butts. Y'all are facing Roger motherfucking Clemens today, and we are going to rock that ass."

Everybody busted out laughing. We loosened up after that, but I was still nervous. It's Roger Clemens. He's one of the best pitchers of our era, of all time.

I knew I'd get at least two at-bats against him, and I wanted to take advantage of that chance. I couldn't wait to see what Clemens's heater was like.

Coming up through the minors, I believed I could turn around anybody's fastball. You couldn't throw it hard enough. Here was my first opportunity to get a quality major league fastball. What would I do with it?

Walking up to the plate, I was thinking, *He better not throw me a first-pitch fastball. He throws me a first-pitch fastball? I'm going to hit it.*

The first pitch he threw me was a fastball, and I smoked it. I hit a double off the top of the center field wall. It was a fraction of an inch from being a home run. Can you imagine the street cred I would have had if I had taken Roger Clemens deep right there?

That double was the only hit we got off him. Clemens went five innings, and we put only three or four balls in play. Tony put a couple in play, and I popped up to the catcher in my second at-bat. Otherwise, Clemens abused our lineup.

We had a tremendous letdown after the fifth inning and got drummed pretty good the rest of the game. Clemens had stuck it up our rear end, but facing him was still the coolest thing any of us had ever done.

My day was made after that first at-bat. I could have struck out three times and it still would have been a happy day. *I just took Roger Clemens off the center field wall.*

I was ready.

CHAPTER 8
Showtime

In July 1993, rumors were flying about who the Braves would trade to get Fred McGriff from the Padres. The Braves needed a cleanup hitter, and to get a guy the quality of McGriff, it was going to take a haul of prospects, including at least one marquee minor leaguer. Ryan Klesko and I were two of the names floating around.

I was a little surprised. I had been told all the way up through the minors that I was untouchable, if not directly, then through what John Schuerholz said in the press clippings. But he said Klesko was untouchable, too. And quite honestly, I thought if the Braves were going to get McGriff, they'd probably have to give up Klesko. Like McGriff, he played first base. He was from Southern California. It seemed like the right fit.

I had no desire to go to San Diego. We had too good a thing going in Atlanta.

Grady pulled Melvin Nieves out in the middle of our game in Richmond the day the trade went down on July 18. One of our starting pitchers, Donnie Elliott, was in the clubhouse packing up. When we came in from the field after the game, everybody was saying, "They traded Melvin and Donnie and one other guy."

I held my breath.

"Well, who's the other guy?" I said.

"Some A-ball guy."

I exhaled. It turned out to be Vince Moore, an outfielder in Durham. Once my relief subsided, the wheels started spinning.

"Wow, for Fred McGriff?" I said.

We just stole Fred McGriff, I thought. Don't get me wrong, Melvin Nieves had big-time power and was a big-time switch-hitter. I expected to see somebody like Melvin put in that deal because he was a good player. I did not expect Donnie Elliott and Vince Moore to be going. Vince Moore was in A-ball. I'd played with Donnie Elliott in Double-A and he was a solid organizational pitcher, but I didn't see him lasting very long at the big league level.

That is probably the best trade John Schuerholz ever pulled off as general manager of the Braves, given the contribution Freddy made to the Braves in 1993 compared to what we had to give up. We plucked him from a West Coast team, so he was familiar with the Giants, the team Atlanta was chasing that year. And McGriff killed it coming down the stretch.

That July, I started to learn the value of not worrying about things you can't control. I'd been driving myself crazy: *Am I going to get traded to San Diego? Am I going to stay here? Am I going to the big leagues? If I go to San Diego, am I going to be in the big leagues or am I going to go to Triple-A?* You go cross-eyed thinking about the possibilities.

I was just glad it was over. Once we got Fred McGriff, and I wasn't a part of the deal, I knew the Braves were going to give me a chance to fail at the big league level.

By September, I was itching for a call-up. A bunch of us were. It was cup-of-coffee time, when teams expand their rosters and call up some of their prospects. It was hard to focus on anything other than when the call might come. The minute the Triple-A season was over, a handful of us figured we'd be packing our bags to join the Braves in San Diego.

Our Richmond team made the playoffs, which just prolonged the wait. In Game 4 of a best-of-five semifinal series, we were down 9–0 to Charlotte and facing elimination. I hit a three-run homer off Paul Byrd; Boi Rodriguez hit two homers for us, and we came all the way back to take the lead going into the bottom of the ninth.

Then Sam Horn hit a two-run bomb for Charlotte off Pedro Borbon to walk us off and it was actually a relief. We should have been devastated. Instead, everybody was sitting in the clubhouse, taking off their shoes, and looking around wondering: "Uh, is somebody going to come say something to me?" "Where's Grady?" "Who's already gotten the word?"

We all wanted to go to San Diego. We didn't give a damn about the Governors' Cup. When you're playing in the Triple-A playoffs, nobody wants to be there, unless you're a thirty-five-year-old guy and this might be your last paycheck.

Finally, I got a tap on my shoulder to come to Grady's office.

"I just want to congratulate you on a good season," he said. "You played outstanding. You're one of the best players that I've ever managed."

"Thank you," I said.

And I waited, with my stomach in my throat.

"One more thing," he said. "You're going to San Diego. Pack your shit. And do your thing; I don't ever want to see you back in the minor leagues."

"You won't," I said, breaking into a smile.

I gave him a big ol' hug and I walked out.

Karin was waiting in the tunnel.

"Going to San Diego!" I said, still in my underwear, pumping both my fists.

Borbon, Klesko, and Brian Hunter were going up, too. All three had already experienced a call-up. It was old hat for them. Not for me. It was a wet-my-pants, this-is-what-I've-worked-for-my-whole-life, earth-shattering moment. I grew up in a town of four hundred that didn't even have a stoplight, living for the Saturday *Game of the Week* just so I could watch big league baseball. I turned around from the TV at the age of four and told my mom I was going to play in the big leagues. Now I was actually *going* to the big leagues.

We flew to Richmond from Charlotte that night, packed our stuff, and flew to Atlanta at the crack of dawn the next morning. I dropped Karin off at home during the layover in Atlanta and went right back to the airport to catch a flight to San Diego. I called my parents from the air.

Dad answered.

"Guess where I am," I said.

"Where?" he said.

"Flying over the Grand Canyon," I said. "I'm on my way to San Diego. I'm in the big leagues."

Dad still gets tears in his eyes when he tells that story. I was too macho then to get emotional. On September 10, 1993, at age twenty-one, I was running on pure excitement. I bypassed the Hyatt in downtown San Diego and took a cab straight to the stadium. I couldn't wait to put on that uniform.

Back then, Jack Murphy was not the plushest stadium, but it might as well have been the Sistine Chapel to me. I was in "The Show." *This is a big league locker room. I am getting dressed right next to Dave Justice, Fred McGriff, Sid*

Bream, the stud pitchers. It was awesome. I was home.

I couldn't have asked for a better environment to walk into, not just the clubhouse itself and all the Hall of Famers, MVPs, and World Champions in there, but a do-or-die situation in September. It gave me a good gauge of what the next fifteen to twenty years of my life were going to be about.

The Braves were a game behind the Giants in an epic pennant race. They were playing the game at a different speed, with a different mentality. *Yesterday, I was playing baseball. Today I'm playing with the cosmic all-stars.* I had the best seat in the house, watching how great players handled themselves in a pennant race, how resilient they were, how focused.

As a rookie, I knew I was supposed to be seen and not heard. If you open your mouth, you don't learn, so I kept my mouth shut as often as possible. As much as I wanted to play, I also had an unadulterated fear that I would mess up. All I could think was *Bobby, please don't put me in a meaningful game. Make sure we're up eight or ten runs so if I screw up, it's not going to kill us.*

We had a twelve-run lead on the Padres the first time he put me in a game, thank goodness. It was my second night in the big leagues. It went by so fast I don't even remember it. Four of us went in as defensive replacements in the ninth inning and nothing was hit my way at shortstop, which was probably a good thing.

The next night, September 12, the game was on the line when Bobby put me in to pinch run for Sid Bream. I remember that time crystal clear. We were down a run to the Padres in the sixth inning. I was at first and Rafael Belliard was at second.

All I was thinking was *Do not get picked off.* Bobby opened his arms wide, a sign for me to take a bigger lead off first. *Yeah, right,* I thought. *You guys have just come back from ten games down in August to catch the damn Giants. I am not about to screw this up. My run may mean something, but I'm not going to be the reason y'all lose this game.*

Otis Nixon flew out and Jeff Blauser struck out to end the inning, and I got stranded at first. We lost the game. But I did not get picked off.

Two nights later back in Atlanta, playing at Atlanta–Fulton County Stadium for the first time, I got my first big league at-bat.

We were up 10–0 against the Reds in the first game of the home stand and Bobby sent me in to pinch hit for Blauser in the seventh. I'd been sitting on the bench waiting for this moment for three hours. I'd been dreaming about it my whole life. The adrenaline flowing through my veins was almost palpable.

Kevin Wickander, a lefty, was pitching. I was standing in the right-handed batter's box looking out at him, thinking, *I don't have a snowball's chance in hell. I can't feel my arms. I can't feel my legs. Just get your three hacks in somehow.*

He threw me a really good fastball first pitch. I pulled off it and hit a little swinging bunt to third. Juan Samuel was playing back because we had such a big lead. Once I saw where the ball was headed, I thought, *That's a knock. He ain't throwing me out.*

But when I came out of the box, I almost fell down. *Oh my god, my legs aren't working.* I was going to get thrown out in my first major league at-bat on what should have been a hit because I didn't have my legs ready. I hadn't stretched. The batting cage was way up the tunnel at Fulton County Stadium. The dugouts were small. There wasn't really a great place to warm up. But so what.

Lucky for me, Samuel double-clutched and never threw to first. I got a hit but I also learned a lesson: Stay ready.

I had three at-bats my first three weeks in the big leagues, so I wasn't surprised when Bobby came up to me after the last game of the regular season and said, "We're not going to put you on the playoff roster."

I nodded. *Makes sense.*

"But I want you to travel with the team," he said.

Really? Awesome.

Then he said, "If somebody gets hurt, we may use you to replace them on the roster."

Internally, I wigged out. The possibility that I might be thrust into a playoff situation? It was too much, too fast.

Luckily nobody got hurt. And the experience I got traveling to Philadelphia for the NLCS was an eye-opener, to say the least. Working out on the field at Veterans Stadium before games, I got to experience what playing in Philly and the Northeast was all about. I saw just how raucous the fan base is up there. And I saw the difference in intensity in my teammates during the playoffs. I saw them flip another switch and take their game to a new level.

I could see the intensity in the Phillies, too, not to mention sheer size. You want to talk about passing the eye test? The Philadelphia Phillies in 1993 had Curt Schilling and Terry Mulholland on the mound; Darren Daulton behind the plate; John Kruk at first; Dave Hollins at third; Wes Chamberlain, Pete Incaviglia, and Lenny Dykstra in the outfield. They had some boys who were large and intimidating.

That was a wake-up call for me. *Now you're playing against grown-ass men. You better get in the weight room.*

Frankly, it was an eye-opener for other reasons, too. The first inkling I had that players might be using performance-enhancing drugs (PEDs) was watching those Philadelphia Phillies. They looked like a damn football team. Every one of them was yolked to the gills. Every one of them hit the ball five hundred feet. At that point you're thinking, *What's going on?*

Steroid suspicions about them didn't become public knowledge until years later, and I don't know for a fact who was on them and who wasn't. But usually where there's smoke, there's fire. I'd like to see a guy like Schilling talk candidly about what went on with that team because they looked different from everybody else.

The Phillies beat us that NLCS in six games. I think it was pretty obvious that the pennant race with the Giants had taken it out of us. We won 104 games that year; the Giants won 103. But we still had a lot to look forward to. Greg Maddux had just won 20 games in his first season in Atlanta. He, Tom Glavine, John Smoltz, and Steve Avery were all coming back. Fred McGriff had a monster second half after the trade. David Justice hit 40 homers that year. All those guys were returning, and a couple of young bucks were ready to break through—myself included.

Coming into spring training in 1994, I figured my best chance to make the team was at third base. Terry Pendleton was starting to slow down and probably wouldn't play there every day anymore.

So that offseason I took a hundred ground balls a day at both shortstop and third. A couple of weeks before we left for West Palm, Ronnie Gant broke his leg in a motorcycle accident. One of the coaches came up to me shortly thereafter when I was working out at Fulton County Stadium and said, "Pack an outfielder's mitt."

We had Deion Sanders in center, David Justice in right, and now Gant's spot was open in left. While I wouldn't ever wish an accident like that upon Ronnie, it was a tremendous opportunity for me. Somebody had to play left field in his stead for the Atlanta Braves. Might as well be me.

Of course, I'd never played an inning at third base or an inning in the outfield, and now, my first big league spring training with a chance to make the team, I had to learn two new positions. It was a little scary. I was so worked up the week before camp I made myself sick. I couldn't sleep. I had headaches and a constant lump in my throat.

I knew there was going to be stiff competition at both positions. Oliva had been our third baseman in Triple-A. He was the logical replacement for TP. And both Klesko and Tarasco, could play left. When I was in Double-A and Triple-A with Tarasco, I thought he was the best prospect we had. He was a true five-tool player. He could hit for average and power. He could run, he could field his position, and he had a cannon. I was more like a four-and-a-half-tool guy because my power hadn't really developed yet. Tarasco had a better arm than me. He was as fast as I was. And he had experience in left. I didn't have any.

The one thing working in my favor was that I was a switch-hitter. I knew the Braves were in love with Klesko, but I also knew they didn't like playing Klesko against lefties.They'd want to platoon him with a right-handed left fielder so that guy could face lefties and Klesko could face righties. The middle of our lineup was already left-hand dominant and Tarasco was a lefty, too, so maybe that would leave Tarasco as the odd man out.

Early in camp, Bobby pulled me aside and said, "I'll tell you what I'm thinking. I don't think Oliva can play every day at third, and I'd like to platoon Klesko in left. I think you're a good enough athlete to play both. So I'm going to play you at third base against righties and left field against lefties."

Pfft. Awesome.

"So what you're telling me is, I've got an everyday job?" I said.

"Yeah," he said. "You think you can handle both positions?"

"Damn straight I can handle both," I said.

All my stress turned to excitement. This was going to be fun. Position changes would just keep me on my toes.

Offensively, I knew I was ready. All my work

in the offseason, with Dad standing forty feet away flinging balls at me, was starting to pay off. I had gained another fifteen pounds, which put me at about two hundred.

My focus was clear. *OK, I've gotten my opportunity. This is not slipping by.*

When you walked into the clubhouse in West Palm Beach, all the lockers were on the far side to the left. The morning of our first spring training game, I looked down to see who all was there, nodded a little "wassup," and walked across to the doorway to the tunnel that went to the weight room and down to the field.

Posted on the wall was that day's schedule—what time we had to be on the field, which pitchers were throwing live BP—and the lineup card for the game. I immediately started scanning names.

1. GRISSOM, 2. BLAUSER, 3. JONES, 4. MCGRIFF, 5. JUSTICE . . . *Wait, what?* I was hitting third in front of Freddy and David? *Is there another Jones on this team that I'm missing? Is Clarence hitting third? Clarence isn't supposed to be playing.*

Clarence Jones was our hitting coach. When it finally registered that I was the "Jones" Bobby was referring to and I'd be hitting third in front of two All-Stars in the first game of spring training, I thought, *Oh shit. Here we go.*

Your number three hitter is usually your best and most versatile hitter, a guy who can hit for average and for power. A number three hitter has to do it all, whether it's hitting a ground ball to second base to advance a runner into scoring position, drawing a walk, or hitting a fly ball with less than two outs to score a runner from third base on a sacrifice. I had hit third all through the minor leagues—with the exception of the first part of 1992 in Durham when I led off. That morning in West Palm, it dawned on me: *They've been grooming me for three and a half years to be the next number three hitter. It's time to go.*

Bobby never said anything to me about it. He just put my name in the lineup, right there in black ink.

I was a little worried about what the veteran guys would say. But nobody said a word. I didn't catch any flak. I never sensed any hard feelings. It was weird. *If nobody is saying anything, nobody is pissed off, then everybody must be OK with it.* That's the biggest vote of confidence I could have received, other than Bobby Cox putting me there in the first place.

As pumped up as I was about the opportunity, I managed to match my excitement at the plate. I had a monster spring. Two weeks from breaking camp, I led the team in homers and RBIs, with five and fifteen, and I was hitting .375. I had the team made.

Playing the outfield is a fraternity in and of itself. Fortunately for me, Deion Sanders took me under his wing.

Deion was beloved by everybody in the club-house. The guy was constant comedy, and he could run a 4.18 40. He was the fastest guy any of us had ever seen.

He never let his "prime time" persona as a two-spot athlete get in the way of being a good teammate. I never heard anything about the Falcons. I never heard anything about football. Whenever Deion was in a Braves uniform, it was all about baseball. And Deion beat me to the clubhouse every day, and I usually got there pretty early.

I think the first time Deion saw me run he accepted me. He knew I was a part of the "Braves Burners," a club we had in the minors for the fastest guys in the organization. Out of about twenty-five or thirty players, Tony Graffanino and I were the only two white guys who made the cut. It was both a badge of honor and a curse. We had to show up early every morning and work on the backfields with Sonny Jackson, our baserunning coach. We were out there trying to read Charlie Leibrandt's pickoff move. (That's what kind of guy Leibrandt is. He was a big leaguer who gave up his time to work with us.) We worked on jumps and talked about how to get an extra step here and there. It was a pain in the neck, but looking back on it now, it helped.

The best 40 time I had ever run was a 4.45 when I was playing football at Bolles. The best 60 speed I ever clocked was a 6.65. I knew I wasn't in the same league as Deion or Otis Nixon in our organization, but I could still turn some heads.

Deion and I stretched together in BP every day. We ran next to each other. There was an ease to Deion's gait that I didn't have. He was in second gear while I was bordering on fourth. When it came to speed, I was in the minors and he was a galaxy all-star.

But I got to play next to him in the "soul patrol," Deion's nickname for our outfield. Playing next to Deion was a blast. I would be in left field and he'd be in center, and in the middle of a game, I'd see him dancing in place. Out of nowhere, he'd start singing, "Chippahh, Chippah Jones," to the tune of "Me and Mrs. Jones" by Billy Paul. That was Deion.

We were playing a night game against the Yankees in Fort Lauderdale. A ball was hit between us early in the game. My first reaction was to look at Deion to see if he had it. My second reaction was to listen because you never knew what was going to come out of his mouth.

Deion had a nickname for his glove. He called it Lucille. The rest of us had our names stitched into our gloves; Deion had "Lucille" stitched into his. When that ball went up in left center field, I looked over at him and he looked at me. He said, "Don't worry, Chipper, Lucille got it." And he loped over and caught it.

The next inning they hit another ball to left center, this time a lot deeper. I looked at Deion and he was looking at me. He started screaming, "Chipper, you got to go! Lucille can't get there!" I was running as fast as I could, but that was easier said than done because I couldn't stop laughing.

That might have been the last time I laughed for a while.

There are some nights you're a little more jacked up to play than others; that spring training game against the Yankees was one of them. It was the first time I ever played against them. They weren't the vaunted Yankees of the late '90s and early 2000s yet, but they were still the New York Yankees. It was our first night game of the spring. We were on TV. I was facing a big leaguer and a good pitcher, Terry Mulholland, who I'd seen pitch for the Phillies in the NLCS.

I got to face them when I was hot. It seemed like I was getting two hits every game. I was hitting homers. Hitting behind Marquis Grissom and either Blauser or Mark Lemke got me a lot of RBI opportunities. *Man, I'm going to drive in one hundred this season.* I was well on my way.

I wanted to make a good impression on people in the American League, too, and this was my chance. I homered off Mulholland in the first inning. *Keep it going.*

Two at-bats later, in the fifth, I hit a ground ball to shortstop. Dave Silvestri's throw pulled Jim Leyritz off the bag at first. I saw Leyritz coming toward me, so I planted my left leg to jump to the outside and avoid the tag. My knee exploded. The pop was so loud the whole stadium could hear it.

I closed my eyes. It was the most blinding pain I've ever felt in my life. I thought I had broken my leg. It felt like the lower part of my left leg was pointed out at a forty-five degree angle. I hopped on my right foot for three or four steps before finally trying to put weight on my left. I opened my eyes and looked down. *OK, both of my legs are pointing forward. It must not be broken.*

Pat Corrales, our first base coach, was yelling, "Go down! Go down!" So I went down to the ground like a ton of bricks. Lying there, I was in pain for about thirty seconds. Then it went away.

OK, maybe I just sprained my knee. I've come down on somebody's foot playing basketball. You hear that pop, you sprain your ankle, you're out a couple of weeks, then you're back. *I'll be all right.*

Pat and our assistant trainer, Jeff Porter, helped me off the field. I could gingerly put pressure on my knee, but there was too much give. It felt like I would fall over if I didn't have help.

Back in the training room, Bubba, which is what we called Porter, rolled up my pant leg. My knee had swelled to the size of a mini-basketball.

"That's why you don't feel any pain," he said. "Your body is going to do what it has to do to protect that area because it's hurt."

They brought in the Yankees' doctor to examine me. He started manipulating the bottom part of my leg. It literally rolled up over the top part of my leg, right out of joint. *Whoa.* There should have been a stopping point, and there was no stopping point.

"I won't know for certain without looking at an MRI, but I'm ninety-nine percent sure your ACL is torn," he said.

"OK," I said. "What does that mean?"

"The anterior cruciate ligament is the stabilizing ligament in your knee," he said. "When you walk, does it feel like the top half of your leg is going to roll over the bottom half?"

"Yes," I said.

"You tore your ACL," he said.

"So, what, a couple weeks?" I said. "A month?"

"You're done for the year," he said. "You're going to need surgery, and you're going to be out for ten to twelve months."

Ten to twelve months?

"You've got to be kidding me," I said.

My mind started going 100 mph. *I've worked my whole life to get right here, and I get hurt? I've never gotten hurt in my life. I've played through broken bones. I've played through sprains. Now I'm two weeks from making my debut as a starter in The Show and I'm done?*

I saw Terry Pendleton standing in the doorway of the training room. He had come in from the field between innings.

"What happened?" he asked Bubba. I could read his lips.

"He tore his ACL," Bubba told him. "He's done for the year."

TP closed his eyes and said, "No way."

He took a deep breath and came into the room.

I had spent all spring leaning on TP. If Deion was my mentor in the outfield, TP was my mentor on the infield. We sat side by side in the locker room. I took ground balls with him at third base every day. When he walked over to me sitting on that training room table, it was like Niagara Falls. I lost it.

Never in a million years did I think I would have lost it like that, but seeing the look on his face and knowing how bad he felt for me opened the floodgates. I was devastated. We sat there and cried for four or five minutes. Eventually, though, he grabbed me by the collar.

"Wipe those tears up right now," he said. "Your wife is outside. She's going to come in here. Don't let her see you crying. You're going to get in that weight room. You're going to bust that ass all year, however long the doctors say, and you're going to be good as new, ready to go, whenever the time comes. Be strong and get your work done and everything will be fine."

I was pretty much beyond consoling at that point, but it meant a lot that he came in and said that. And I took his advice. I took a deep breath and pulled myself together.

I was on crutches when I walked through the glass doors at the Marriott in West Palm. The lobby was packed with autograph seekers. They took one look at me and left me alone.

I needed twenty-four hours to get my thoughts together, to mourn. I hadn't gotten an MRI yet, so there was always hope the doctors were wrong and it was just a sprain. But as I lay in bed in pain, looking down at my leg, I knew it was far worse than a sprain. I cried. I got it out. It was probably three or four o'clock before I went to sleep.

When I woke up the next morning, I was done being upset. I tried to prepare for the worst, and if it was better news, then great. Karin and I flew to Atlanta and went straight to Piedmont Hospital for an MRI.

After about an hour, Dr. Marvin Royster—one of the Braves' orthopedic surgeons—came in to see me with Dr. Joe Chandler, who was the dean of our team doctors. They put the MRI results up in panels on the wall.

Lit up in a sequence of images was a 360-degree look at the inside of my knee.

"Your ACL is in two different pieces," Dr. Royster said. "You completely tore it."

I'd had a full day to get used to the sound of that. So I just said, "OK, what's the next step?"

Dr. Royster wanted me to wait a week or two to let the swelling go down before he did the operation. In the meantime, he wanted me to strengthen my quadriceps, which would help after surgery. The stationary bike and the leg-press machine at Piedmont Hospital became my refuge.

There were so many unknowns. ACL tears weren't all that common in baseball at the time. I was scared to death I would not be the same player I had been or that I wanted to be. I didn't just want to make it to the big leagues and have a nice career. I wanted to be great.

Would I still be agile enough to play shortstop? Would I still be able to steal bases? Would I be fast enough to beat out infield singles and turn doubles into triples? Or had one misstep on the first base line just ruined everything I was determined to do with my life?

My surgery was scheduled for April 4, the day the team opened the season in San Diego. Opening Day was supposed to be a benchmark that I had arrived as a big league player. Instead, I spent the day in a bed at Piedmont Hospital.

Dad and I were alone in my hospital room for a few minutes before I was wheeled into surgery.

"Everything we've worked for may have been for nothing," I told him.

He welled up. I was already on my way.

I never would have said something like that to Karin or to a friend or teammate. I may not have even said it to my mom because she might have slapped me upside the head and said, "I don't ever want to hear you say that again." But in that moment I needed some compassion, and I knew I'd get it from Dad.

The Braves were on TV in my room when I came out of surgery. I was still groggy, but I didn't want to see it. Klesko had started in left field, and all I could think was *It should be me.* I told Dad to turn it off.

Dr. Chandler told me if I was diligent with my workouts I'd be as good as new, if not better, when I came back.

I did some research. Danny Manning, who was playing for the Los Angeles Clippers, had come back from ACL surgery. I spoke with Doc Rivers, who was with the Knicks then, and he'd been through it. Once I had the confidence that basketball players had come back from ACL tears, it was just a matter of getting in my mind that I wasn't going to let it slow me down.

Dr. Royster had used part of the patellar tendon in my left knee to repair the ligament. I had a six-inch incision in the front of my knee from where they removed the patellar tendon. I had another two-inch incision on the side where they threaded it through to repair the ACL. They had drilled holes through the bone in the top and bottom of my leg where they inserted screws. My knee was stabilized by a brace with hinges on both sides.

They woke me up at seven o'clock the morning after surgery—eighteen hours out—and told me, "You're going to bend your knee to a ninety degree angle now."

"You crazy?" I said.

It took me thirty minutes to do it, and I was dripping sweat when I was done, but I did it. For the first ten days after surgery, that's all they wanted me doing. At first I did it once a day. Then twice. Soon enough, it was three or four times a day and before long I was doing sets of 10 four or five times a day.

Once I got some range of motion back, they let me get on a stationary bike. I've never been so happy to get on a stationary bike in my life—it was like having a chocolate sundae—and I hate stationary bikes. But that was a big step; it meant

I had enough range of motion to start my rehab.

I wanted to get back in my element. I'd been working out at Piedmont with fifty-year-old guys with torn rotator cuffs, doing their Dr. Jobe exercises with resistance bands. I wanted to have my finger on the pulse of what was going on with the team. I wanted to shoot the breeze. I wanted to walk into the lounge. I wanted my fraternity back.

So the trainers let me move my workouts to Fulton County Stadium, and it was good therapy. The Braves wanted me to travel with the club the rest of that '94 season. They had me locker next to Terry Pendleton, not just in Atlanta but on the road. That was no accident.

TP was a great support system. I literally had to take his shoes off for him at times because his back was so bad he couldn't bend down. But I got to learn what it was like to play major league baseball. Bobby knew where I was going. He was going to get me as mentally prepared as I could be.

I did as much as I possibly could in my rehab. By September, I was hitting from both sides of the plate. I was running the bases, taking ground balls, throwing. I wasn't doing it all at game speed—nothing can simulate game speed—but I was chomping at the bit to get back in there. I felt like I was ready to play.

Then in August, major league players went on strike. It was probably a blessing in disguise. I think the Braves brass and training staff were relieved they wouldn't have to keep the collar on me. I had no choice but to wait.

The Braves sent me to instructional ball during the strike, but they wouldn't let me play in games. I'd proven to them in spring training I could play left field. They already knew I could play short. But I wanted to show them I could play second and third, too. I wanted to do everything I possibly could to make sure I was on the team the next spring. But all they let me do was work out.

Sitting out that season humbled me in a lot of ways. During the strike, I was flat-ass broke.

After three years in the minor leagues of traveling, rent, food, and getting married, the only money I had left from my signing bonus was for a down payment on a house. I'd bought one in the Atlanta suburb of Kennesaw that April of 1994, thinking I was going to be making a couple hundred thousand dollars a year in the big leagues. But because of the strike, we ran out of money shortly after the new year in '95.

I had a radio gig on 790 AM in Atlanta during the strike, but it didn't pay much. Karin got some temp jobs teaching, but she was still trying to get her foot in the door.

It got to the point where we couldn't make payments on the house. We had to skimp on car repairs. We were spending fifty dollars at the grocery store when normally we'd have spent two hundred. We were putting five dollars' worth of gas in the car at a time.

Eventually, Karin and I had to go to her uncle and ask if we could borrow some money. As hard as it was to do, he was really nice about it. He loaned us $10,000 and told us to come back if we needed more.

Luckily in April, everybody came to their senses and we were able to go back to work. Glavine, who was our rep with the players' union, called me, and said, "You've got to be ready to go to spring training on a dime." As soon as we got off the phone, I was packing up the truck to go to Florida.

I've never been so relieved. I was going to have a steady paycheck, which would take a lot of stress off Karin and me. We'd been going at it pretty good.

The end of the strike also meant the injury was behind me. My career could start. My childhood dreams could play out.

I'd spent the previous few months making peace with the injury. I stopped feeling sorry for myself. I learned that you don't start growing until you struggle a little bit. I knew the next time I had a play like that at first base, I would run right through the first baseman. I might slide or dive to avoid a tag but never would I plant on one leg.

By the spring of 1995, I could trust my knee again. I had my confidence back. I was ready.

CHAPTER 9
Going Deep

My dad always said he'd know I'd arrived when he heard my name announced over the loudspeaker on Opening Day. It's a rite of passage. It means you've made it.

Atlanta–Fulton County Stadium was only about half full on April 26, 1995, for our season opener against the Giants. Coming off the strike, fans wanted to make a statement. It didn't feel right, but I wasn't going to let anything ruin my first Opening Day.

I hadn't played in a big league game for over a year, and I was nervous. I was replacing an MVP at third base and one of the leaders on the team. The last thing I wanted to hear was "Terry Pendleton would have made that play" or "Terry Pendleton would have gotten a hit there." I wanted to take charge out there, maybe a little too badly.

Maddux was pitching, and with two outs in the first inning, Barry Bonds hit a pop-up on the infield, sky-high, a little on the first base side of the pitcher's mound. I came in hauling the mail, with my flip-downs on to shield the sun, screaming, "I got it! I got it! I got it!"

Next thing I knew, I was flat on the ground. My flip-downs were in my mouth. Freddy McGriff had caught the ball over both Maddux and me, and I had completely flattened our ace and soon-to-be four-time Cy Young winner. I had kneed him in the calf. McGriff was standing there giggling. As soon as he caught his breath, Maddux started cussing me up one side and down the other.

"Settle the fuck down, you motherfucking rookie," Maddux yelled. "Stay the fuck away from me."

He proceeded to verbally chastise me for the next three or four innings. He didn't try to hide it either. It was on the field; it was in the dugout. Everybody else was laughing their asses off. Not me. I had just run over the $12 million man in my first start. Needless to say, I pulled the reins in a little bit after that.

I wanted to redeem myself right away, and I got the chance in the bottom of the first inning.

Terry Mulholland was pitching for the Giants, as in the last pitcher I saw before I blew out my knee against the Yankees. Only in baseball would this happen.

With runners on first and third, I hit a bullet through the right side of the infield for a base hit to knock in the first run of the year. I got to first base and thought, *Here we go.*

The first six guys in our lineup got base hits. We

first and third-ed them all day. Freddy McGriff hit a couple of homers. We scored twelve runs. If there was any indication of how good our team was going to be that year, it was our first six at-bats on Opening Day. We took off.

Thirteen games into the 1995 season, I made my first trip to New York City. It was a culture shock. Being from small-town America, I was intimidated by concrete and steel. Flying into LaGuardia and looking down into Manhattan from twenty thousand feet, I couldn't believe how big and expansive it was. It was incredible, overwhelming.

I had put New York on a pedestal because of everything I grew up hearing about Mickey, the Yankees, and New York. Dad always told me if you can be successful on that stage, you can be successful anywhere. I'd always dreamed of going to New York and meeting that challenge. We were playing the Mets that series, but it didn't make any difference to me. It was still New York.

My first game in Shea Stadium I proved to myself I could hit in the big leagues. It was May 9 and one of those cold piece-of-crap early spring nights in New York.

Bret Saberhagen was pitching for the Mets. He was the first Cy Young winner I ever faced, a guy I had pulled for, growing up. I was a big George Brett fan, and he and Saberhagen played together on the 1985 Royals team that won the World Series. I loved Brett and Sabes, and a bunch of their other guys, too: Willie Wilson, Steve Balboni, Frank White, Buddy Biancalana—best name in the game. Saberhagen was their ace. Whenever he pitched, they won. Now here I was sixty feet six inches from him, and he was trying to get me out. He may not have been the pitcher in New York that he was in Kansas City, but his stuff was still really good.

I struck out my first at-bat, but the second time facing him I settled down. I got ahead in the count and waited for the first pitch where I thought, *I can handle that*.

I got it 3-1, a fastball out over the plate, and smoked a line drive single to center. I rounded first base telling myself, *Game on, boys. I belong here. You better get used to it because you're going to see it for a long time.*

Little did I know that night would set the tone for having a lot of success at Shea Stadium. And I didn't stop with a base hit.

Two at-bats later, with the game tied 2–2 in the top of the ninth inning, I led off against a right-hander named Josias Manzanillo. I'd faced him a couple of times in Triple-A with Norfolk. Real good slider, threw hard, mid-90s, but straight as an arrow. If he fell behind in the count, you were going to kill him. If he was getting ahead and mixing in that slider, he was tough.

I took his first two pitches for balls and at 2-0 I knew, *I'm taking this dude deep right here.*

I knew I was going to get a fastball. It was the perfect storm. He was a young kid trying to impress. Fred McGriff and David Justice were coming up behind me. The last thing he wanted to do was walk the rookie in front of two bona fide left-handed power hitters to lead off the ninth in a tie game.

Sure enough, he grooved a 93, 94 mph heater, and I killed it. I thought it might have a little too much topspin to go out, but when it got halfway there, I knew. *That ball is gone. We're going to win this game 3–2.*

The ball landed five or six rows deep in the second level of seats down the right field line. I don't think my feet hit the ground the whole time I was rounding the bases.

I thought about my parents back in Pierson. *Mom is bawling. Dad is fist pumping.* As I rounded third, Freddy McGriff was waiting on me at home plate, with a smile on his face. *This is so cool. I'm in Shea Stadium in New York City, Fred McGriff is waiting for me at home plate, and my first major league homer is going to be a game winner.* It was surreal.

I high-fived David Justice going back to the dugout, where all my teammates were waiting on me. I took a little guff from Avery and Maddux as I walked by. Then I felt this sudden wave. *I'm going to lose it right here.* I rushed down into the tunnel.

Karin was watching on TV back home in Atlanta, worried that I went down in the tunnel to throw up. Nope. I was about to cry. I went down and just stood there for a few minutes with tears in my eyes. I had waited a long time for that moment—through the knee injury, the strike, the work it took to get back.

I probably watched every late-night episode of *SportsCenter* on ESPN that night in my room at the Grand Hyatt. I had finally made a highlight, and it was a game-winning homer. I called everybody I knew, Mom and Dad, the wife. I was getting calls from all my high school buddies, my hometown buddies, and my best friend, B.B. It was 3:00 or 4:00 A.M. before I finally settled down enough to sleep.

You hit that first home run and all of a sudden you relax. I got another one off Pete Harnisch the next night in New York. I came back home and hit my first one in front of the crowd at Atlanta–Fulton County Stadium off Jose Rijo. Then another one off Pete Smith, then Curt Leskanic. I hit five home runs in eight games. They were coming fast and furious.

I'd been all of three days without a homer when I faced one of the nastiest dudes in baseball, Florida Marlins closer Robb Nen, in the ninth inning of a 7–7 game at Fulton County Stadium.

I was absolutely terrified of Nen. He wasn't known for his command back then, and the guy threw 100 mph. He'd be out there grunting and he had a little stutter step in his delivery that messed with your mind.

His ball cut, too. Early in his career, I'm not even sure if he knew when it was cutting and when it was straight. I knew the only chance I had against him was to get the bat head out. Walking up there, I thought, *All right, just bail and whale.*

I basically stepped in the bucket—Dad would not approve—and started swinging when he took that little stutter step. I would have probably swung no matter where the pitch was, but he grooved it. He threw a fastball middle in, right where my bat was swinging, and I got out in front of it. It was all reaction. Complete and utter luck.

My mentality in that swing was just *let it eat*—let loose as big a swing as you've got. And when you're six foot three and 190 pounds and you connect with a pitch coming in at 100 mph, it feels really good. When I hit it, it was a no-doubter. It cleared the first section of seats.

I'd never hit a walk-off home run before, at any level. It was so cool. The house was packed that night and all my teammates were waiting on me at home plate. I had turned around 100 mph to win a game and cap off a ten-day period when I turned the corner as a professional athlete. I went from questioning if I belonged to knowing I did.

I didn't exactly light it up at the plate like that for the entire season by any stretch of the imagination. I hit .265 my rookie year. But Bobby knew what he was doing. I was a good fastball hitter, and as a rookie hitting in front of sluggers like McGriff and Justice, I was going to see a lot of fastballs.

I set a couple of trends early on in my rookie year: I held my own against the Mets. And I had no shot against Hideo Nomo.

Nomo was the first Japanese player to make the jump to Major League Baseball and stay there. Nomo was our generation's Fernando Valenzuela. I was nine years old and a Dodger fan when Fernando-mania swept Los Angeles. I actually homered off him once in Triple-A when he was rehabbing with the Orioles. When Nomo arrived in LA in 1995 it wasn't nearly as fun for me. He was an enigma to a lot of hitters, and I was at the top of the list. I went 0-for-27 before I got my first hit off the guy. He threw a perfect game against me!

Nomo was the first Japanese pitcher I'd ever faced. I took one look at his windup and thought, *Oh. My. God.* It was unconventional, with a hesitation at the top. And he threw everything with the exact same arm angle and arm speed. He was some kind of tough.

He threw 93, 94 mph with probably the best forkball I've ever seen. When a pitcher throws a forkball, his fingers are spread a little farther apart than with a split-finger fastball grip, so the ball squirts out of his hand. A forkball acts more like a knuckleball; it comes out slower than a splitter and dances around a little bit. With the split, the pitcher has a better grip on the ball and he's relying more on rotation so the bottom just drops out.

The first time I saw Nomo's forkball, we were facing him in Atlanta a week before the All-Star game in '95—which he started, by the way, as a rookie. It was Nomo vs. Smoltz, and the electricity in Atlanta–Fulton County Stadium was palpable. It was one of those special games with more on the line than your normal mid-July game. It was a playoff atmosphere.

Nomo dominated. He had ten strikeouts in seven innings—including a pair against me—and we had only two hits before he left the game with the score tied 1–1.

It was still tied 1–1 in the bottom of the ninth inning and we were down to our last out when I came up with runners on first and second. Pedro Astacio had gotten the last out of the eighth inning, and Dodgers manager Tommy Lasorda sent him back out to start the ninth. But he went

2-0 to me, and Lasorda came to get him in the middle of the at-bat. You could tell Astacio was none too happy about it.

Then Lasorda brought in Rudy Seanez, a future teammate of mine, but at that point, I'd never seen him before. David Justice called me over to the on-deck circle.

"Base hit wins this game," he said. "We don't need no three-run homer. We need just a good at-bat, a good solid base hit right here."

So I went back to the plate thinking, *All right, just put a good swing on it, get your base hit, and let's get out of here.*

At 2-0, I knew what I was going to get, especially with the guys hitting behind me: a heater. And I did. I got the head of the bat out, put a good swing on it, and I nutted it. Walk-off number two. I got the three-run homer after all.

"I wasn't trying for it," I told David afterward.

"Yeah," he said. "That's usually when it happens."

To send all those people away happy from such an important game—I'll remember that homer for a long time.

Nomo edged me out for National League Rookie of the Year in 1995, and that created a bit of a controversy. Nomo turned twenty-seven in August of that year. He'd pitched for more than four years as a professional in Japan. But by Major League Baseball rules, he was as much a rookie as I was when I was twenty-three and had eight major league games under my belt coming into the season.

I had no problem with it, though. While I understood the argument against him, he was new to the National League, and I've never seen a more dominant first season by a pitcher. He led the league in strikeouts, and we're not talking about a bunch of schmucks. Pedro Martinez was in the league in 1995. Curt Schilling. Maddux. Nomo also finished second in ERA (2.54) to Maddux (1.63). Sure, I was leading some rookie categories offensively, but compared to the rest of the league, I was middle of the pack.

Maybe there should be a rookie pitcher of the year and a rookie player of the year, I don't know. But I've said it a hundred times: I will gladly trade Rookie of the Year for the douse of champagne I got at the end of the season.

In a lot of ways, my rookie year was a blur. I played the entire season on adrenaline. All I focused on was being one-ninth of the equation every day to help us get to the postseason. Once we got there, I wanted to be the difference that brought us our first World Series title after the near misses in 1991 and 1992.

My first playoff game was in Colorado, and it might have been the best game I ever played given what was at stake.

The playoffs had just been expanded to include a Division Series round and the first-ever best-of-five playoff series. The way MLB first set it up, having home-field advantage meant we "got" the last three games at home. It wasn't really an advantage, though, because we had to play the first two games in Colorado. In such a short series the first two games are critical. We had the best record in the National League and the Rockies were the wild card team, but we could have easily been down 2-0 by the time we got back to Atlanta.

The Rockies had a scary lineup, with guys who could not only hit but hurt you. Eric Young. Walt Weiss. Dante Bichette. Larry Walker. Andres Galarraga. Ellis Burks. Vinny Castilla. Joe Girardi. They were tough whether we were playing them in Colorado or Atlanta, but Colorado was worse because they could turn the lineup over in three minutes in that light air. Once they got rolling, there was no stopping them.

Their pitching staff wasn't bad either. Kevin Ritz started Game 1, Lance Painter pitched Game 2, Billy Swift Game 3, and in Game 4 they had Saberhagen, who had gotten traded there from the Mets in July.

Seeing all the media at Coors Field for the first game, my eyes lit up. I wanted to make a splash. We were the marquee game on prime time TV that night, and I knew everybody was going to be watching. From the moment we walked on the field for BP, I could feel the cameras on me; people were waiting to see how I'd perform.

I had a rush of nervous energy like I used to get on Friday nights before I ran out on the football field at Bolles: It was 20 percent scared, 80 percent I want to kill somebody. Being out in Denver in October, it was pretty cold. But it could have been ten degrees and I wouldn't have known the difference.

I was amped up in my first at-bat and hit into a double play. I lined out in my second. But in my third, I homered off Ritz to get us, within a run, down 3–2 in the sixth inning. *Whew, OK, I got this.* We tied it up that inning and took a 4–3 lead going into the bottom of the eighth. That's when the Rockies put runners at first and third with nobody out for the Big Cat, Andres Galarraga.

Greg McMichael was pitching, and it was not a good matchup for us. Not that I ever liked the matchup when Andres came to the plate, but McMichael's sinker and changeup would tail down and in to Galarraga, and he was a good low-ball hitter.

On McMichael's first pitch, a strike, I had Big Cat played pretty much straight up. But right before the 0-1 pitch, Blauser whistled at me from shortstop. Being new to third base, I always wanted to know when something off-speed was coming so I could cheat closer to the line or toward the hole. Mac didn't throw a lot of breaking balls, so I knew that meant Blauser had seen Javy put down the sign for a changeup. The pitch was going to be down and in, and if Big Cat did what he should, he was either going to hit it out of the park or down the third base line. So I moved over two steps toward the line.

Sure enough, Galarraga hit a frickin' rocket down the line. I completely laid out and the ball stuck in the webbing of my glove. I don't know how I caught it. There was no skill involved whatsoever, other than putting myself in position to make a play. It was blind luck.

I saw Dante Bichette hold at third, so I threw to second to get the out there. Burks, the next batter, followed with a double to score Bichette, and the Rockies tied it up 4–4, but if you give up ones in an inning in Colorado instead of fours and fives, you've got a chance.

I was still jacked up from making that play when I came to the plate in the top of the ninth. There were two outs, nobody on, and Curt Leskanic, one of their closers, was pitching. He threw hard, and when he was right, he had one of the best sliders I ever faced. He'd throw you fastballs in to try to get you to speed up your bat, then drop the bottom out of a little back-foot slider. You had to cheat to get the bat head out for the fastball, which left you hard-pressed to square up the slider.

At 2-0, I was sitting dead red. I had everything started, gearing up for the 95 mph fastball. Of course, he threw me the slider. Lucky for me, it was a hanger, belt-high, right in the middle of the plate. I was able to lag the bat just enough to catch the ball out front.

I thought I had just missed it. But then I got to first base and saw Mike Kingery climbing the wall in right center. *You've got to be kidding me.* No way that ball would have gone out at Fulton County Stadium. Then it hit me. *You just won the game.* Mark Wohlers was the best closer in baseball at that point in his career, and if we got the ball to Woh in the bottom of the ninth, we won. My emotion kicked in, and I threw both hands up in the air.

If I had done that in June, I'd have probably gotten drilled between the numbers. But I was a twenty-three-year-old kid who'd been waiting for that moment his entire life.

In a short series like that, momentum is everything. If Galarraga's ball had gotten past me, and they had blown the game open, the Rockies easily could have taken the momentum and gone on to win that series. But we crushed their spirit that night. We took their best shot and we had an answer at every turn. Personally, I took some momentum from that game, too. I knew I could handle the magnitude of the moment.

I did some pretty cool things against the

Rockies and then in our four-game sweep over the Reds in the NLCS. I got a hit in each of my first eight postseason games and batted over .400 with three homers along the way. I like to think that I was a big reason why we made it to the World Series.

Once we got there, though, I didn't do much. You saw the cream rise to the top. Glavine and Justice, Doggie—"Mad Dog," a.k.a. Maddux—and Smoltzie took over. It was my turn to follow their lead.

CHAPTER 10
Our Time

The night before we opened the World Series at home against the Indians, I couldn't sleep. Not only was the first game of the World Series the next day, but also it was Opening Day of deer hunting season in Georgia.

My mom and dad were stopping in South Georgia on the way to Atlanta for Game 1 so Dad and my old Little League coach could deer hunt. I was torn. Dad was getting ready to deer hunt without me.

Why can't I do both? What better way to burn off some nervous energy the night before the World Series and kill some time than getting out in the woods?

"Hey, I can't sleep, I'm nervous as heck," I told Karin. "I'm going to drive down to Macon and go hunting in the morning."

"You're going to do what?" she said.

She didn't like it, and if I were her, I probably would have felt the same way. But I knew hunting would be therapeutic for me. I got in my truck around midnight.

It was 2:00 A.M. by the time I pulled into their hotel parking lot in Perry, Georgia. Nobody

181

was at the front desk, so I couldn't get a room. I parked my truck in front of my parents' room, put the seat back, and went to sleep. At five in the morning, Dad came out to get coffee. He knocked on my window.

"What are you doing?" he said.

"Let's go hunting," I said. "I'm ready."

"You're playing in the World Series tonight," he said.

"I know," I said. "I got it. I'm good."

Hunting that day might not have been the best decision, but it helped me relax and get my mind right. I sat in the tree that morning thinking, *I'm going to face Orel Hershiser in the first game of the World Series tonight.*

We hunted until about eleven o'clock and then I drove straight to the ballpark. I got there about one o'clock, curled up on the training table for a couple of hours, and woke up ready to go.

Cal Ripken was in Atlanta to throw out the ceremonial first pitch. It had been six weeks since he broke Lou Gehrig's record, and Major League Baseball was honoring him. I was starstruck.

Growing up, Mickey Mantle was all I ever heard about, but Cal was my guy. He was somebody I could actually lay my eyes on. And he was a shortstop like me.

Interleague play didn't exist yet, and who knew if we would ever play against the Orioles in a World Series? I wanted to meet the man, and I wasn't going to let the moment pass. I was determined not to be tongue-tied like I was at the card show with Mantle. I walked right up to him as he was coming off the field and asked him to sign a ball for me.

When I got back to the dugout, I looked at the ball—it had orange stitching and his number 8 stamped in black—and he'd written: "You're off to a great start, now the hard part begins."

Cal Ripken has been paying attention to me? Cool. His message was a good one. He wanted me to keep that fire burning. But if he had known me well, he would have known I'd had fire in my belly since I was eleven years old and it wasn't going anywhere any time soon.

Game 1 was a dream pitching matchup: Maddux, who was almost untouchable that year, against Hershiser, one of my guys growing up a Dodger fan.

Hershiser was thirty-seven years old by then, but his location was as impeccable as ever and he was still pretty damn good. He was the number one starter for a World Series team, and you're talking about a pitching staff with Charles Nagy, who was an All-Star the following year, and Ken Hill, who had been probably the best pitcher on a really good Expos team in '94. Everybody talks about Cleveland's lineup that year. Their pitching was no joke either. Their starting staff led the American League in ERA.

In my first at-bat against Hershiser, I took the first pitch. *Eh,* I thought. *I can hit this.* Four pitches later, I lined into a double play, but I walked away with confidence thinking, *All right, I just squared you up on a sinker.* That was Hershiser's bread and butter. If you saw six or eight pitches during the course of an at-bat, four or six of them were going to be sinkers. All I needed to do was make him get that sinker up a little bit. Anything that started just above the knees was going to be too low. Anything that started waist-high, whack it.

I ended up going 0-for-4, but I knew I'd had a good game plan. And it was OK because we won Game 1, 3–2.

The Indians' lineup is what got all the publicity and understandably so. It was stacked. They had the best leadoff hitter in the game in Kenny Lofton. Omar Vizquel was one of the best number two hitters out there, not to mention a perennial Gold Glover at shortstop. Carlos Baerga, their second baseman, who hit third, was a .300 hitter from both sides of the plate and a jack of all trades. He could hit the long ball and was still a .400 on-base percentage guy. Albert Belle, an intimidating man and a professional hitter, hit fourth. Eddie Murray, a Hall of Fame switch-

184

hitter, hit fifth, and my old Triple-A rivals Jim Thome and Manny Ramirez followed in the sixth and seventh spots. Then it was Sandy Alomar or Tony Peña in the eighth spot—no slouches behind the plate.

The Indians had a lot of good young position players much like we did. Most of them were homegrown prospects, meaning they were drafted by the Indians and brought up through their organization: Baerga. Belle. Lofton. Manny. Thome. That World Series represented two organizations reaching their potential. What gave us the advantage was we had a longer sustained run of success up until that point. It was our time.

At every crucial moment during that series, something good happened for us. We made the right pitch. We made the right play. We got the big hit. It seemed to happen in every game.

We won back-to-back one-run games to take a 2-0 lead in the series. In Game 1, Kenny Lofton made an impact with his speed, but Doggie dealt. In Game 2, Javy hit a two-run homer off El Presidente—Dennis Martinez—and we won, 4–3.

We lost Game 3 up in Cleveland, but it was one of the most exciting games I ever played in. Jacobs Field was raucous. It was adrenaline to the nth degree. If the Indians lost the game, the series was basically over. They'd have to run through the Maddux-Glavine-Smoltz gauntlet just to get it tied. Standing near their dugout at third base, I could sense their panic. I could hear them willing themselves to win, and they did. We made a late comeback, but they tied it in the eighth and Murray got the better of Alejandro Peña with a walk-off hit in the eleventh inning.

Heading into Game 4, I don't think anybody expected Steve Avery to (a) pitch and (b) pitch as well as he did. Everybody thought Maddux would come back and start Game 4 on three days' rest and all of a sudden the Indians got Avery? He'd made one start in a month and just wasn't the same dominant pitcher of '91 and '92. But Bobby trusted him. And Avery didn't need the fastball velocity he used to rely on; he got the Indians out in front of his changeup and he basically shut down the best lineup in baseball. The Indians had to be thinking to themselves, *These Braves pitchers are unbelievable.*

We won Game 4 to go up 3–1 in the series, and the writing was on the wall.

Hershiser got the better of Maddux in Game 5, but we still felt that we had the momentum up 3–2 in the series. We were fighting for something we felt was ours for a long time. They were fighting an uphill battle the entire six-game series. And we were going back home. We knew we would get it done at home.

Waiting for us in Atlanta was a fan base that

would be as riled up for Game 6 as any we saw at Jacobs Field in Cleveland. We had David Justice to thank for that.

I didn't hear what DJ said to reporters after our workout on the off day in Atlanta. I read his comments in *The Atlanta Journal-Constitution* the morning of Game 6, just like everybody else.

The headline JUSTICE TAKES A RIP AT BRAVES FANS certainly got my attention, as it did for people all over town. Basically, he took Braves fans to task for not being as boisterous as Indians fans. And while I probably wouldn't have said some of the things he said, in a lot of ways, he was right.

It had been almost eerie to see the difference in the two fan bases the first five games. In Atlanta, it was like just another game. We could have been playing in August. When we went up to Cleveland, it was like playing in a circus. It was dizzying. From start to finish, you could not hear yourself think. The drummer who plays in the bleachers? Could not even hear him from two hundred feet away. I didn't know he was there until we went back to Cleveland in interleague play a few years later.

Experiencing the two extremes is probably what led David to say what he said, and I don't think he meant anything malicious by it. But much like me, when David had something on his mind, he was going to say it. Saying it on the eve of a potential World Series clincher made him a target. He had the weight of the world on his shoulders for Game 6. He heard it from our fans, the media, you name it. Our own fans were booing him from the minute he walked onto the field for batting practice.

Dave was usually happy-go-lucky, and he wasn't saying a word. He was intent on making an impact.

We all knew what had to be done. We knew Glav would pitch well and give us a chance to win. It was just a matter of who was going to get the big hit. Who was going to do something special?

If David had been trying to send a message to the fans, the message was received. Fans showed up in force for Game 6. The atmosphere at Atlanta–Fulton County Stadium was crazy. It was awesome. It was how it should be.

I tried to control my nervous energy by focusing on the matchups, the cat 'n' mouse. The Indians had made the adjustment on Maddux in Game 5, moving up in the box to try and catch his sinker earlier. *Now what are they going to do with Glavine?* Glav is a little bit harder to make an adjustment on because he's so deceptive. How do you adjust to what you can't see? Glavine's changeup looked exactly like his fastball. His arm action was the same. Everything was the same.

Most changeup pitchers try to turn the ball over. They bury the ball in their palm and when they release it, you can see their last three fingers. Plus, it's got screwball spin. Hitters can pick that up.

Glav's changeup was all about grip pressure. He could throw you a two-seam fastball at 88, 89 mph, then make a subtle grip change for his changeup. Rather than turning the ball over, he just let it roll off his fingers. It looked like the same two-seam spin of his fastball, only it was coming out 6 to 8 mph slower.

With that kind of deception, his usual good command, and a generous strike zone that night, Glavine was in complete control. The Indians couldn't barrel him up. With every swinging strike or weak ground ball, you could see their frustration mounting. Every time we got the third out of an inning, I chuckled. *He's doing it to 'em again.*

Glavine was getting strikes called quite a bit off the plate—don't get me wrong—but so did everybody else. That's one of the reasons Dennis Martinez didn't allow any runs either. Was the strike zone Eric Gregg–esque, like what Livan Hernandez got against us in the '97 NLCS? No. But it was a big zone. You weren't going to walk your way to a win that night. You better get the bat off your shoulder and swing it. Fine by me.

Quite honestly, I was licking my chops to face

El Presidente because that series he didn't have anything to get me out. If he was getting his big hook over early in counts to get you off his fastball, you were going to have trouble. If he got predictable, you could do some damage, and of my six hits in the World Series, four were off Martinez. But other guys must not have felt real good against him because we didn't score many runs in his two starts. It took a home run by Javy in the sixth inning to win Game 2, and Presidente threw five shutout innings in Game 6. We got to him early in some innings, but he kept pitching his way out of jams. It's one thing to hit around those wily veterans, but to actually push runs across is another story.

Game 6 was still scoreless when we came back to the dugout after the third inning. Nobody was saying a word. The intensity was almost palpable. Then Glavine broke the silence.

"Come on, boys," he said. "All I need is one."

It was his way of saying, "I got this." And it immediately set everybody at ease. We went back out on the field focused on doing our jobs and just trying to get him one run. Who better to heed that call than David Justice?

With two outs in the fifth, Martinez was done and the Indians brought in a lefty, Jim Poole. He got Fred McGriff to end the inning and, with two more lefties due up, went back out to face David leading off the sixth.

With the count 1-1, David connected on a fastball from Poole. We all jumped up from the dugout bench and went to the rail. It was going to be close. Baseball players know the sound of a home run, but until you get out in the open and look at the flight of the ball, you're never really sure. When we saw the ball disappear behind the right field wall, everybody went absolutely nuts. I threw my hands in the air.

I greeted David at the top of the dugout steps for a high five and swiped him on the helmet as he went by. If I had stood directly in front of him, he might have killed me. He was jacked up. And he should be. He had just silenced the naysayers with the biggest home run of his life.

Settling back down in the dugout, I thought, *Whew. We got one*. I looked down at Glavine. He raised his eyebrows and gave me that shit-eating grin of his as if to say, "It's over. They ain't scoring off of me."

I think Glavine got a little gassed in the sixth and seventh innings but he gutted out eight innings to get the ball to Woh in the ninth. Glavine and Maddux were always incredibly honest with Bobby. They'd say, "Skipper, I'm done. I got nothing left." I can't say I would have done the same in that situation, but not only was Wohlers fresh, he threw 100 mph with a split and a slider and could control all three pitches. We had the utmost confidence that if we just got through the eighth with a lead, the game was over.

Of course, the top of Cleveland's order was due up and those three outs in the ninth were the biggest of our lives. I was thinking back over not only what I had been through personally with my knee but what my teammates and Braves fans had been through with so many near misses over the years. *We are this close to winning it all.* I was so jacked up I probably would have thrown the ball twenty rows deep.

The always dangerous Kenny Lofton led off the ninth and Woh got him to pop up. Rafael Belliard, who had come in for us on defense at shortstop, made a nice running catch. One down. Paul Sorrento pinch hit for Vizquel and flew out to center. Two down, one to go. It was all up to Baerga. All I was thinking was *I don't want to see Albert Belle come to the plate.* That's who was on deck.

Baerga hit a fly ball pretty well. I thought, *Oh no, that's in the gap.* But I'd momentarily forgotten we always overshifted in the outfield. We played everybody to hit to the opposite field, no matter who was hitting. Our pitchers were so good at locating on the outside corner that if a hitter did what he was supposed to do and went with the pitch, our defense was standing there waiting.

I turned and saw Marquis Grissom headed for

the gap. *He's got it in his hip pocket.* I started inching toward the mound to go crazy with my teammates. Grissom ran the ball down in left center and we had our championship.

Javy sprinted out from behind home plate and jumped into Wohlers's arms. I was the next one there. Guys rushed out from the dugout, ready to unleash the frustration of one near miss in the postseason after another. I was trying to make sure I didn't get blindsided, but I still got absolutely smushed. Somebody in the bottom of the pile was yelling, "Get off me!" but it is the best pain you'll ever experience in your life.

Skip Caray's call on that night's broadcast summed it up: "The Atlanta Braves have given you a championship." You can hear his broadcast partner Joe Simpson in the background going, "Yes! Yes! Yes!" They were saying what everybody in Atlanta was feeling. *Finally.*

Our 1–0 win to clinch the World Series had to be the biggest moment in sports history in the state of Georgia, the city of Atlanta, and the Southeast. None of Atlanta's other professional sports teams had won a championship—not the Falcons or the Hawks. Both the University of Georgia and Georgia Tech had won national championships in college football, but they didn't unite our entire city and state. The 1996 Olympics were still a year away from coming to Atlanta.

That World Series win resonated well beyond

state lines. We were on TBS then—the biggest superstation in America—and people from all four corners of the United States had tuned into that game because they were fans of ours. We were America's team.

We dogpiled. We patted each other on the back and told everybody how much we loved each other. Then we went back inside the clubhouse and got "World Series Champions" T-shirts, hats, and some of the bubbly. But it wasn't long before we came back out on the field because none of the fans wanted to leave the stadium. They were going to soak this moment up as long as possible, and we wanted to share it with them.

I was determined to find Mom and Dad. I spotted them up in the seats, but I couldn't get to them from the melee on the field, so I raised both arms and opened and closed my hands trying to get their attention. Finally they saw me, and I blew them a kiss.

Dad raised his hand in the air, and I choked up. When we won the state championship my junior year at Bolles, my dad and I embraced right there on the field, and that was a special moment for us. The 1995 World Series was that times a hundred. Even though we were standing probably a hundred feet apart, in that moment after the game, I needed Dad and Mom to know how thankful I was that they helped me get there, to the pinnacle of baseball.

CHAPTER 11
Raising the Stakes

My agent, Steve Hammond, called me up the winter after we won the World Series and said, "The Braves want to sign you to a long-term deal."

"For what?" I said.

"Four years, thirteen million dollars," he said.

"Sign it," I said. "Right now."

He said, "Well, let's talk about things . . ."

He wanted me to think it through, and maybe I should have, but all I could think about was that I wouldn't have to worry about money. The year before, I'd been borrowing money from Karin's uncle. Now the Braves were offering me $13 million. *Thir-teen mill-ion dollars.* Talk about security. I could buy a new house. I could buy a new car. I would get stability at twenty-three years old, knowing I could almost bank on getting at least one more multi-year deal later on with a shot at big money. We did some negotiating, but not a lot. I signed for four years, $13 million, with an option for a fifth, and I was more than content.

I took my share of criticism for the contract, but if some blowhard agent wanted to bad-mouth it, that was fine. From where I was sitting, it was a great deal. I didn't want to play anywhere else. I had security. And I was flattered. The Braves wanted to keep me in Atlanta for five more years. None of the other guys I'd come up through the minors with—Klesko, Tarasco, or Javy—had that assurance. And the money was nothing to shake a stick at. I went from making $109,000 a year to $750,000. That made me the highest-paid second-year player at that point. And not too many guys have made that kind of money their second year in the big leagues since.

I had inked the deal; now I was ready for the big league life. Karin and I bought a house in Country Club of the South, an upscale neighborhood in the northern Atlanta suburbs where a lot of my veteran teammates lived. Karin was happy. We weren't arguing over money anymore.

I felt a new kind of freedom, as if the contract gave me the right to come and go as I pleased and buy and do whatever I wanted. I could hunt when I wanted to hunt, hang out with the fellows when I wanted to hang out with the fellows. Needless to say, that bred contempt between Karin and me.

She could come and go as she pleased, too, but she wanted to be on my arm 24/7. Karin had been a fixture in the wives section at the stadium my rookie year. She traveled with me so much the

Braves made a rule that wives could only fly on the team charter twice a year. I think everybody called it the Karin Jones rule.

I loved Karin, but there were times I felt suffocated. Part of that was just being twenty-three years old and wanting to be independent. Part of it was living in the public eye. By the beginning of the '96 season, we were fighting nonstop. Then it was even easier to let all the attention I was getting from playing baseball seep into the marriage.

It was probably fitting that Bobby Cox, who had made me the number one pick in the draft and batted me third as a rookie, also named me to my first All-Star team. Bobby was the National League manager for the 1996 All-Star game by virtue of our World Series win the year before. He called me into his office in early July with a little shit-eating grin on his face and said, "You've had a great first half and you deserve to go. I'm taking you to the All-Star game."

I was hitting around .300 with 17 homers at the break, about the same as Giants third baseman Matt Williams, but I didn't have his track record and fans voted him in over me. But I was one of six Braves Bobby took to Philadelphia, including Fred McGriff, who was voted in, Smoltzie, Maddux, Glavine, and Wohlers. Leading up to the game, Williams got hit in the elbow, so Bobby named me the starter at third base with Ken Caminiti backing me up.

I got to experience so many cool things that let me know I was in the presence of greatness. Just taking ground balls was a treat. That's how I first got to know Caminiti during batting practice at the old Veterans Stadium.

He and Matt Williams were the measuring stick at third base. I was the new kid on the block, aspiring to be where they were. Cammy was on ESPN every night, falling over backwards, throwing guys out from the seat of his pants, hitting homers. He could do it all—hit third, hit for power and average. Matt could rival Cammy power-wise and RBI-wise, although maybe not average-wise, and he played steadier defense. Matt didn't hit third for the Giants—Barry Bonds did—but he was Barry's bodyguard in their lineup for a long time. He made sure Bonds saw plenty of fastballs because of the threat he provided coming up behind him.

After I took grounders with Cammy, I went over and took some more with Ozzie Smith and Barry Larkin, who along with Cal were my three favorite shortstops of all time.

Barry and I stood there and watched Ozzie take ground balls. Barry was a kid watching the master, and I was a toddler watching the kid watch the master. Ozzie would field a ground ball, and as he turned to talk to Barry and me about ten feet behind him, he'd flip the ball to second base without looking. After a while, that got old, so Ozzie asked somebody to cover first. On his next ground ball, he threw a big ol' rainbow to first base, without looking, and hit the guy in the chest.

He gave it about five seconds, listened for the guy to catch the ball, looked at me, and said, "Did that ball hit him in the chest?"

"Yep," I said.

It's one of the most incredible things I'd ever seen. I glanced over at Barry.

"Don't look at me," he said. "I can't do that."

That 1996 All-Star game was a wake-up call for me. There were people on this planet doing things I couldn't even fathom. I was on deck when Mike Piazza hit a ball off Charles Nagy into the upper deck. To see and hear him crush a baseball like that and then listen to everybody in the dugout behind me yelling, "Holy shit!"— that was fantasyland for me at age twenty-three. Piazza was Superman.

I was just glad to take my base hit to center off Nagy later that inning. I got a little reassurance that I could hang with the big boys.

Just rubbing elbows with some of the elite players in the game was a big part of the fun of going to an All-Star game. Some of them made good impressions, like Tony Gwynn. Some didn't. I was sitting at a table in the clubhouse BS-ing with Gary Sheffield and Dante Bichette before batting practice when I had my first real interaction with Bonds.

Barry, who was usually the center of attention wherever he went, sat down with us. He had just signed something like a $40 million contract, and Sheff was poking fun at him about it. "You still can't win no championships," he said.

Barry said, straight-faced, "You know how many World Series rings you can buy with forty million dollars?"

I sat there stunned, thinking, *So you want to buy your World Series ring? Wow, what a crappy thing to say.* I cut my eyes over to Dante, and Dante gave me the same look back, like "That's Barry." We quickly changed the subject.

That All-Star game was also a reality check. There was a difference between the way I looked at six foot three, two hundred pounds and the way Caminiti looked. You had to wonder.

I didn't find out for sure that Caminiti had used steroids until much later. And I had no way of knowing Matt Williams would be linked to them at the end of his career, too—he has admitted to buying HGH and steroids while he was with Arizona in 2002. I wasn't going to assume anything about either one in 1996. If I had been in the same locker room with them and saw what was going on, I might have felt differently, but I didn't.

I couldn't persecute somebody for taking steroids back in the day. It crossed everybody's mind. I couldn't help but wonder what kind of numbers I might have put up if I had taken steroids.

I actually had a conversation with Karin about it.

"A lot of people I know are doing stuff illegally," I said.

"What are you talking about?" she said.

"Steroids," I said.

She said, "Well, it's wrong."

"Yeah," I said. "But it's hard to sit here and play this game knowing that people who are winning MVPs, Gold Gloves, and batting titles and beating me out for All-Star teams are cheating."

These were guys who played my position.

Karin started reeling off reasons why she was against it.

"I would be so disappointed in you," she said. "We haven't had kids yet. Steroids have a way of causing deformities and breaking your body down. You could do all kinds of damage. It wouldn't be right. And think about what your mother and father would say if they knew you were on steroids. Your dad would be so disappointed if he ever found that out. You've carved your niche doing it the right way. It'd be a shame for you to take a shortcut now."

She was right. And I needed to hear it. That was probably the single best conversation she and I ever had. I was seriously thinking about it at the time. It's not like I thought steroids were going to take me from 30 to 60 homers or make me the greatest player of all time. But I was open to it.

I thought a lot about what she said. She opened my eyes to the repercussions. That conversation was 90 percent of the reason why I never touched the stuff.

I was coming off a 30-homer, 100-RBI season in 1996. People kill for that kind of production. And I knew I still had room to improve without taking performance-enhancing drugs. I hadn't reached my peak yet.

CHAPTER 12
World Series Ghosts

Standing between us and a trip back to the NLCS in 1996 was my old nemesis Hideo Nomo. We had won the first two games of the Division Series against the Dodgers while I went hitless and now I was facing a guy I was 0-for-12 against, including a triple play I'd hit into earlier in the year. I needed a break against the guy, and I finally got one.

Watching video of Nomo heading into Game 3, our hitting coach, Clarence Jones, figured out Nomo was tipping his pitches out of the stretch.

Most pitchers who throw a split start with that split grip and change it at some point if they're going to throw a fastball. When Nomo came set out of the stretch, he wiggled his pinky finger on his glove hand whenever he changed his grip to a fastball. If he didn't wiggle it, you were getting the split.

I knew if I faced him three or four times in the windup, I was in for a tough time. But if I got him in the stretch, meaning we had runners on base, I'd have a shot.

I managed to single off him and draw a walk in my first two at-bats, even with nobody on base.

My third time up, Lemke, better known to us as "Lemmer," was on second base. Nomo was in the stretch, so I would know what was coming. First pitch, Nomo hung me a split, and I was waiting on it.

My two-run homer to right center gave us a five-run lead and put the game out of reach. We were going back to the NLCS. I went 2-for-2 off Nomo in that series, which gave me some consolation for going 2-for-35 against him in my career.

Waiting for us in the NLCS were the St. Louis Cardinals.

We didn't like the Cardinals very much that year. They had taken on their manager Tony La Russa's personality; all his teams did. La Russa was a very good manager, a Hall of Fame manager, for a reason. His teams were well disciplined and fundamentally sound. But La Russa was a hard-ass. He was not coming to the ballpark to make friends. He was coming to whup your butt. And I respect that. But there were times I wanted to wring his neck.

There was a game in Atlanta one time when Mike Remlinger, one of our relievers, knocked down Jim Edmonds, their center fielder. Remlinger might not have liked Edmonds diving out over the plate, or he might have been sending a message for a high-and-tight pitch by one of their guys earlier in the game. I have no idea. But

Tony started screaming at me from their dugout.

"You better go talk to your pitcher or you're going to get it," he yelled.

I looked over there and he was looking right at me and pointing at his head.

"I'm not pitching," I yelled back.

I didn't have any say over what happened on the phones between our dugout and bullpen. I didn't know if that was a message sent by Bobby or Leo Mazzone, pitching coach, or if it was done by Remlinger himself. I was focusing on my job. I always tried to play the game with class and respect my opponents. La Russa's antics were out of bounds in my opinion. Nothing ever came of our exchange; the Cardinals never knocked me down or hit me. Ultimately, I think it was just window dressing for La Russa to let his team know he'd scream at the other team's player on their behalf.

Very seldom did Cardinals players talk to you on the field. Even guys you knew who went to play for the Cardinals became standoffish and wouldn't look at you, even during time-outs. Adam Wainwright, who came up through the Braves system, was like that. Mike Matheny, their catcher who eventually replaced La Russa as manager, was like that. Edmonds would talk a little bit. Albert Pujols you couldn't shut up. He broke the Cardinals' rule that it was a faux pas to fraternize. I always knew what kind of mood

Albert was in. If he wasn't happy, he would tell me why. If he was happy, he'd tell me that, too. To each his own. But that cool indifference was much more typical of the Cardinals throughout the years, and the '96 team had it in spades.

I think La Russa and Dennis Eckersley, their closer, were separated at birth. The only way their moms could tell the difference was that Eckersley grew a mustache. Eck was just as cocky as Tony and just as intense.

It was the playoffs; you have to be intense—I get it. But Eck got way too emotional for my taste, and it turned that NLCS series around. The Cardinals were kicking our butts, up 3–1 after Eck nailed down a 4–3 win in Game 4 in St. Louis. He got the last four outs and after he struck out Marquis Grissom to strand the tying run at second base and bring the Cardinals within a win of the World Series, Eck gave a full arm swing and looked right into our dugout, yelling, "Yeah!!!"

We were the defending World Series Champs, and they were trying to make a point. OK. But celebrate with your teammates. Celebrate with your fans. Walk off the field and get ready for the game tomorrow. Do not wake a sleeping giant. And that's what he did.

I was fuming. I didn't know if anybody else felt the same way—this was my second year in the league—but I was pissed. When we walked back into the visiting clubhouse at Busch Stadium, David Justice was one of the last guys in. He shut the door behind him.

"Did y'all see that right there?" he said. "They're over there putting nails in y'all's coffins right now."

He said "y'all" because he'd been out since May with a shoulder injury.

"But I'll be damned if Dennis Eckersley is going to do that to me," he said. "They ain't scoring another fucking run this whole series."

Fuck yeah, I thought.

We had a bunch of good leaders in that clubhouse, but David had the balls to say the words nobody else would say. That's why I like David so much. He's a lot like me. A lot of times we should probably keep our mouths shut, but speaking our minds is who we are.

Our team walked out of the clubhouse that night almost like we had just won the game. We were so fired up to get to the park the next day. And the ass whupping that took place after that was epic.

We didn't want Dennis Eckersley to take the mound for the rest of the series. The way to do that was by never giving him a lead to protect. Our pitchers were right there with us, like "We got this."

I wanted to beat them 15–0 every game. If Alan Benes hadn't thrown well in Game 6, we might have. We outscored them 32–1 over the next three games.

Poor Todd Stottlemyre and Donovan Osborne. Stottlemyre didn't make it out of the second inning in Game 5, gave up seven runs, and we won 14–0. The series was going back to Atlanta, and I think everybody between St. Louis and Atlanta said, "Oh shit, here we go. It's going to get crazy."

There were a few thousand empty seats at Fulton County Stadium for the first two games of the series, but by the time we got back for Game 6, the place was rocking. Atlanta fans have taken their knocks throughout the years—and some of it has been warranted—but when we have absolutely, positively needed them, the fans have been there.

Doggie outpitched Alan Benes in Game 6, and we won 3–1. Then we blew the doors off in Game 7. We scored six runs in the first inning off Osborne, including a bases-loaded triple, from Glavine, of all people.

I was one of the guys who made an out in that first inning, but I had a good series. I thought I was going to win the MVP—I had eleven hits with a couple of doubles—but Javy had thirteen hits with a couple of homers. Goodness. The Cardinals couldn't get him out either.

From Game 5 of that NLCS until Game 3 of the World Series—a five-game stretch over eight days—we were the hottest team on the planet. Then all of a sudden, we weren't.

The '95 World Series had been a blast, but it went by so fast. In '96, with a year under my belt, I was relaxed enough to take in a lot more sights and sounds.

The World Series was in New York, which amped it up times ten. Nothing against Cleveland because those fans were out of control, but the difference between a World Series in Yankee Stadium and a World Series in Jacobs Field was night and day. There's just something special about reaching the pinnacle of your season and seeing how you measure up against a New York team.

I was a small-town boy playing in Yankee Stadium for the first time. I wanted to make my mark in the house where Mickey, Babe Ruth, Don Larsen, and Whitey Ford played, not to mention guys I watched growing up, like Catfish Hunter, Ron Guidry, Dave Righetti, and Donnie Baseball. If you love the history of the game, nothing beats playing in a World Series in the old Yankee Stadium. It's the most fun you'll ever have playing baseball.

The only problem was we had to wait out a nor'easter before it started. We spent three days sitting in our hotel rooms and it felt like a week. We'd go to the park and hit in the cages, but that was it.

The clubhouse at old Yankee Stadium was nothing glamorous, but it was like walking into a haunted house. It was spooky. All I could think was *My goodness, how many studs walked through this door? How many studs sat down in this chair that I'm about to sit in?* The clubhouse guys were like a window into the past. They probably saw Ted Williams walk those halls.

Walking along those two-tone blue-and-white walls to head out for BP the first time, I got about thirty feet from the dugout and looked out. All I could see on the field from that vantage point were legs and feet.

It was a throng of people, and I think every one of them had a camera. With all the flashes going off as I walked up those dugout steps onto the field, you would have thought I was Elizabeth Taylor. It was the first and only time I was almost overwhelmed by all the media.

I couldn't get to the batting cage without somebody tapping me on the shoulder: "Hey, can you take a picture? Hey, can I get an interview? Hey, just a couple questions." There was no way to accommodate everybody. Yankee Stadium is where I first learned how to say no to the media.

The next time I walked down the tunnel to the field, it was easier to focus; it was game time. That was my forty-five seconds to take a deep breath and get mentally prepared, because once you got there, it was chaos.

The 1996 Yankees were itching to get back to prominence. Their roster was so stacked it was almost laughable. They had good young homegrown talent—Derek Jeter, Jorge Posada, Mariano Rivera, Bernie Williams—mixed in with a who's who of Hall of Fame–worthy players they'd gathered up along the way—David Cone, Darryl Strawberry, Cecil Fielder, Wade Boggs, Tim Raines.

I caught myself looking over into their dugout thinking, *Wow, that must be a cool clubhouse to be in, all those guys interacting together.* We had some pretty good names on the backs of our jerseys, too, and top to bottom, I thought we had the better team, but those Yankees were almost like a World Baseball Classic team. They had it all.

I don't know how awestruck our guys were, but even Glavine, Maddux, Smoltz, Justice, McGriff—the guys who were on top of their game—had never been to Yankee Stadium. They might not have admitted it then, but being there was pretty cool for everybody.

Walking to the plate under the bright lights and hearing Bob Sheppard announce my name for my first at-bat was the most nervous I'd ever been—more nervous than my first at-bat in the World Series the year before. I did not want to strike out and get that crowd on me. I wanted to serve notice immediately.

Andy Pettitte made a mistake and I hit a rocket

to right center field. I thought it was a double, but Paul O'Neill ran it down. Still, as I rounded first, I thought, *Whew, OK, I got this.* Watching replays of it later, when the camera panned to Pettitte, I could read his lips saying to himself: "You're lucky to get that one back."

My next at-bat, I was more relaxed. *It's just baseball. Same game. Tune everything out and keep going.* Our nineteen-year-old phenom out-fielder Andruw Jones had introduced himself to the world by hitting the first of his two home runs that night, and we were up 2–0. I had runners on second and third, with one out. Luckily, the Yankees decided to bring the infield in, which made it all-or-nothing for their fielders. *You've got to put the ball in play right here.*

With two strikes, I knew Andy was going to his bread and butter: his cutter. Sure enough, he threw me a cutter down and in, but it was over the plate enough that I could shoot the hole between short and third. Both runners scored to put us up 4–0. I took second on the throw home, and I wasn't finished.

While angry fans buzzed in the stands, and the Yankees met on the mound, I stood there thinking. *All right, we've got one out; Freddy McGriff's up. Pettitte's a tough matchup on our lefties, so why not make life easy on Freddy? If I can get to third with less than two outs and Freddy drives me in, we'll make this a five-run lead and Game 1 is over. If Pettitte gives me one look and throws home, I'm going.*

Pettitte had an unbelievable pickoff move. Bobby and the coaches had told us in the scouting meetings: Don't move off first base until you literally see Pettitte step toward home plate. But they also said Pettitte paid very little attention to runners on second. He hadn't shown our scouts an inside move all year.

Pettitte gave me one look then went into his big high leg kick. I had taken six steps before he ever delivered the ball. I stole third easily. Then Freddy singled to make it 5–0, and the flood-gates opened. Three batters later, Andruw Jones homered again.

We beat the Yankees 12–1 that night, and their faithful were none too happy about it. Our lead was big enough where I could relax a little and actually pay attention to what was going on around me. I looked down around third base and there must have been two dollars in change lying in the dirt. I had been so focused on what was going on between the pitcher and the hitter I didn't notice nickels and quarters flying in front of my face. I did have a guy throw a piece of chewed-up bubble gum at me when I caught a pop-up near the stands behind third base. The umpire was standing right there and threw him out of the game.

That's one thing about New Yorkers; they're going to get their money's worth. If their team wins, they're cocky and talking smack. If their team is getting an ass whupping, they will rag on you all night. They'll get drunk and talk about your mama and your wife and kids.

It didn't bother us that night. We'd come to New York with a goal of splitting the first two games. Then we would reclaim home-field advantage because three of the remaining five games would be in Atlanta. Now we'd already guaranteed the split, so all the pressure was on them.

Game 2 was a better indication of what the series was going to be like—a dogfight—but we won that one, too. None of us had seen Jimmy Key before, but McGriff drove in three runs and we won 4–0. Maddux dealt. He pitched eight shutout innings, allowing the Yankees maybe a half dozen balls out of the infield. It might have been the best game Doggie ever pitched, to shut the Yankees out in that atmosphere, with that much on the line.

I don't think anybody expected us to take the first two games in New York, especially in such dominant fashion. But after our comeback against St. Louis, we were peaking. Our offense was clicking. Glav and Doggie were pitching well. We were going back home with the world by the tail.

Game 3 wasn't that big of a hiccup; we just got beat. David Cone and Tom Glavine both threw well, and Bernie Williams homered off McMichael in a 5–2 loss. Then everything changed in Game 4.

We had the game all but won. We knocked Kenny Rogers out in the second inning and were up 6–0 through five innings. But Denny Neagle, as good a number four pitcher as we ever had, started to let things get away. By the eighth, our lead was down to 6–3, and Bobby brought in Wohlers. Sometimes a save comes in the eighth inning.

Any closer will tell you, the rule of thumb in crunch time is if you're going to get beat, get beat with your best pitch. Wohlers broke it. He hung a slider—his third-best pitch, behind his fastball and split—to Jim Leyritz, and Leyritz jumped all over it for a three-run homer.

The game was tied 6–6, and whatever control we had of both the game and the series was lost, just like that.

The game went extra innings, and in the tenth Wade Boggs threw up an epic at-bat against Steve Avery with the bases loaded. Boggs kept fouling off pitches, and after a couple of marginal calls, Avery walked him to give up the winning run. We lost 8–6.

I by no means fault Ave; that was a Hall of

Fame hitter throwing up a great at-bat. That game was not won or lost right there. It came down to one swing of the bat by their backup catcher in the eighth inning. I think we could have stomached Leyritz's homer if he'd hit it off of one of Wohlers's 100 mph fastballs. But give Leyritz credit; he was still able to adjust, slow his swing down, and barrel up a slider—pretty impressive.

After we lost that game, the series was tied 2-2; but you could feel it slipping away. We'd been poised to win the World Series in five games, and instead we lost it in six.

In Game 5, we didn't expect to repeat what we did against Pettitte in Game 1, but we didn't expect what he did to us either. He and Smoltz dueled like Smoltz and Jack Morris in Game 7 of the '91 World Series. And like the Twins, the Yankees won, 1–0.

The Yankees were up 1–0 when I led off the ninth. They had brought Pettitte back out, and I couldn't believe it. I knew I'd have a better shot against a tiring Pettitte than a fresh John Wetteland, their closer. I just knew I was going to give Atlanta hope that we could turn things around.

I turned on a little cutter from Pettitte and hit it down the left field line. Strawberry, as a left-hander, had to come around the ball in left field, get turned, and throw. I knew I was going to second regardless. Once I got there, I turned to our dugout and growled. Everybody was jacked up. *We're going to get this sucker tied up.*

I took third on a groundout, so with one out, all we needed was a fly ball to tie it up. Javy hit an absolute rocket to third base, and Charlie Hayes snagged it. I went from *We're going to win!* to *Oh shit.* Now Wetteland was coming in.

Luis Polonia threw up an incredible at-bat and squared a ball up. When I saw its trajectory toward right center field, I thought there was no way Paul O'Neill was catching it. He kept gaining on it, though, and when he made the catch, we were done. It was like somebody popped our balloon. We were down 3-2 in the series and headed back to New York.

We lost in Game 6 3–2 at Yankee Stadium. When Lemmer popped up with runners on first and second to end the game and strand the tying run in scoring position, I was on deck. I never got a chance to face Wetteland, that day or the rest of my career. I was one out away from being able to live out the backyard dream in the biggest baseball cathedral of them all. I felt cheated.

"New York, New York" was blaring on the sound system as I turned and walked back to our dugout. Missing a chance like that felt worse than striking out with the bases loaded. From that day on, I vowed to make the most of every opportunity, especially late in games with the winning run on base.

The '96 World Series loss stung. There's no doubt in my mind we had the best team in baseball that year and we started the series like a house on fire. For whatever reason, the spark was extinguished.

Had we won that World Series, those '90s Braves teams would have been spoken about differently. Instead, our '95 World Series title was our last, and the Yankees went on to win three World Series in the next four years. If you win back-to-back championships, you're put in a different category. We had the chance. We had it right there. And I never got that close again.

Already "suited" for baseball at age one.
Jones Family

Best buds since we were kids. That's B. B. Abbott (right) at age eight and me at age six, hanging at the Joneses' house in Pierson, Florida. *Jones Family*

The Pierson Cubs was the first team I ever played on at age eight. Our uniform was baby blue T-shirts, Levi's, and black cleats. Horrid, right?
Jones family

Taking a left-handed stance for my DeLand Babe Ruth All-Star team, age fourteen.
Jones family

Bolles baseball portrait
my senior year, 1990.
Jones family

Dad and I
embrace after
we won the state
championship
my junior year at
Bolles. That was
a big moment
for Dad and me.
Jones family

Sharing a laugh with my boys (from left: Shea, Tristan, Matthew, and Trey) and with my parents (Larry and Lynne) behind us the night the Braves retired my number 10 jersey.
Jones family

On our wedding day, with the queen of my castle, Taylor Jones. *McClanahan Studio*

CHAPTER 13
Inside the Clubhouse

Even though I played in two World Series my first two years in the big leagues, my teammates made sure I kept my head out of the clouds.

Not only did they nail me in the annual rookie prank once—dressing me up in ridiculous clothes on a road trip—they got me my second year, too. It was always in Montreal. That was the only city where we went through customs. We had to walk through the airport terminal instead of busing out onto the tarmac, which guaranteed embarrassment.

Our last trip to Montreal in '96, I thought, *This is great. I get to watch the rookie dress up instead of being a part of it.* But I came in after the last game of the series and waiting in my locker were a pair of red polyester pants, a candy cane–striped blazer, a white butterfly-collared shirt, green platform shoes, and big Harry Caray glasses.

"What the fuck?" I said to anyone who would listen. "You guys got me last year."

"We don't remember" was the response. "We're getting you again."

I bitched about it for ten minutes, but they weren't giving my street clothes back. So through customs I went, wearing the Pee-wee Herman outfit, pissed off.

My teammates had their little ways of sending me messages. Avery, Glavine, and Kent Mercker, another one of our really good starting pitchers early in my career, were always scheming. As long as they weren't pitching, they were up to no good. Ave, Mercker, and Maddux were usually the ringleaders. They would run the idea by Glavine and he executed everything.

One of their old standbys was the flaming shoelaces trick. You'd be sitting on the bench and somebody would crawl up behind you and light your shoelaces on fire. You wouldn't realize it until your ankles started getting hot. You'd look down and see a flame and wig the fuck out. Then you'd be kicking off your shoes while everybody else was laughing their asses off.

They were big on shaving cream in the toes of your shoes, Icy Hot in the crotch of your shorts, bubblegum bubbles on your hats, all the typical stuff. I think Ave actually invented the idea of wearing snow goggles during champagne celebrations. He's from Michigan, and he took part in a lot of celebrations, so it makes sense.

Ave was a little kid around the clubhouse. But he was a different animal when he pitched. He hardly said a word during his starts, which is why one game he pitched against the Mets in New York in 1996 stands out so much in my memory.

It was the third inning and Jose Vizcaino was on second base for the Mets. Todd Hundley, their catcher, homered off Avery, and Vizcaino turned and started waving both his arms at the ball, yelling, "GO! GO! GO!" He had his back to the mound, but Ave was watching. When the ball went out of the park, Vizcaino gave it a big "Yeah!"

This was early June, not the stretch run in September. Vizcaino had been in the league for half a dozen years. He knew better. I was taken aback by his antics, and I wasn't the only one. Ave came back in the dugout, sat down next to me, and nonchalantly said, "Was Vizcaino doing what I think he was doing?"

I raised my eyebrows and nodded.

Ave didn't say another word about it.

"Wow, that guy really hit that ball a long way," he said, referring to Hundley.

"Yeah, he got it pretty good," I said.

As fate would have it, Vizcaino came up the next inning. The first pitch he saw from Ave hit him in the side of the kneecap. Vizcaino was done. They had to come get him off the field. He was out the rest of the series. Dallas Green, the Mets manager, went nuts.

Avery didn't flinch. After the inning was over, he came back in the dugout, sat down, and just as nonchalantly as before, said, "Hey, was Vizcaino doing cartwheels when they were carting him off the field?"

The whole bench erupted in laughter.

Then, of course, Ave led off the next inning. He and Dallas Green started jawing at each other while Ave was at the plate. It must not have bothered Ave much because he proceeded to hit a ball 410 feet off the center field wall. He got to second base, turned, and looked at Dallas Green like "What are you going to do about it?"

That's the kind of guy Ave was. You pushed his buttons, you made him better. He'd shut you out and get three or four hits to rub it in. And he was a really good hitter for a pitcher, the best out of that starting rotation, and all those guys could handle the bat a little.

Maddux is a different cat, man. He has fun, and what he deems fun is grossing people out.

Doggie was a very good athlete, but he didn't look it in street clothes, especially before he got LASIK and had to wear glasses. Because of that, I think he got his jollies being a shock jock.

In our clubhouse, his locker was right by the basket of clean sanitary socks. Every day when he came in, usually after playing eighteen holes of golf, he'd drop trou, wipe his ass with a sanitary, and put it back in the basket. Then while he got dressed he'd wait for the next guy to walk in and take some socks. Sometimes that guy was me.

Doggie got the biggest kick out of it. He'd just sit there and giggle. Sometimes he would wait until a guy actually put them on before he told them.

Doggie was also big on loogies. He'd hock one onto the dugout ceiling, then watch it land on some unsuspecting teammate's head. Or he'd take aim at a chain-link fence and see how many links he could get the loogie to drip down while staying in one piece. Sometimes if we were somewhere cold, the loogie would still be there the next day, frozen.

I was the butt of quite a few of Maddux's pranks over the years. He used to find something important to talk to me about in the shower after a game. I'd be locked in, engaged in conversation—I mean, you're talking to Greg Maddux—and everybody would start snickering. I'd look down and he'd be pissing all over me.

You couldn't get mad, though. He would bust out in uncontrollable laughter, and everybody else would, too. Trust me, whenever Doggie was around, the mood was jolly. Very seldom did Doggie and I ever get confrontational, and if we did, it was over a card game on the plane.

I don't want to get all bromantic, but I cherished my time with him. I knew Greg Maddux was the best in the business. He came as close to being a unanimous first-ballot Hall of Famer as only a handful of players in the history of the game—he had the eighth-highest voting percentage when he went in. And I think it's pretty cool that I count him as one of my friends.

Doggie was all about wins. He wanted to be our generation's wins leader. One time he asked me, "Would you rather go 20-20 or 19-2?"

"I'll go 19-2," I said. If you go 19-2, chances are, with that many more no-decisions than losses, your team won more games. "You're going to say 20-20, right?"

"Yep," he'd say. "I won more games than you."

That was just his mentality. His record of 15 wins or more in 17 straight seasons was ridiculous. Nobody is ever going to do that again. How many guys are going to have a career that long, much less stay healthy and be that dominant for so long?

If Doggie was really honest, he would probably say he should have retired a couple of years earlier than he did. But as long as Roger Clemens was still pitching and they were neck and neck in wins, Doggie was going to keep pitching. He was not going to retire until he knew he had Roger Clemens in the rearview mirror. I don't know that he'd ever admit it, but I knew. And once that finally happened, Doggie rode off into the sunset with 355 wins. Clemens had retired with 354.

I've got no problem saying Maddux was the

best pitcher of our era, over Clemens. Early in his career, Roger got by on intimidation—with that "don't-mess-with-me, I'm-going-to-shove-it-up-your-rear-end" aura about him. And it worked. But once he started to lose a little on his fastball, he learned how to pitch, and he was even harder to hit.

At that point, you didn't know if you were going to get a fastball. You might get a cutter, some splits, or maybe even the hook that you never expected to be a strike. Clemens had great angles. He could throw a pitch on the outside corner that looked like it was off the plate. Then boom, it was right on the corner. Or it looked like it was going to be low. Boom, right at the knees. You had to work your ass off to put the ball in play against him. That's when he became more like Doggie.

Greg knew how to pitch from day one. He took his lumps his first year or two in the big leagues and realized something had to change. That's when he learned how to sink and cut the ball on both sides of the plate. That and the fact that he's got probably one of the best two or three changeups the game has ever seen. Doggie was a surgeon. He didn't do it with 95, 96 mph. He did it with 90 to 92, movement, change of speeds, and most of all, by outsmarting you.

You can't outthink Doggie. He knew exactly what a hitter was thinking just by his reaction to a pitch and then he formulated a game plan to make him look bad for the rest of the night.

I faced Maddux nine times after he left Atlanta, and each time it was like a chess match. I managed three hits off him, so apparently I had learned a few things from nine years of playing cards with him and talking baseball. Every opportunity I got with him, I listened and learned.

Sometimes, though, you just had to scratch your head. One story, in particular, made its way into Atlanta lore. Doggie was facing Luis Gonzalez in a one-run game with a couple of guys on and a base open. Gonzalez owned Doggie, and Doggie was behind in the count, but he didn't like walking anybody intentionally or otherwise. Leo came out, and we were meeting on the mound.

"Bobby wants you to walk this guy," Leo said.

"Nope, not walking him," Doggie said. "I'm going to throw him a changeup away, then a cutter on his hands, and he's going to pop up to Chipper."

I looked at Doggie. I looked at Leo. Leo looked at me. I'm thinking, *Huh?* The right play was to walk him, get a ground-ball from the next guy, and get out of the inning.

Leo shrugged and said, "All right." He turned and went back to the dugout.

First pitch was a changeup, three or four inches off the plate for a ball. Then came the cutter in, and Luis popped it up to me. The whole time the ball was in the air, I was standing under it with my glove up, thinking, *You gotta be shitting me.*

I caught the ball and gave it back to Doggie. When we came off the field, Leo was laughing his ass off in the dugout.

"Just the way we drew it up, huh, Chip?" he said.

Unbelievable. Maddux had just told us not only what he was going to throw but what the hitter was going to do with it. We've laughed about that one a hundred times over the years. But Maddux knew if he executed his pitch what Gonzalez would do with it. That's not just playing the game; it's knowing the game inside out.

All of our "Big Three" Hall of Fame pitchers played the game at a different level, which made them fun to play behind. And they had three completely different personalities. Doggie was the brainiac. Glavine was all business, all the time. Smoltzie was straight clown, 24/7.

Doggie knew what people were thinking, and he had the arsenal to expose their weakness at any time. Glav didn't have the greatest stuff, but he gutted out every single inning. And Smoltzie pitched like his hair was on fire; he threw everything as hard as he could. All three ways worked.

Of the three guys, I probably got along the best with Doggie. Glav didn't let his hair down much, didn't like a lot of company. I was close to Smoltzie for a time, but when it came to going out to eat on the road or riding to the ballpark, I always went with Doggie. He took care of me, too. I never paid for a thing when Doggie was around.

Every once in a while I filled out their golf foursome. Back then, I didn't play a ton of golf during the season. I was anal about how it might mess up my baseball swing.

Smoltzie was the most competitive of the three. It didn't matter if they were reading an article in the newspaper at the same time; Smoltzie wanted to finish first. The guy is like a ten-year-old kid. Smoltzie would play as many holes of golf as it took until he won, and he usually did. But when he lost, he lost big because he'd get down and keep pressing.

Glav was just as poised on the golf course as he was on the mound. He wasn't going to let you see if something bothered him, but he has one of the ugliest golf swings I've ever seen in my life, like a left-handed Jim Furyk—no disrespect to either one of those guys. Jim is a friend of mine and he's obviously one of the best golfers in the world.

Maddux was the least physically imposing of the "Big Three," but he was afraid of nobody. I know this because I was sitting next to him in the dugout in Tampa after our shortstop, Walt Weiss, got hit by a pitch twice in a game. The second time Tanyon Sturtze had drilled him in the back of the neck, and Bobby Cox was pissed.

I was right there when Bobby walked past Doggie and said, "I want you to hit the first motherfucker who comes up the next inning. I don't give a fuck who it is."

After Bobby walked off, Doggie said, "Larry, who's leading off next inning?"

"Canseco, bro," I said, as in Jose Canseco, six foot four, 250 pounds, and ripped up.

Maddux stuck out his bottom lip, as if to say, "Oh, OK."

"Sure you don't want to hit the second guy?" I said.

"Nope," he said. "Got to hit the first guy."

So I started to strategize.

"OK, if he charges the mound, run toward second and I'll come in from the side and take out a kneecap," I said. "I'll get him off his feet until the cavalry gets there. You won't have to worry about any of it."

He just laughed.

"He won't charge," he said.

I'm not sure how he knew that, but he was right. Second pitch the next inning, Maddux drilled Canseco in the hip. Jose chirped, but he didn't come out. The benches cleared, and words were exchanged, but that was it. Maddux never got warned, ejected, nothing. He just kept pitching, and before it was all said and done, he had pitched a complete game.

I get asked a lot, if I were playing in a Game 7, which of the "Big Three" would I want on the mound? You can't go wrong with any of them, but if you were to put a gun to my head, I'd probably have to say Smoltzie.

Smoltzie had a way of digging deep, and he had the most swing-and-miss ability. That's probably why he was the most successful of the three in the postseason. When it's cold, it's hard for hitters to get loose, so it's easier to overpower them than to finesse them.

Smoltzie's approach probably hurt him at times during the regular season, but it helped him in October. It didn't matter if it was spring training or Game 7 of the World Series, Smoltzie was trying to strike you out. Because of that, he didn't go as deep into games as the other two. He'd throw 120 pitches in five innings and wonder why he couldn't throw a complete game. But come postseason, his approach worked better than the other guys'.

Maddux and Glavine wanted to throw three-hit shutouts on 95 pitches in two-hour games. In the regular season, you love to see pitchers being economical and taking advantage of hitters' contact. But in the postseason, the more balls you put in play, the more pressure you put on defenses and the greater your chance to generate offense. If you strike out 10 or 12 times against a guy, offense isn't going to come easy.

The pitch that really set Smoltzie apart was his slider. He could do a bunch of different things with it. A good slider comes out of the pitcher's hand looking like a fastball, and when it gets halfway to home plate it starts doing something else. Most sliders sweep across the plate, like a David Cone slider, or a Laredo.

Smoltzie could make his slider sweep or drop straight down like a hard curveball. Then he had one slider that did both—swept across and dropped down at a forty-five degree angle. While that was probably the pitch he made the most mistakes with, it was also the pitch he had the most success with. The only time I did any damage when I faced him in spring training was when he tried to throw that pitch for a strike and hung it.

He would tell you before the ball ever got to home plate whether it was good or not. If a slider came out of his hand wrong, you could actually hear him say "uh-oh." I faced Smoltzie in a couple of simulated games down in West Palm, and I hit one of my favorite home runs ever on one of his hanging sliders. As it came out of his hand, I heard him say "uh-oh," and I hit it out of the park. I never let him live that down.

I never did face Smoltz in a major league game—he finished his career with the Red Sox and Cardinals—and I was glad. If either of us had one at-bat to go on, whether he got me out or I got a base hit, it would have been absolute hell for the other guy.

Smoltzie and I had a big brother–little brother relationship. We would fight like sibling rivals and then we'd be fine. I can't tell you how many games of backgammon he and I played in the clubhouse, or how many hands of cards.

Smoltzie was a cutup. He had fun playing the game. That's one thing I always loved about him. Don't get me wrong; when he pitched, he was there to beat you. But the second the game ended he was doing the "marching band" in the shower. He would be butt naked in a pair of flip-flops and start stomping on the ground and beating his chest and thighs to a certain beat. You didn't even have to be in the shower. Whenever somebody said Smoltzie was doing "marching band," everybody came running from all over the clubhouse. The whole team would stand around him, clapping their hands and stomping their feet.

Smoltzie would literally be red with handprints on his chest and thighs from beating them so hard. Everybody loved it, especially one time when the floor was extra soapy. Smoltzie stomped, and his foot went out from under him. He landed flat on his back. Everybody gasped. But he just rolled over and got back up. Everybody started dying laughing again.

We had some real characters in our clubhouse, and I'm not just talking about the players. Frank Fultz, our strength and conditioning coach for a lot of years, was a clown. He provided endless hours of entertainment.

He had a really dry sense of humor, and there was nobody better at initiating young guys. He'd have three or four veterans in the weight room, and some young pup would walk in and Frank would say, "What do you want to work on today?"

"My hamstring is a little tight," the guy would say.

"Oh, I've got the perfect remedy," Frank would say. "Let me show you these hamstring exercises."

He'd go over to a forty-five-pound straight bar and start giving instructions.

"OK, now, I want you to pick up the straight bar to your waist," Frank would say. "Then I want you to flex your butt cheeks."

We're sitting there listening to this.

"I want you to get up on one tiptoe," he'd say. "And I want you to hop."

We're all about to bust out laughing. The guy would be clinching his butt cheeks before he realized he'd been had. By then the whole room was erupting.

You've got to be able to laugh at yourself in a big league clubhouse. The same goes for the bench. As seriously as we all took the game, things happened from time to time that you couldn't help but lose it over. It happens to everybody.

We were playing a game in Florida early in my career when I forgot the number of outs. That's one of the most embarrassing things a ballplayer can do, whether you're on the bases or in the field. Somebody is going to see you. Everybody saw me that day. I made one of those swinging-bunt bare-handed plays at third base, slung it to first for an out, and ran off the field in complete "dig-me" mode.

I got all the way into the dugout, put my hat and glove on the step, sat on the bench, looked out on the field, and realized everybody else was still out there, staring at me. Smoltzie and Glav were sitting next to me in the dugout, dying laughing. There's nowhere to hide either. I had to go back out onto the field, obviously. So I gave a little tip of the cap to my teammates as they welcomed me back.

You do that once in your career? You don't ever do it again.

When you live with twenty-four other guys in a clubhouse day in and day out, some guys are going to rub you the wrong way. And that's fine. One good thing about the Braves—if they deem you a bad apple, you're not going to be around very long. So we didn't have very many. I rarely had problems with guys we had long-term.

One guy who didn't like me all that much when I first got to the big leagues was Jeff Blauser. I had a lot of hype and I was next in line for his job at shortstop. To be honest, I probably wouldn't have liked me either. Blaus made fun of me from time to time, which I didn't particularly like, but once I moved to third base, we made our peace. Playing side by side on the infield, our respect for each other grew. He was always prepared to make the smart play. And he gave you steady offense in what was still predominantly a defensive position at that time.

Blaus helped me get over the hump the first time I hit 30 homers. I'd been stuck on 29 for more than a week my second year in the big leagues, pressing. Finally, Blaus walked up to me and said, "You want to hit thirty or not?"

"Yeah," I said. "I want to hit thirty."

"Then stop worrying about it," he said. "Just play the game, dude. You got to twenty-nine just playing the game. Now you're all freaked out and jacked up because you want so bad to get to thirty. Immerse yourself in the game. Trust me, you're going to hit thirty."

He was right. I got my 30th within a game or two of that conversation.

There weren't too many guys I played against over the course of my career that I had much of a problem with either. I wasn't "big leagued" very often. The one time I remember somebody looking down his nose at me, it was Barry Bonds.

We were playing the Giants early in 1996 and I asked one of the clubhouse guys to go over to their side and ask Barry if he would sign a couple of balls for me. Bonds told the clubhouse guy to have me come talk to him during batting practice. Every once in a while, if a player thinks clubhouse guys are taking advantage of him—that they're getting the autographs for some ulterior motive—he will ask you to come to him directly. Fair enough.

So I went up to Barry during batting practice and asked him to sign a couple of balls, one for me and one for charity.

"Man, you ain't even got the *r* from behind your name yet," he said.

He was basically calling me a rookie. He'd arranged this little meeting to tell me no.

"You're exactly right," I said. "I got no right to ask you for an autograph." I walked off thinking, *Don't worry, it will never happen again.*

Major League Baseball players, especially the really good ones, have egos. I've got an ego. But I would never disrespect another player like that.

You can call it rookie hazing, but I wasn't a rookie anymore. I never would have asked him my rookie year. That wasn't the proper etiquette. By '96, I felt that I had earned the right to ask for an autograph. We had won the World Series. I was hitting third for the best team in the National League. Apparently, in his eyes, I was wrong. I was navel lint as far as he was concerned.

Now, whatever my thoughts of him personally are, Barry Bonds is the best all-around player I ever saw don a uniform, in person, in my life. That still does not give a guy the right to disrespect another player. It made a very bad first impression with me, and quite frankly, I never forgot it.

Over the years, I got the feeling Barry started to respect my game. He'd get to third base when we were playing the Giants, and I wouldn't even walk over there. A couple of times late in his career, he'd say, "Man, you don't even talk to me no more."

I'd be thinking, *What do you want with little ol' me?*

I played professional baseball for twenty-three years, nineteen in the big leagues, and I never turned another player down for an autograph, regardless of my status in the game, regardless of his. That is the ultimate compliment you can receive from another player. You have to swallow some pride to ask a player on another team for an autograph. You must think an awful lot of that player. Apparently, Barry didn't see it that way, and that's baffling to me.

The Braves actually came within a hair of trading for Bonds when he was with Pittsburgh in the early '90s. I don't think that relationship would have lasted very long. We didn't have guys like that in our clubhouse. We had a bunch of guys who cared more about being one-ninth of the equation than trying to be the greatest to ever play the game. That's the way—thank goodness—the Braves brass thought a team should be put together. And you can't argue with the success we had.

CHAPTER 14
The Perks

As a player, you have to portray a certain amount of necessary arrogance. When you're walking to the plate, you need a strut in your step that says, *I'm going to get you.* But there's a time, even during the game, when that wears off. There's a time when, during a pitching change, you can walk over and exchange pleasantries with an ex-teammate or say hello to a third base coach. There's nothing in the rule book that says you can't be a good dude and still have an edge.

I'm the classic example. Nobody wanted to knock a pitcher's head off more than me. But when I wasn't either hitting or gearing up midpitch at third base, I'd like to think most people on other teams would say, "That Chipper is an all right dude. He came over and said hey to me, told me I was a good player."

Getting a compliment from an established player can do wonders for a young player. And I don't think there's anything wrong with giving somebody on another team an encouraging word. Our pitchers could get them out no matter what I said.

Cal Ripken did it for me. So did Tony Gwynn. Some of my best friends in the game were guys I never played with. Do you think Derek Jeter is too big to autograph something for me? He would walk over after I hit a two-run double in the gap and say, "Hey, man, swinging it. Way to go." Those are guys I respect. Those are guys I could sit down with at an All-Star game and have a beer with.

Meeting Cal in Game 1 of the '95 World Series broke the ice for me. The next time I saw him was two years later when we played the Orioles in the first year of interleague play. With a couple of years under my belt, I felt better about walking up to somebody of Cal's stature and saying, "Hey, what's up?" But Cal had made me feel like I belonged from the get-go. It was the same way that series.

I was standing at third base during a pitching change and Cal came over to me. I was like a little schoolgirl, inwardly giggling and hee-heeing. *Cal is talking to me.* We massaged each other's egos for a minute, but typical Cal, he did away with the pleasantries pretty quickly and got right into baseball talk.

He had just made the move from shortstop to third base that year. He started asking me where I took my cutoff throws from left field. I thought, *You're asking me for advice, really?* But he was dead serious, so I backed up and showed him.

"Right here," I said.

"OK, I can see that," he said, and then went on. "Let me ask you something. Wouldn't it help if you were back a little more towards the catcher? That way when you've got that runner coming around third, you can keep him in your peripheral vision longer. And you can already tell if the throw needs to be cut or if it's on line. You can cut more bad throws."

I'm thinking, *Man, this guy has been playing third base for a shorter period of time than I have and he's coming up with this great piece of advice.*

"That makes perfect sense," I said. "That's awesome. Something so simple, I never even thought about that."

From then on, I played as deep as I could toward the catcher on cutoffs. I never even had to listen for the catcher to tell me when to cut the throw because I already knew. And I had a much better shot of getting outs, either by throwing a guy out trying to take an extra base or letting a ball go through for an out at home plate. I got all that from one conversation on the base paths with Cal.

I had a couple of funny conversations standing on deck throughout my career, too. The most memorable one was with President Bush, the elder one, H.W.

He was sitting right behind our on-deck circle at Minute Maid Park in Houston during Game 1 of the 2001 Division Series. Big Astros fan. I couldn't help but cut my eyes over there as I stepped out of our dugout. President Bush was looking right at me.

Straight-faced as hell, he said, "Don't you do it."

The game was tied 3–3 and Astros manager Larry Dierker had brought in Billy Wagner, their closer with the 100 mph fastball, to face me in the eighth inning. It was the right move. I was 0-for-9 with seven punch-outs off Wags at that point, hadn't gotten so much as a base hit off him.

But I had a little shit-eating grin on my face.

"Mr. President, I've got a job to do," I said. "You of all people should understand that."

"I do," he said. "But I'm really nervous about this at-bat."

"I'm glad to hear that," I said.

I think he actually helped relax me. I remembered something I had heard one of the Cardinals hitters, Eduardo Perez, say in passing by the cage, about facing Wagner. He said he always tried to swing an inch over the ball. Wags threw kind of uphill and everybody swung under his fastball. I figured I'd try it.

First pitch, Wagner threw me a heater middle in. I tried to swing an inch over it, and I barreled it. It landed in the first row in the Crawford Boxes out in left field.

After I crossed home plate and celebrated with my teammates, I looked over to President Bush. He had his hand on his head and his eyes wide, as if to say, "What?!"

I gave him that shit-eating grin again as I went back to our dugout. We won 7–4 and went on to sweep the series. That was pretty cool.

Playing major league baseball had perks. You get to meet a lot of cool people. For me, Muhammad Ali was at the top of the list.

I met The Champ in Houston. He scared the shit out of me.

I was with Karin and a baseball card dealer, who introduced us. I walked up to Ali and his entourage.

"How you doin', Champ?" I said.

He cocked his head and said, "Did you call me a nigger?"

He said it with a straight face. His whole entourage looked dead serious. I took a step back. Finally, somebody in his entourage started cracking up. Eventually, Ali cracked up.

"Ah, look at that. White boy got scared," somebody in his entourage said.

He loved getting that kind of reaction out of people. Karin and I laughed as soon as we could breathe again.

"Don't ever do that again," I said. "You just scared the shit out of me."

Ali just laughed and let me take a picture with him.

He put my fist up to his jaw, so it looked like I was right-crossing him. He signed a couple of gloves for me. I thought that was killer.

Then there was the time I got to meet Christie Brinkley. She was down in spring training at West Palm shooting photos of baseball players for *Beckett Baseball* magazine. She was actually the one taking the pictures, with some guidance from another photographer. She'd been in front of the camera for so long, I guess it intrigued her to be behind it.

She took pictures of a couple of us with the Braves and Expos. One of the ones she took of me ended up on the cover of *Beckett Baseball*.

As soon as I saw it a couple of weeks later, I knew it was going to drive Bobby Cox crazy. He's a stickler for how you wear your uniform, and there I was with my sleeves rolled up, my shirt unbuttoned, and my hat on backwards. But hey, she did with me as she pleased. What am I going to say?

Christie Brinkley was still married to Billy Joel at that time. Guys like me had fantasized about her for years in that black dress in the "Uptown Girl" video.

The shoot was fun. Not only was she gorgeous

but also really nice and easy to talk to. She wanted to play catch with me, and she signed a baseball to me that I still have.

I got to meet some pretty amazing celebrities during the course of my career, but a lot of the "everyday" people I met because of baseball made just as big an impression on me, if not more. Matthew Bowles was the prime example.

Early on in my career, I was looking for a charitable organization to support, something that I felt a personal connection with. Nobody in my family had cancer, multiple sclerosis, or Lou Gehrig's disease, by the grace of God. I didn't even lose my first grandparent until I was forty-three years old.

I was still searching for the right fit in January of 1997, when I met Matthew at a celebrity hunting event outside of Selma, Alabama. He was an eleven-year-old from South Georgia.

We were introduced through Jackie Bushman, a big name in the hunting industry, who started the Buckmasters Classic to give Make-A-Wish kids a chance to realize their dreams of hunting.

Matthew had cystic fibrosis, a life-threatening genetic disease that can affect your lungs and pancreas. His days were numbered.

You could tell he was sick. He was gaunt, and he had to have an oxygen tank with him all the time. But he had a fervor, this spice for life, and he wasn't going to let his sickness dampen his spirits. It was awesome to witness.

When I got into camp, Matthew already had a truckload of deer. He had shot himself out of ammo.

"Man, you had a day, didn't you?" I said, nodding toward the back of his truck.

"Chipper," he said. "I sat there and emptied my gun. I shot three or four deer and I had a blast. But after I ran out of bullets, this big buck walked out. Man, I really hope you kill that deer."

He didn't say, "Man, I wish I hadn't run out of bullets because I really want to go back and harvest that deer." He wanted me to do it, and he was genuine about it. That tugged at my heartstrings.

"He's this big nine-point, with a big ol' round rack," Matthew said. "He's got big twos and threes [referring to the G2 and G3 antlers], a big frame. It's the biggest deer I've ever seen in my life. What's the biggest deer you ever killed?"

"A one-hundred-and-twenty-inch seven-point," I said.

"Oh," he said. "Then he's the biggest deer you'll ever see, too."

That got my attention.

A couple of days later, I was in a tree stand when I saw the deer Matthew had described. I knew it from the second I laid eyes on him. I got him with one shot.

The first person I ran into back at camp was Matthew Bowles. When he caught a glimpse of the deer in the back of my truck, his face lit up like a Christmas tree. He gave me a big hug. Then he walked over to the tailgate and picked up the deer's head.

"I would have had you if I'd had one more bullet," he said.

I sat there beaming like a proud father. This was such a cool kid. Everybody who ran across Matthew was drawn to him. I don't know if I would have been as happy-go-lucky as he was, making the most of every single moment like he did, if I knew I was going to die soon.

Within a week of the Buckmasters Classic, Matthew relapsed and went in the hospital. His dad told me they knew he didn't have much time left. One of Matthew's dreams had been to kill a deer and have it mounted on his wall, so they put a rush on a mount from one of the bucks he killed in Selma. When his dad walked into his hospital room carrying the mount, Matthew's face lit up. He put his arms around that mount and hugged it.

Not long afterward, Mr. Bowles got up to get a Coke from the vending machine down the hall. Matthew passed away while he was gone.

It's a tough story, but one I always tell at all the golf tournaments and charity events I host to explain why I support 65 Roses, the Cystic Fibrosis Foundation.

At various times in my life I've felt as if God has tapped me on the shoulder and said, "Whoa, watch yourself." I've also felt as if God has tapped me on the shoulder and said, "I'm putting this here for a reason. If you're smart enough to listen, you can get a lot out of it."

Meeting Matthew Bowles was one of those moments. The Bowleses gave us the mount from that nine-point deer, and my parents put it over their fireplace. It's a monster.

A week before the 1997 season started, when I walked into our clubhouse in spring training in West Palm, something felt off. The mood was somber.

I went to my locker, which was between David Justice and Marquis Grissom, and tried to mind my own business. Out of the corner of my eye, I noticed DJ's locker was packed up. All his clothes and gear were in Braves duffel bags. David was nowhere to be found.

Marquis was sitting on the other side of me, shooting the breeze with some guys.

"Where's David going?" I said.

"We're going to Cleveland," Grissom said.

Cleveland? Then it hit me that he had said *we.*

"*We're* going to Cleveland?" I said.

"You ain't," Grissom said. "But me and David are. We got traded."

"Shut the fuck up," I said.

"Yeah," he said. "We got traded for Kenny Lofton and a left-handed pitcher."

You could have hit me with a two-by-four right between the eyes, and I wouldn't have been more shocked.

I didn't understand. We went to two World Series with these twenty-five guys. Why would we break it up?

Two of my best friends weren't going to be here anymore? David had taken me under his wing from day one. Marquis was the consummate professional and a great teammate. I had played the outfield with both of them. I loved hitting a couple of spots behind Marquis because the threat of him stealing meant I saw a lot of fastballs. David gave me some of the best protection of my career hitting a couple of spots behind me.

And David was my big brother, my mentor. He was the one guy who didn't care as much about hazing me as he did preparing me to be "the man" in our lineup one day. After all my at-bats my rookie year, he would sit down next to me and say, "OK, what'd he do? What's his go-to pitch? What do you think he's going to get you out with the next time? What approach are you going to take?"

Even as he was making fun of me for being the "Golden Child," he was preparing me.

"You're good-looking, and you got game," he said. "You're going to be here forever, Chipper."

When David showed up at his locker that morning, he had tears in his eyes.

"Man, I've got to get out of here before I start bawling," he said.

Our goodbyes were short-lived. I was getting choked up, too.

That trade gave me my first real taste of the business of baseball. We had Andruw Jones and Jermaine Dye waiting in the wings, and the "Big Three" were all due extensions. The left-hander we got from Cleveland turned out to be Alan Embree, the guy I'd hit the bull off of in Durham. He was a good pitcher but, by virtue of his role, didn't stay long. And Lofton, as good a player as he was, had no desire to be in Atlanta. He could hit .330 with a toothpick if he wanted to, and he was a Gold Glove center fielder who could fly. But he had found a home in Cleveland, and he got traded against his will. For whatever reason, Lofton never had much success as a Brave and lasted only one season. He signed back with Cleveland that winter.

Shortly after the trade first went down, David Justice said something in the paper about how "the club is Chipper's now." I read it. I didn't agree with it. The quickest way to piss off the powers that be who were still in that clubhouse was to walk around like I was some kind of top dog.

Our pitchers were our leaders. They might

have acted like ten-year-olds off the field, but they were still "the man" when they were on the mound, and I wasn't ready to assume that leadership role yet. You have to grow into that. I still had a lot to learn.

CHAPTER 15
Leading a Double Life

The 1995 season had changed my life. I went from being a rookie with a lot of promise to a celebrity.

The combination of playing on TBS and winning the World Series brought us a crazy amount of attention, both locally and across the country. I didn't pay for a meal or a drink for a long time. When you walked into a restaurant or supermarket, everybody knew who you were. It was fun, hearing the whispers, "That's Chipper Jones," and having people come up and ask me for autographs. I ate it up.

I tried to go to the mall to Christmas shop that winter and got crushed. Just trying to do a little window shopping made me feel like a new panda at the Atlanta zoo. People followed me, wanting to take pictures. I had to sign autographs on the go. If I stopped, I got trapped. After that day, I learned to shop online.

Karin was very protective. She never left my side. She wanted everybody to know that I was taken and by whom.

She went to almost every home game, and quite a few on the road. Every appearance I had, she was there. Every picture I took, she was in it. It was like I was ten or twelve years old and she was the doting mother. At first I had no problem with it—we were in love—but then the honeymoon phase wore off and I needed some space.

We got into a fight one time over a picture in the paper. We'd been at a function and got our picture taken together. The next day in the paper, she had been cut out. You could see her hand through my arm and that was it, and she was pissed.

"So your picture wasn't in the paper," I said. "Big deal."

My comment started a fight, and that's when I realized just how much her identity was wrapped up in being Mrs. Chipper Jones.

We struggled with the attention baseball brought me and the money. Both of us did. Ultimately, I think Karin wanted our lives to head in one direction, and I wanted my life to head in another. I felt like she was trying to change me little by little.

Karin wanted me to be social. She wanted me to get dressed up and go to black-tie events and hobnob with high-society people. That's not me. I've always been the same guy at heart. I'm a pretty simple country boy. I loved my career and playing baseball, but in the offseason I loved to hang out with my buddies, play golf, and go hunting. I love spending time with my family around the holidays. That has never ever changed. That is the crux of who I am.

We were left with two strong personalities that clashed. We fought like cats and dogs the whole offseason after the 1996 World Series. And for the first time in five years of marriage, I went to spring training in '97 without her. I wasn't in a real good place.

I couldn't walk by an attractive lady in the grocery store or at a restaurant bar in those days without getting the eye. And I was willing to give it back. Granted, temptation had always been there—in the minor leagues, big leagues, offseason, spring training, you name it—but most of the time, you had to put yourself out there to run into it.

In the spring of '97, I went looking for trouble. Frankly, I was glad to be away. Karin only came down to West Palm a couple of times that spring, and I cherished the time by myself.

I was twenty-five years old and it was starting to hit me that I hadn't experienced everything a guy in his twenties should have before settling down. I had gotten married too soon.

I would lie in bed at night thinking, *Do you see yourself being married to this girl five years from now?* The answer was always no. I didn't even particularly like her at that point. I knew it wasn't going to last, and that was eye-opening. But I was so young and so immature. I was scared to call it quits and walk out. That was where I messed up.

I actually thought to myself, *OK, screw it. I'm going to go out and make myself happy. Maybe some clarity will come to me—either "Hey, I need to get divorced" or "Hey, I need to clean up my act."* That became my justification when I started to stray in my marriage.

I went out to Hooters one night late that March with my buddy Brad Clontz and a couple of the guys on the team. We went there for three things: basketball games on TV, bar-and-grill food, and good-looking women.

There was a hostess up front who caught my eye. She wasn't decked out in the orange shorts or the white crop top, but she was gorgeous. I batted my eyes at her when we walked in, and after a while she came over to our table and started talking to us. Her name was Jennifer.

I told her we were heading to a country bar down the road and she should come hang out with us. She didn't give the vibe that she was terribly interested—she said she was going out later with some friends—but lo and behold, a couple of hours later, she showed up at the club.

I was so nervous at first. I was looking over my shoulder, left and right, thinking Karin was going to walk around the corner at any moment. But as the night went on, I felt more and more relaxed. I let my collar down and had fun. I felt what it was like to woo somebody again and have somebody be interested in me, that exhilarating first-date feeling.

One of the guys had rented a house in PGA National, a resort in Palm Beach Gardens, and we all went back there to hang out. Jennifer was easy to talk to, down-to-earth, like one of the guys.

She and I made out a little bit. Nothing much, but I knew that there was a connection. I was attracted to her. She was attracted to me. There was no denying we were going to see each other again. And we did, maybe once or twice more that spring, before we lost contact.

A little more than a month into the season, we were playing Pittsburgh and she showed up out of the blue. Karin wasn't on that trip. She wouldn't have been caught dead in Pittsburgh. She saved her trips for places like San Diego, Los Angeles, and Chicago.

This was before everybody had cell phones, and one of my teammates called up to my hotel room and said, "There is a blonde named Jennifer from West Palm in the lobby. She said she knows you and asked me if I would pass it along. You can do what you want with it."

I was thinking, *Are you kidding me? In Pittsburgh?* I went downstairs and there she was.

That night the two of us hooked up for the first time. That was the start of my infidelity. And once I took the leap with Jennifer, it became a lot easier to take the leap with other girls.

I got more and more daring. I had girls in Atlanta. I had girls in three or four cities around the league. I'd met a girl in a country bar in Macon called Whiskey River on a hunting trip that offseason. We hung out and nothing really happened but we'd kept in touch and after the season started, I acted on it. She did some modeling out in Los Angeles and San Francisco, and when I went out there, we hooked up.

It was fun, and it was also out of hand. I lost control there for a while.

I was leading a double life. I maintained the facade of faithful husband, but I was living the jock-fantasy sports life.

I didn't have anybody in my ear saying, "Back it down." I didn't have a guy like Terry Pendleton, who would have grabbed me by the collar and said, "Straighten the fuck up." He was playing for the Reds by then. David Justice was in Cleveland.

Usually people are afraid to really get in my face. Every once in a while Mom or Dad will say something to knock me down out of the clouds, but sometimes when it's coming from Mom and Dad, I let it go in one ear and out the other. And they obviously had no idea what I was up to.

• • •

In June, we went to Toronto for an interleague series. Jennifer lived right outside Detroit, so a jaunt across the Canadian border wasn't that big a deal. She let Clontzy know she was going to be at the game and wanted to meet up with me afterward.

That was a big series for us. For a lot of guys, it was our first trip to Toronto. SkyDome was a really cool place. Playing indoors under the retractable roof with the hotel built into the outfield made it feel as if you were playing baseball in a museum.

Roger Clemens was pitching the first game, and I was jacked to the gills. Facing him in Triple-A was a little appetizer; now I was getting the main course. I was going to see what Roger Clemens was all about. He was thirty-four, but he was still Roger. He was about to win his fourth Cy Young Award.

Charlie O'Brien, my ex-teammate, hunting buddy, and locker mate with the Braves, was catching for Toronto, and that helped. He and I jawed at each other a little bit, which took my mind off the fact that one of the baddest dudes who's ever chucked a baseball was out there on the mound.

I went to the plate telling myself, *OK, I already faced this guy. I know what his heater does. Don't let him strike you out. Put the ball in play three or four times against him.*

Roger Clemens was one reason why I believed I could center anybody's fastball if I knew it was coming. Facing him in that rehab assignment had been a big mental hurdle for me. If you made me think about two or three other pitches, you got in my head. When I had only two options, like fastball and splitter from Clemens in those days, I had you eating out of my hand.

My first at-bat, I was looking for the fastball and got a base hit to right.

In my second at-bat, he threw me a split in the dirt, and I asked the umpire to check the ball. Charlie O'Brien snapped his head up at me.

"Do you know who that is out there?" he said.

"I don't care who that is, man," I said. "Check the ball. It bounced. You think I'm going to give him a scuffed-up ball to throw?"

O'Brien started laughing.

"Oh, OK," he said.

The next pitch was 97 mph chin music. After I backed out of the way and realized I was still among the living, I turned away from home plate with a shit-eating grin on my face. Charlie was the only one who saw it, though, because the grin was gone by the time I turned back around. No way was I going to let Clemens see it. I ended up flying out in that at-bat, but I'll always remember that fastball.

My third trip to the plate, I figured they probably thought I was looking for a fastball away. I'd gotten the base hit in the first inning on a fastball inside, so I wouldn't expect another one in there, right? But I knew: *He's Roger Clemens, he's not going to do what you expect him to do.* He's got an ego just like I do. He's probably thinking, *OK, you got me inside once. You're not going to do it again.*

Sure enough, he threw me a fastball inside and, man, I nutted it. It was a measure-your-dick kind of moment between Clemens and me, and I homered to right field.

We won the game 3–0. Neagle threw a shutout. I went 2-for-4 with a single and a homer and scored two of our runs.

Charlie told me years later that he had called for a fastball away in that third at-bat and Clemens shook him off. Then Charlie called for a backdoor breaking ball, and Clemens shook that off, too. "I told him pregame not to throw you a heater in," Charlie told me. But Clemens shook off every sign until he got one for a heater in, threw it, and I nailed it. That's where the stubbornness of a Hall of Fame pitcher gets in the way of a catcher who watched me play for a year-plus.

That was one of the top three or four homers of my career. Winning a battle against Clemens is what you play the game for. I was sky-high. I felt like celebrating, and Jennifer was there in Toronto to celebrate with me.

• • •

She and I had sex that night. No sooner were we finished than the phone rang in my hotel room. It was Karin.

"You're so busted," she said.

"What are you talking about?" I said.

Jennifer was sitting right there.

"This girl you've been having an affair with in Los Angeles—her husband found your number and gave me a call," Karin said. "As a matter of fact, he's on the phone right now."

She had put me on a three-way call with this girl I'd met in Macon and her husband.

"What's my wife doing with your phone number?" the guy said to me.

"I have no idea," I said.

I was in deny mode. If you don't have pictures and video of me, I'm denying. *Deny, deny, deny.*

"Do she and I know each other? Have we met? Yes," I said. "But nothing's happened."

"Then why has she got your phone number?" he said.

"I don't know," I said. "I think I left her some tickets in LA or something."

Karin wasn't buying it. I knew it was just a matter of time before the house of cards fell. And that phone call was only the half of it. Unbeknownst to me, Jennifer got pregnant that night.

• • •

When we left Toronto for Philadelphia, I thought my marriage was over. The cat was out of the bag, and I figured there was no way we were going to work this out. Instead of begging my wife for forgiveness and trying to work it out, I threw my hands up in the air and just said, "I'm out."

I went right back out on the town, doing the same things I'd been doing. I was going to let loose as much as I could before I got back home and faced Karin. I had a girl in Philly I saw quite often. We went out. We had sex. We had fun together, like we always did, and I didn't give it another thought.

A few weeks later, shortly after the All-Star break, Clontzy sat down next to my locker in the Braves clubhouse, frantic. "You really need to call Jennifer," he said. "She needs to talk to you."

I hadn't talked to her since Toronto. I'd had to shut a lot of that down after the phone call from Karin. Clontz was my middle man. Girls knew if they wanted to get in touch with me, they called Brad, and Brad would get the word to me.

I called Jennifer after the game.

"What's up?" I said.

"I'm pregnant," she said.

Oh no. We both knew the shitstorm that was coming. There wasn't any getting out of this one.

A couple of days went by and I was just starting to realize that this baby was going to happen, when I got a call from the girl in Philly.

"I think I might be pregnant," she said.

That's just great. As if I wasn't going to get enough scrutiny from my wife—and maybe the rest of the world here soon—I'm a big enough dumb ass to let this happen again?

I know this sounds terrible, but I would have done just about anything to make it go away. The girl was a model. She had her career to think about, and it just didn't make sense for either of us. I sent her money to cover an abortion, if that was what she decided she wanted. Frankly, I wasn't sure she was telling the truth about being pregnant in the first place.

I was already getting lambasted at home, and Karin didn't even know about the affair with Jennifer or that a baby was on the way. There was only so long I could keep it on the back burner before the truth about that came barreling out.

CHAPTER 16
Coming Clean

My world was crumbling, and I was the only one who knew the full extent of it. I'd look up into the crowd at Turner Field and see signs kids had made for me. All I could think was *I'm not worthy of that.* I felt like a hypocrite. And I was playing awful.

I'd be in the batter's box or at third base thinking about my personal life. I knew I was going to have to tell Karin, but trying to figure out how consumed me for weeks.

We were playing the Marlins one night in August, and Kevin Brown was pitching. He was one of the toughest guys I ever faced. His delivery was all elbows and kneecaps and he had phenomenal stuff. If you were not mentally focused, he could embarrass you.

I stepped into the box, got both feet set, and started thinking, *How am I going to tell Karin?*

I stepped out of the box and called time. *Bro, this dude is filthy enough. You've got very little chance with a clear brain, much less thinking about Karin and your relationship.* It was like Crash Davis in *Bull Durham* when he's trying to get Annie out of his mind. I had that Kevin Costner moment.

I couldn't play baseball at the major league level with this hanging over my head. Coming clean would change my life forever, but I had to do it. Two weeks went by before I finally got up the nerve. It took a disaster of a game against the Reds to get me to the breaking point. I went 0-for-4 and made an error in extra innings that cost us the game. I was plain horrible.

I sat in my locker afterward thinking, *I'm living a lie. This is not healthy. I've got to get it off my chest. I've got to tell her.*

I had no intention of walking into Bobby's office that day, but for some reason, on my way down the back hallway, which I took to avoid the media, I turned left into his office. I shut the door and sat down.

"What's going on, Chip?" he said.

"Skipper, I want to apologize to you," I said. "I'm playing like crap. But my life is falling apart. I'm probably going to get divorced. I've got a lot of shit going on."

"Are you OK physically?" he said. "Nothing to do with drugs or anything?"

"No, no, no," I said. "It's nothing like that. I feel like the weight of the world is coming down on me, and I've got to get out from underneath it right now. You're probably going to hear some stuff in the next few days because I'm coming clean on everything today when I get home. If I show up with black eyes tomorrow, don't worry about it."

He gave that a little chuckle and said, "Well, whatever you need to do to get your life in order, baseball is secondary. Get your family and your personal stuff in order and then we'll worry about baseball."

That was really comforting to me. I hadn't even told Mom and Dad yet, but Bobby had my back.

"If you need a day just to clear your mind, let me know," he said.

"No," I said. "I don't want to miss any games. I just wanted to come in and apologize to you for the way I've been playing. But I'm about to fix it, and I promise you it's going to get better."

The entire ride home up Georgia 400, I was thinking, *How do I start this conversation? How do I look somebody in the face that I supposedly love and tell her the hurtful things I'm going to have to tell her?*

I decided not to beat around the bush. I would get it all out, and whatever happened after that, happened. It would probably get violent, and she'd probably never want to see my face again. Not that I'd be able to blame her. I just knew I had to take whatever came.

When I walked in the front door, she was in

the kitchen. I picked up a box of Kleenex on the counter, walked over to the dining room table, and sat down.

"Come here," I said. "We need to talk. You need to have a seat."

She sat down and started welling up right away. She knew what was coming; she just didn't know the depth of it.

"Karin," I said. "This is killing me and I've got to get it out, so let me get it *all* out. I've been having affairs with three girls: the girl from LA; a girl from Atlanta; and a girl from Detroit, who I met in spring training. I've been having these affairs since the beginning of the season."

For some reason, I didn't tell her about the girl in Philly. Maybe it was because I thought she might be lying to me about being pregnant. But I got it out that I'd had three affairs and then I lowered the boom.

"The girl from Detroit, Jennifer, is pregnant," I said. "And she's going to have the baby."

There was a long silence, followed by uncontrollable sobbing from both of us. Eventually we got up. I needed to gather myself. I heard something behind me, and when I turned around, I saw she had picked up a vase. She threw it at me, and it hit me on the side of the head.

It didn't break until it hit the floor and I wasn't cut up or anything, but what was I going to say anyway? I deserved it. The only thing I could do was walk out of the room and give her time to cool off.

I went into my office and shut the door. I sat on my chaise longue and sobbed. I could hear her through the door sobbing uncontrollably and screaming. This probably went on for about thirty minutes. Then there were about ten minutes of silence.

She walked into my office and sat on the arm of the chaise longue beside me. She leaned into me. We sat there in silence for a long time.

"I'm so sorry," I said.

"I don't know where this is going to take us," she said. "I love you and we'll see what the future holds."

Ultimately, Karin decided she wanted to stay married, but she couldn't coexist with the child in the picture. I didn't fault her for feeling that way. A child would be an everyday reminder. She was being honest about her feelings. To ask her to bury those feelings would be even harsher. I knew coming into our conversation, I'd probably have a decision to make—her or the baby—and she basically made it for me.

I was scared to get divorced, and I'd already hurt her so badly. I didn't want to hurt her anymore. I felt that I owed it to her to give it a try. So I decided to recommit to the relationship and not to see my child. I would do what

I needed to do to take care of Jennifer and the baby, but I was going to stay with Karin.

I knew I had to tell my parents. That was just as hard as telling Karin, if not harder.

Mom answered the phone.

"I've got something to tell you," I said.

My voice got really low as I tried to find the words. When I got it all out, she let me have it.

"We didn't raise you to treat women this way," she said. "We didn't raise you to treat anybody this way. I thought I taught you to respect women. This is a slap in my face."

My dad had picked up the phone, too. They took turns at me with a lot of cut-to-the-bone comments.

I didn't say much. I listened. And I cried.

Once they said their piece, there was a long silence. Dad took a deep breath, and with a shaky voice, he said, "We are extremely disappointed in you, but you're our son and we love you. You're going to learn a valuable lesson from all this. If you need us, call us. We're here to talk."

When I hung up the phone, I took comfort in knowing that no matter who turned their back on me, I could count on my parents. It took Mom longer to forgive me than Dad, but I knew they had my back. That started my healing process. For the first time in weeks, I had something to feel good about.

I should not have made the decisions I made, and consequently I ended up hurting the three people in my life that I loved the most. I was not happy in the marriage, and I should have gotten out.

The second I unloaded everything on Karin, a huge weight was lifted off my shoulders. I had cleared my conscience. I cut off all contact with the other women. Karin and I started going to counseling two or three times a week, and for a while, it was OK.

But every argument—no matter what it was about and whether it was a 1 or an 8 on the Richter scale—led back to "You cheated on me." Before long, it was every single day.

I remained recommitted, even though things weren't going well. I was not going to rock the boat. I knew it had to be torture for her, sending me back on the road to those same cities and trying to trust me after what I had done.

I wasn't going out anymore, but I looked forward to road trips. They were my sanctuary. I didn't get beat over the head with my transgressions every day. I dreaded going home.

Karin and I floundered through the 1998 season but I had a good year baseball-wise. I had learned how to compartmentalize my job from my personal life and that helped. I took out my frustrations in the weight room and tried to forget about my home life while I was at the ballpark. But Karin and I continued our downward spiral.

We got into an argument at my twenty-sixth birthday party that April. I had invited some high school teammates and friends from Pierson up to our house. A bunch of Karin's girlfriends were there, and so were some of my Braves teammates.

It was late. I was liquored up. We all got a little blurry.

I was talking to one of Karin's friends, and Karin construed it as flirtatious. She didn't even know what we were talking about—we were talking about this girl's husband—but it set her off, and we got into it.

"Are you frickin' serious?" I said. "You think I would do that right here in our own house? We were just having a conversation."

I let her storm off, and I stayed out by the pool. We had a DJ playing music in the basement, and after a while, I looked in and saw Karin and Pedro Borbon, one of my teammates, dancing. They were rubbing up on each other.

I went barreling into the house.

"What the hell is going on here?" I said.

She started yelling. I told her to shut up. Next thing I knew, Pedro sucker punched me.

Slowly, I turned back around. Somehow I had the presence of mind to grab something to wrap around my right hand—there weren't going to be any broken bones this time. I came over the top and smoked him. Pedro went down. All hell broke loose.

I flew on top of him, and everybody started jumping in. My buddy Stacy Jones from Pierson and his wife, Sonya, tried to break up the fight. I had no idea who had me. I was seeing red. I went after Pedro with everything I had. Unfortunately, in the process, I broke Sonya's nose. I felt just awful.

Clearly, the party was over. Karin and I were, too. We just didn't know it yet. We tried to make it work for the rest of that season. For what reason, I don't know.

Karin's mom is an ordained minister. She and Karin sat me down one day and her mom said, "Whenever something bad happens, God comes along and spreads grace over it. Karin and I think the way that you can help cleanse everything and we can get some closure is for you to come out publicly and own up to your mistakes."

I have no problem owning up to any mistake that I make, but deep down, I didn't think my personal life was anybody's business. They convinced me that it would help Karin heal. My parents, my friends, and my agent were all against it, but I did it anyway.

There was one guy in the media I trusted to tell the story word for word and that was Bill Zack, the Braves beat writer for the Morris News

Service. With Bill, I could say something off the record and it wouldn't show up in his stories. And when I said something on the record, he printed what I said. So I had Bill out to the house, and Karin and I sat at our kitchen table and told him about my infidelities and that there was another woman with a child on the way.

This was well before social media, so I didn't get much of a sense of people's reaction until I went on an Atlanta radio station shortly after the story came out. I sat in the studio for three hours and got lambasted on live radio. I answered to all of it.

Some callers told me they'd never root for me again. Atlanta is in the Bible Belt, and obviously a lot of people frowned upon what I did. I didn't really know what to say except "All right. That's your decision."

Some callers asked, "Why are you doing this?" My answer was to clear my conscience because I felt like I was living a lie, which I was. But what I wanted to say was "Because my wife is making me."

After we went public, I lost all my marketing deals. Coke dumped me. Lowe's, too. We were done with the Wendy's contract anyway, but by spring training, it was all over.

There was a certain part of telling everyone that was therapeutic. I no longer carried the burden of living this hypocritical life. My secret was out.

Everybody could make their own judgments, and I could live my life and go play baseball.

But going public turned out to be the beginning of the end of my marriage. There was just too much damage, too much pain. For every one step forward, we took three steps back.

A little before Thanksgiving in '98, Karin went to Texas to hang out with Staci Borbon, Pedro's wife. Karin was the godmother of their kids. I thought it was all pretty innocent until I tried to call her. Two days went by and I didn't hear back from her. So I called Staci.

"Where's Karin?" I said.

"She's not here," she said.

"Where is she?" I said.

"She went to the store," she said. "She'll be back in a little bit."

I called an hour later, two hours later. Staci finally picked up again.

"Where's Karin?" I said.

"She's not here," she said.

I found out later during our divorce proceedings, she'd been out on a date. At the time, I just knew something was up. Karin finally called me back after about three days and said, "I'm not coming home until you're out of the house."

It was like bells going off in my head. Lightbulbs came on. I didn't even say goodbye. I just hung up the phone. Then I picked it back up and called my mom and dad.

"I need you here tonight," I said. "I'm moving out of this house first thing in the morning."

I called a moving company. I took everything that was mine and left anything she could have an argument about, and I was out of there by noon the next day. As I was pulling out of the driveway, Karin's mother pulled in.

"Don't do this," she said, bawling. She and I had a great relationship.

"She was very clear," I said. " 'I'm not coming home until you're out of the house.' What do you want me to do?"

I rented a condo in Buckhead, in the heart of Atlanta, and I never looked back.

We'd been playing this charade for almost a year and a half and it wasn't getting any better. At some point you've got to fold your cards.

I'm sorry for the way things happened. It was my fault. If I had it to do all over again, we would have divorced two years earlier. But when I slammed that phone down, I started the next chapter in my life.

The next call I made after asking Mom and Dad to help me move was to Brad Clontz. I wanted to know if he'd been in touch with Jennifer.

Thanks to Brad, I knew I had a son. Jennifer had named him Matthew, which means "gift from God." Jennifer and her mom had taken

279

Matthew to one of Brad's minor league games in Toledo to meet him.

Matthew was eight months old now and I wanted to see him. The disappointment of not being a part of his life had been eating at me. But Jennifer was on the lam. She wasn't in Detroit anymore. She wasn't in Florida. I hadn't realized that when the shit hit the fan, people in the media tried to get ahold of her, so she got as far away as she could. I had to hire a private investigator to find her.

When he tracked her down, she was living in Seattle, Washington, with another guy. That complicated things a little bit, but she sounded upbeat about wanting me to see Matthew.

We had to cut through some red tape to get them to Atlanta, so it didn't happen until February. But Jennifer flew in with her mom and Matthew, who was eleven months old by then.

No Game 7, no Opening Day, no first day in the big leagues ever made me more nervous than I was that day, waiting for them to arrive from the airport. I hadn't seen Jennifer in two years. On top of that, I was going to meet her mom, which was a little awkward. And most importantly, I had an eleven-month-old son I'd never met before. *Is he going to be shy? Will he take one look at me and start bawling?*

I planted myself by the front door. Every time I heard the elevator ding I looked out my peephole. When Matthew finally waddled through the elevator doors in a little red sweat suit and looked up at me with these big blue eyes and blond curly hair, life as I knew it changed on a dime. Seeing those big ol' chubby cheeks and that big ol' smile, I was staring at myself at eleven months. It brought tears to my eyes. In an instant, I knew I was going to be as big a part of this little boy's life as Jennifer would let me.

Before that day, I hadn't been 100 percent sure if divorce was the right way to go. As soon as I met him, I knew it was.

Now I could focus on getting to know Matthew. He and I spent our first couple of hours together messing around on the floor, rolling a little ball back and forth. I pushed him around my condo on an ottoman that had wheels on it. I bounced him on my knee. I did whatever I could to make him smile. I wanted him to know who his daddy was. And I spent the next couple of years trying to make sure that no matter who Jen was with, he knew who his proper father was.

Jen got married a couple of years later, but she let me move all of them to Atlanta so I could be close to Matthew. I bought them a house down the street from Country Club of the South, and I got to see Matthew pretty much whenever I wanted to.

They were in Atlanta for a year or two before she got homesick for Michigan. I'm sure some of it was pressure from the husband and also the fact that she didn't have family down here. I was gone a lot, and I couldn't always be around for her. I understood.

A friend of mine from Florida roomed with me that winter in Atlanta. I needed a running mate, and he had played college football, so he was in great shape. He was single, didn't have kids, and could be at my beck and call to work out whenever I needed him. We ate together, hung out together, and worked out constantly.

We took a break over Christmas and he went home to Pierson with me. We went out one night to a country bar on the north side of Orlando called Eight Seconds that had a mechanical bull in the back. We got there around midnight. I wasn't really in the mood to talk to anybody, and it must have been written all over my face. A couple of girls actually came up to me and said, "Dude, cheer up. You're out having beers and you look miserable."

I loosened the collar a little after that. My buddy was talking to some girl, and I was people watching when a buxom blonde walked by.

"Oh my god," I said. Not only had I thought it, apparently I'd said it out loud.

She didn't hear it but the girl my friend was talking to did and took it upon herself to go tell the blonde, "You need to come talk to this guy." She brought her back over and introduced us. Her name was Sharon.

I was so embarrassed.

"Look, I can mow my own lawn," I whispered in her ear. "I realize you're with people. I'd love to buy you a beer later on if you're up for it."

She smiled and said OK and walked off. About fifteen minutes later she came back and we started talking. We talked all night. We exchanged numbers.

As we left, I dropped her off at her truck. It was a Toyota with forty-inch Bogger tires on it. *Wow. I didn't see that one coming.* She was this ninety-eight-pound petite blond-haired, blue-eyed girl, and she went mud bogging and rode horses. She was a redneck! I couldn't get her out of my head.

I called her the next day and we set up something for Christmas Eve at another country bar in Downtown Disney. We hit it off.

She wasn't a real big baseball fan and didn't have much of a clue who I was. She deemed herself a football fan. That was fine by me. We were both smitten, and it wasn't long before she moved to Atlanta with me.

I had a new spark in my life, when I was least expecting it. I was just beginning to go through a divorce, so it was complicated, but I looked forward to seeing somebody again. After three years of fighting with Karin, I was ready for some fun.

Sharon and I were from the same part of Florida; we were a year apart in age, and we grew up the same middle-class way. I'd found somebody a lot like me. That's what I told friends and family who thought I was jumping into yet another relationship too soon. I liked having Sharon in my life. I never liked being alone. And I wanted that support system because I had a lot going on professionally. I was facing some major damage control in my baseball career.

I knew my image would never be the same. I had disappointed a lot of fans who thought I was throwing away the gifts I had been given with a series of bad decisions. That motivated me to go home that winter, shut everybody out, and say, *This is not going to affect the kind of baseball player I am.*

I had no idea how people within the Braves organization were going to react, much less the fans. So I conditioned myself to block everything out. I knew there would be hecklers, and I couldn't do anything about that. But for the fans who might still be unsure about me, I was determined to win them back by having the best year I could possibly have. If the bases were loaded with two outs in the bottom of the ninth, and we were down a run or two,

I wanted every Braves fan to want me at the plate. I was twenty-seven years old and coming into my prime as a baseball player. It was time to take the next step.

Not only could I use working out to make myself a better player, it became my release. Normally, when something is bothering me, I clean out my closet. I reorganize the garage. I prune and burn trees. But that entire offseason, I went to the ballpark. I went to the weight room. I exercised.

Other than a few nights out over the holidays, I was a recluse. I didn't want to read the newspaper. I didn't want to listen to the radio. I didn't want to have to look people in the eye until I was ready, and I wasn't going to be ready until spring training.

I either worked out with my roommate or I met up with Frank Fultz, our strength and conditioning coach at Gold's Gym. Under Frank's guidance, I started "maxing out" more often when I lifted weights. I'd always focused on staying long and lean by doing a lot of reps, not piling on the weight. Now I was throwing two manhole covers on each side of the barbell and throwing up 275 like it was nothing. We got up to 350 on the bench that offseason, which is territory I never thought I would see.

I still did some of my old routine. I did my Jobe exercises to keep my shoulders in check. I did the "curls for the girls," with the biceps and the triceps, too. But for the first time since I blew out my knee in '94, I concentrated on my legs. Frank convinced me I needed to build up my base.

I went from doing 700 pounds on the leg press to maxing out at around 1,000 pounds. I had every weight in the whole place on that leg press machine.

By the time we opened spring training, which was our second year in Disney, I was in as good a shape both physically and mentally as I'd ever been. Normally, I came to camp weighing about 215 pounds. In 1999, I was 225. I was ready for April 1 on February 14.

When you're an established major leaguer, spring training at-bats are generally pretty meaningless. The games don't count. Nothing is on the line. But after all my personal turmoil played out on the front page of the sports section, my first at-bat of the spring was huge; I'd been thinking about it for months. I was scared to death of how the fans would respond.

I knew the quickest way to make people forget was to come out rolling.

CHAPTER 17
The Worm Has Turned

For all the ways I planned to make myself over as a hitter in 1999, there was one thing I hadn't thought of, and it took Don Baylor all of one day as our new hitting coach that spring to nail it. When I met first him in the cages at Disney, he asked me what my approach was right-handed.

"I get turned around a lot late in games," I said. "So usually it's a big at-bat with guys on base. I don't need to be up there trying to hit three-run homers and striking out. I need to hit the ball up the middle and the other way and get base hits."

"Fuck that," he said.

Now, Baylor is a big man, an intimidating guy. He hit more than 300 homers in the big leagues. He commands respect when he walks into a room.

"You hit third and play third base for the best team in the National League," he continued. "You need to strike fear in people's hearts— from both sides of the plate."

He was looking me dead in the eye the whole time.

"What's the difference between striking out and hitting a two-hopper to shortstop?"

He had no plans to wait for an answer.

"Not a goddamn thing," he said. "You're still 0-for-1 either way. I want you to have the same mentality right-handed that you do left-handed. You might not have enough at-bats to hit thirty homers right-handed like you do left-handed, but I want your ratio to be the same."

Baylor had been one of the opposing managers who turned me around late in games in his previous job with the Rockies. He knew the havoc I could cause if I hit for power from the right side like I did the left. He knew what I was capable of better than I did.

"I don't care if you strike out two hundred times," he said. "I want you to make people pay for turning you around."

At that point in my career, I was a much better hitter left-handed than I was right-handed. I got more than twice as many at-bats against right-handed pitchers as I did lefties and put in a lot more work on my left-handed swing. When teams turned me around to hit right-handed, I just tried to set the table for McGriff and Justice with base hits. The most homers I'd hit in a season from the right side was six.

My dad had tried the hard-ass routine to get me to be more aggressive from the right side. "I'm fricking tired of you swinging the bat like a pussy," he'd say between BP pitches during the offseason.

"Hit the fucking ball out of the ballpark," he'd say. "I don't want you filleting shit to the opposite field. I want you to knock those fucking walls down."

I would whale away for eight or ten swings, then we'd start talking fundamentals again and I'd fall back into my old habits.

Sometimes the message comes better from a third party, somebody who doesn't know you from Adam's house cat.

Don wasn't going to take any shit from me. And it didn't stop with our initial conversation. After I took my usual swings left-handed that first day in the cage, I started packing up. We didn't have a left-hander throwing.

"Where are you going?" he said. "Get your high-priced ass back in the cage and take some swings right-handed. I don't care who's throwing."

Bobby gave us a lot of latitude when it came to preparing ourselves for the season. But Don served notice that day that I wasn't on my own schedule; I was on his.

I'd been staying in Pierson, eighty miles up the road, the early part of camp because it was before position players officially had to report. The back door hadn't shut behind me at my parents' house that afternoon before I told my dad, "The worm has turned."

I'd never had a hitting instructor tell me flat out who and what I was. Baylor lit a fire under my ass. And I could see it paying dividends from day one.

I started to let it rip right-handed in batting practice, and the way the ball was jumping off my bat, I knew Don was right. I knew I might strike out more, but it wasn't going to be a ton more. I still had a good enough eye to put the ball in play more times than not.

All that was left to do now was clear a couple mental hurdles, starting with my first at-bat of spring.

Walking to the plate in our first exhibition game against Georgia Tech, I listened for boos. I heard some, but there were a lot of cheers, too. It sounded a lot like the same pretty loud ovation I normally got to start spring training. I took a deep breath. *OK, that's it. I won't think about it again. Just go play.*

I had the perfect mind-set heading into the 1999 season. I was confident because I had put in the offseason work. I was determined to put my personal turmoil behind me. I was strong. I was healthy, and I was in complete control of my swing. Combine that with a hitting coach who was meant for me; it was the perfect storm.

My first home run of the season was right-handed. I got it on a hanging slider from Randy

Johnson, no less. My first thought rounding the bases at Turner Field? *Ruh roh.*

"You're fixing to see something right-handed you ain't seen before," I told Dad when I called him after the game.

I hit my third homer of the season right-handed, too. It cleared the left field bleachers in Colorado. I loved how our broadcaster Don Sutton, the Hall of Fame pitcher, put it: "The only question was whether it would come down in Colorado or Wyoming."

I went from hitting three or four homers a year right-handed to hitting fifteen that year. It didn't matter if the pitch was two inches off the outside corner or on the inside corner. If I was looking in one of those two spots, I was going to take you deep, from foul pole to foul pole, from either side of the plate. Instead of hitting my usual 30 homers, I hit 45 that year.

After every home run, I came back to the dugout looking for Don. It was the pupil coming back to the teacher for affirmation. Don was a lot like my dad. He wasn't going to hand out a whole lot of attaboys. But the way the year was going, he almost had to. I got a lot of Cheshire cat grins, which was fine by me. I could tell he was enjoying it.

I was scuffling a little bit when we got to New York in early July. I had gone thirteen at-bats without any damage, just a base hit and that was it. When I got to the park for the series opener against the Mets, it felt like it was 100 degrees. We'd had the night off coming in from Montreal, but I was still dragging.

Don came up to me and said, "Don't even pick up a bat today. No BP. You're off. Show up at 7:05."

"Are you serious?" I said. "You run this by Bobby?"

"I got it," he said. "Don't worry."

Sweet. I went to the training room, stretched out on a table, and slept through BP. I woke up feeling refreshed and got something to eat.

We were facing Masato Yoshii that night, a righty who followed Nomo over from Japan. First at-bat, I hit a bomb to left center. A couple of innings later, Pat Mahomes, also a righty, threw me a hanging slider, and I hit another bomb to right center.

Don had sensed me pressing and defused the whole situation. It was his way of was telling me: "Get out of your own head. You're thinking too much. Sit in here and watch *SportsCenter.* Play cards." Boom, two bombs.

Two days later, I homered off Orel Hershiser. From that point on, if a pitcher made a mistake, I hit it out of the ballpark—for the rest of the year.

I had 21 homers in the first half, but it felt like I had hit 10 or 12. I knew there was more there.

You can have a monster second half, I thought.

My first half, and that July series against the Mets, told me my focus was right where it needed to be. I'd ventured into the teeth of enemy territory and come out unscathed. The amount of ammunition I had given fans in New York and Philadelphia with my personal situation must have seemed like Christmas. I knew they couldn't wait to rag on me, and I couldn't blame them. I'd have done the same thing.

I wore cotton in my ears from time to time on the road that year to muffle some of the voices. When I did hear hecklers, it was usually when I was on deck. Every once in a while, I'd ease some tension by interacting with the guy in the fourth or fifth row.

He'd say, "Hey, Larry, let's go to Hooters after the game." I'd turn around and shake my finger and say, "Nah, I don't think so tonight, guys."

If they said, "Why did you cheat on your wife?"

I'd say, "Yeah, that was stupid, wasn't it? I can't believe I did that."

The look on their faces would say, "Huh?" Then it was over. They had nothing else.

When I stepped into the batter's box, it had to be me and the pitcher or I was done. And there wasn't a single instance in '99 when I was in the box that I heard anything going on outside of that span of sixty feet six inches. It's hard to explain, but I saw a tunnel between the pitcher's mound and me—all year. I told my dad, "If he releases it in that tunnel, I'm going to hit the ball out of the ballpark."

I was also playing in my first real pennant race. In 1993, when we were neck and neck with the Giants, I was just getting a cup of coffee. In my first four full seasons in the big leagues, we drummed everybody. It was a shock if a team was within ten games of us in September. The '99 season was different. We were nip and tuck with the Mets the entire second half, and this time I was on the front lines.

I can't tell you how much fun it was to come out of the All-Star break knowing that every at-bat and every play you made in the field was going to mean something. Playing with that level of focus, you find out what you're capable of.

In late September, we had a one-game lead on the Mets with twelve games to go. We hadn't played them in three months, and we were about to play them six times in ten days. The buildup was tremendous, but I was tired of it. Chirp is cheap; I was ready to play.

Turner Field was electric for the series opener, and Smoltzie was pitching. He and I had this agreement where he would come up to me before he pitched and say, "I only need one tonight." That's when I knew he was locked in; he could win with one run. Other times he would say, "Think you can give me three?" and I knew we were in for an uphill fight.

Before the first game against the Mets, Smoltz came up and said, "Just give me one," so I knew he was feeling good. We just had to break the ice. Whoever scored first was going to win.

Rick Reed was pitching for the Mets. He was a poor man's Greg Maddux. He didn't throw as hard and his movement wasn't quite as good, but he could locate all his pitches and he could sink it and cut it on both sides of the plate.

He'd struck me out a bunch with that front-hip comeback fastball. Most pitchers like to throw it late in the count, with two strikes, to lock you up. For some reason I thought the Mets might do something different that night and pitch me backwards. I'll be danged if they didn't.

I decided in my first at-bat, if I saw a pitch in, whether it was a ball or strike, I was swinging. I wanted to get Reed off that pitch. I wanted him to know I was ready for it.

Right on cue, Reed came inside early in the count. He didn't get it as far in as he wanted, and I barreled it—home run to right center. That put us up 1–0.

Smoltzie had his "one" in the first inning. But the Mets tied it up 1–1 in the third inning, and Smoltzie came back up to me. "Think you can get me one more?" he said.

I came up empty my next two at-bats, but I got another chance in the eighth. Mets manager Bobby Valentine decided to turn me around to hit right-handed. He brought in Dennis Cook, a quality lefty reliever I hated facing. Cook was an older guy who never really gave me much to hit. He dotted fastballs away and painted sliders both in and away.

My confidence was at an all-time high, though, and I'd faced him enough that I knew his repertoire. Cook's go-to pitch was a four-seam fastball an inch or two off the outside corner. I knew he was going to throw it at some point during the at-bat. *Be ready for it,* I told myself. *Move up on the plate a little bit and make sure to get the bat barrel to it. Don't try to pull it. Drive it in the gap somewhere.*

Sure enough, with the count 1-1, he threw me the fastball away, and I nutted it out to left center. I had a home run from each side of the plate.

Smoltzie came up to me and said, "You're frickin' awesome."

Our fans wanted a curtain call, but I was sheepish. I'd never done one before. I'm thinking, *Hey, this is Atlanta. We don't do curtain calls.* My teammates had to push me out there.

I had homered from both sides of the plate only three times in my career—all in '99—but all I cared about was that we had just struck the first blow in a playoff-type atmosphere, where momentum was everything. We were up 2–1, and it might as well have been 8–1.

I knew the game was over. We had the upper hand on the Mets in those days. It always felt like we took the field expecting to win and they took it hoping to win. Smoltzie had thrown so well, he should have had a complete game shutpiece. And now we had Rock—our closer John Rocker—ready to come in, and he was on top of his game.

The first homer I hit off Rick Reed had set the tone for the series, and I was just getting started.

Winning the series opener guaranteed we'd at least be tied for first place in the NL East when the Mets left town. So our mentality was: Take one of the next two games and we win the series. That would give us another game in the standings and some breathing room.

Hershiser was pitching Game 2. Between facing him in the '95 World Series and hitting a homer off him in July, I didn't have the awe factor of facing a boyhood hero working against me anymore.

I had a runner in scoring position my first at-bat of the game; Bret Boone—our second baseman—was on second base. Orel started me with a little cutter middle in that I swung through. That pitch told me all I needed to know. Hershiser was one of the best sinkerball pitchers in the game and he wasn't confident enough to stick with it and throw it to me on the outside corner.

It also told me the Mets weren't convinced I could hit a fastball in, at least not left-handed. They were trying to tie me up inside, which was pretty smart. My strength was getting my arms extended and hitting the ball out of the ballpark the other way.

But their mistake was pitching me the same way over and over. I prided myself on making adjustments. If you show me time and time again you're going to pitch me in, I'm going to get you. If you show me time and time again you're going to stay away from me, I'm going to get you there, too. The pitchers who had success against me never pitched me the same way twice.

After Hershiser saw me swing and miss that little cutter, I thought, *OK, he's going to his cutter again. I'm going to sit here and wait on another one.* I got it the next pitch. It wasn't nearly far enough in. I got my hands inside it and drove it to deep right field for a two-run homer. For the second straight game, I gave us a first inning lead with a homer, this time 2–0. Granted, it was still early in the game, but you could feel the noose slowly starting to tighten around their necks. If the Mets lost again, they'd be three games behind us in the standings with the prospect of going down four the next day.

Glavine took advantage of the early lead, threw great, and we won 5–2. No way had we come into the series thinking sweep, but after winning the first two games, it was right there for the taking.

I didn't think I was going to get much to hit after three home runs in the first two games, and I didn't. After my homer off Hershiser, I got walked every open base, every big at-bat. But I still wasn't finished yet.

Al Leiter was pitching the finale. He's one of the toughest nuts I've ever faced. He and Andy Pettitte are clones. They would go hard cutter, hard cutter, hard cutter, backdoor curveball, hard cutter, hard cutter. It never stopped. You saw nothing straight. They were just trying to bury that ball in on your hands.

In my first at-bat, first base was open so Leiter intentionally walked me. In my second, he struck me out on a strike-'em-out-throw-'em-out double play. When I came up again in the fifth, the Mets were up 2–1, but we had runners on first and third with one out. Leiter had to pitch to me again.

The electricity started to build among the crowd before I even got to the plate. Heck, I was thinking what the fans were thinking. *Man, if I get a base hit or hit a home run right here, the frickin' roof is going to come off this place.*

I focused on putting the ball in play to get the runner in from third. The best way to do that was to hit the ball up the middle. That was easier said than done off Leiter because he buried every pitch in on your hands, so it was hard to stay inside the ball. I kept telling myself, *Just stay up the middle and hopefully get the barrel to it.*

With the count 1-0, instead of throwing me the cutter up and in on my hands, he threw me a cutter down that had a little more break, almost a hybrid slider. Any hitter will tell you it's a lot easier to get the barrel to a pitch down. I dropped the head of my bat and hit that cutter out of the park to left center for a three-run homer to put us up 4–2.

It was a pitch I'd fouled off my front foot a thousand times, but I stayed inside of it that day. When I touched it off, I thought, *No freakin' way that just happened.*

I was trying to stay composed, but inwardly I was trash-talking, *Yeah!!! That's right.* I gave Hubby—our first base coach, Glenn Hubbard—a fist pump as I ran by him. John Olerud, the Mets first baseman, was looking at me like "Unbelievable."

After I rounded first, I looked back at home plate, and their catcher, Mike Piazza, had his hands on his knees like he was thinking, "I cannot believe it." Al was staring off into left center field. His cutter was probably the best pitch of all the ones I homered off of in that series. It was down and cutting in on me. But I semi-anticipated where he was coming and got the bat head to it.

When I rounded second, it hit me what I had done and how excited the fans were. I glanced up into the stands, and there must have been a dozen fans waving brooms behind the third base dugout.

Rounding third, I gave some dap to my third base coach, Ned Yost, and then I turned to see what was going on at home plate and in our dugout. It was sheer pandemonium. I did my best to soak in the moment.

I'd hit four homers in the biggest series of the year, and all four put us in the lead. It was like having my Altamonte Springs Little League game in the stretch run of a pennant race. And this time we won.

The fans gave me my second curtain call in three days. They'd been chanting "M-V-P" all series long. The four home runs put me at 45 for the season, a career-high for me.

Some of my teammates looked astonished. Jorge Fabregas, one of our backup catchers, said, "I've never seen anybody have that good a series in that big a spot." Ozzie Guillen, who backed up Walt Weiss at shortstop that year, came up to me and said, "Hey, kid, you're a stud." Big Cat, Andres Galarraga, had been out all year battling non-Hodgkin's lymphoma, but he was in the dugout that series. He didn't speak a ton of English but didn't need to that day. After we did our little handshake, he flashed me one of his Chiclet smiles and said, "Man, you're a bad mofo."

Getting that kind of affirmation from my teammates was the ultimate gratification, but I knew I had to laugh it off because we still had work to do.

CHAPTER 18
Lar-ry

Riding the momentum of our sweep over the Mets, we went to Montreal and swept the Expos, too. We clinched the division before we even had to go to New York to face the Mets again. The series was hardly short on drama, though. The Mets were still fighting for a wild card spot. Our two teams didn't like each other anyway, and for me, the rematch in New York was going to be personal.

Bobby Valentine and some of the Mets players—I heard Hershiser was among them—had speculated in the New York papers that during our series in Atlanta I'd been tipped off about what pitches were coming.

It was a pretty horseshit thing to do. We never tipped pitches and for them to suggest it screamed "poor loser" to me. You made a bad pitch. I hit it. Own up to it. And I was hot at the plate. A month or two earlier, I might have flown out to right field on those pitches. But it's not like I was a seven-hole hitter who coincidentally picked the biggest series of the year to hit four homers. I had 40-plus homers. I had hit 30 homers twice in the first four years of my career. I was a .300

hitter. A little credit for being clutch was due, and they didn't give it to me.

I'd had four days to think about it by the time I stood in front of my locker in New York and answered questions about their allegations. I'd had time to figure out how to keep my feelings fairly close to the vest.

We got our payback that night anyway in a 9–3 win against Hershiser.

We put runners on the corners five or six times and Hershiser was gone before the first inning was over. It was like a merry-go-round. The Mets tried to come in on me again and I drove in the first of our four runs in the first inning with a base hit. Nobody was sitting on the big apple out in center field at Shea Stadium tipping pitches for me.

I was fired up that series, maybe a little too fired up. I let the Mets fans get under my skin. We were coming off the field after winning the series finale—and all but burying the Mets in the wild card race—and Mets fans were leaning over our dugout screaming: "Your mom this . . ." "You stink . . ." "You suck . . ."

I had done such a good job all year of keeping my head down, my mouth shut, and not letting what fans said get to me. But then I saw a guy wearing a jersey split down the middle and a hat with two bills—half Mets, the other half Yankees.

That absolutely flew all over me. You can't be both a Yankees fan and a Mets fan. It's like being a Pittsburgh Steelers and Dallas Cowboys fan. This so-called Mets fan was yelling, "There's no way you'll beat the Yankees in the World Series . . ."

I was still fired up when I told a pack of reporters around my locker, "Now all those Mets fans can go home and put their Yankees stuff on."

If I had been a fifteen-year vet, I'd have just laughed at the guy and let it roll off my back. I might have told him what I thought instead of telling the whole world through the media. That's the difference in my maturity level at age twenty-seven and at thirty-five.

I was a brash young kid who ran hot sometimes, and I shot off at the mouth when I shouldn't have. That one came within an inch of biting me in the ass.

Lo and behold, the Mets, who had been down two games in the wild card with three to play, won out while the Cincinnati Reds lost two of their last three. The Mets then beat the Reds in a one-game playoff to win the wild card.

If we had to go back to Shea Stadium in a league-championship atmosphere, I would be in the crosshairs of New York fans. They would be all over me.

Everybody in Atlanta—myself included—said a collective "Oh shit. Here we go." It didn't matter who each of us played in the first round; we all knew it was going to be the Braves vs. the Mets in the NLCS.

Nobody in our clubhouse wanted to see the Mets again. We knew how evenly matched we were. We didn't like each other. We hated playing in each other's ballpark. We wanted to see the other team's fans suffer. We were archrivals.

Right on cue, we played a hell of a Division Series to beat the Astros in four games, and the Mets beat the Arizona Diamondbacks in four games to bring us face-to-face again, this time for the right to go to the World Series.

I kept a pretty low profile the first two games of the NLCS in Atlanta. I'd never been one to shy away from the cameras, but to say I had learned my lesson from my comments in New York was an understatement. I was not going to have a verbal sparring match through the papers with Bobby Valentine.

We won the first two games in the series, which made my first trip back to Shea Stadium a lot easier, but the New York faithful were ready for me. Mets fans started chanting my given name, "Lar-ry," any time I had a bat in my hands.

The first time I heard forty thousand people yell my name in sync was unnerving. But it was a compliment, too. Barry Bonds always said forty thousand people don't yell your name at the same time if you suck.

Mike Piazza had been calling me Larry for a while. I think Doggie, Smoltzie, or Glav must have told him at an All-Star game, "Hey, Chipper doesn't like being called Larry." Piazza told me one time, "Hey, bro, I can't call a grown man Chipper, so if you hear me calling you Larry . . ." Whenever I walked to the plate and Piazza said, "Hey, Larry, what's up?" I just said, "Hey, Michael, what's up?" It wasn't that big a deal.

But somebody told me later that Ed Coleman, one of the Mets broadcasters, had interviewed Hershiser on the radio after they beat Arizona, and Hershiser said he heard I hated being called Larry. Ed suggested Mets fans use that to their advantage. Obviously they picked up on it.

Some of the Mets fans kept a running tally of my strikeouts in the series by holding up head shots of Larry from the Three Stooges for every whiff. Bobby Valentine was not going to let me take the bat off my shoulder anyway. Every chance the Mets got with a base open, they pitched around me. They walked me nine times in a six-game series. I got five hits. And Al Leiter hit me once. I only hit .263 during the series, but I reached base 15 times in 29 at-bats. That's a .517 on-base percentage. I also stole a few bases, so I was putting pressure on them in other ways.

As hostile as that New York atmosphere was, it

was still fun, even when we lost an epic game on what was dubbed a grand slam single by Robin Ventura in Game 5.

I had hit a ball down the right field line off Octavio Dotel in the thirteenth inning that almost won it. Keith Lockhart had been running from first base on the pitch, so if my ball had made it all the way to the corner, the game was all but over. But for some reason it checked up. Melvin Mora rounded the ball off in right field and made a great relay throw to Edgardo Alfonzo, who threw out Locky at the plate.

Eventually the Mets wore us down that night. With the bases loaded and the game tied in the fifteenth inning, we had a young kid, Kevin McGlinchy, pitching against a fifteen-year vet in Ventura, and the kid was probably scared to death. It wasn't the right recipe for us.

Ventura hit a grand slam—the ball cleared the fence—but it was ruled a single because the Mets mobbed Ventura before he got to second base. I walked off the field thinking, *It sucks that we lost, but that was frickin' awesome.*

I didn't have that *uh-oh* feeling because we were still up 3-2 in the series and the last two games were at our place. No way would the Mets beat us both games at home. Right?

We lit Leiter up to start Game 6 and jumped out to a 5–0 lead. Smoltzie came on in relief. He'd pitched seven innings as the starter in Game 4 three days earlier, and none of us realized how much his elbow was bothering him. He gave up four runs within what seemed like thirty seconds, including an opposite field homer to Piazza. Then it was *Oh shit.*

We went from making plans to play the Yankees in the World Series to fighting for our lives. I had a flashback to the '96 World Series. *This cannot be happening.*

The game was tied 9–9 in the bottom of the eleventh when Gerald Williams doubled off Kenny Rogers to lead off the inning. We bunted him to third to put the potential series-winning run ninety feet away. Rogers intentionally walked me and Brian Jordan to bring up Andruw Jones with the bases loaded and one out.

The count went to 3-2, and I stood on second base thinking, *There's no way this is going to end on a walk. Andruw is going to be swinging.* He swung at everything. That was Andruw's MO. So when Rogers went to home plate, I was running. But Andruw surprised everybody and took a pitch up and away.

I give him all the credit. The pitch wasn't even close, but that's probably the biggest walk Andruw ever took in his life.

I don't think anybody on either side wanted to see the game and the series end on a bases-loaded walk. The Mets had utter despair on their faces.

I was relieved. I had learned a valuable lesson about keeping my mouth shut that series, and I was just glad to be done with the Mets. The Yankees were coming to town, and then it would be right back to New York.

CHAPTER 19

Playing the Villain

I was sitting at my locker at Turner Field a couple of hours before Game 1 of the World Series when one of our security guards came in and said, "Sharon is here."

I looked at the clock. It was 6:00 P.M. *That's weird. She's not supposed to be here yet.* I met her in the tunnel.

"What are you doing here so early?" I said.

What I was thinking was *It's the first game of the World Series. We're playing the Yankees. I'm facing El Duque in an hour. You don't need to be here right now.*

Then I realized she was trembling.

"Are you all right?" I said.

"I'm pregnant," she said.

You could have knocked me over with a feather.

"Are you happy about this?" she said.

"Yes, I'm so happy," I said, putting on my best "I'm so happy" face. But all I could think was *Oh shit, I'm not divorced yet.* I wanted to have kids. I wanted to be a full-time dad, but I wanted to close the last chapter before I started this one. My divorce with Karin wouldn't be final for three months.

I loved Sharon. I wanted to be with Sharon every moment I wasn't at the ballpark. We'd been living together for almost a year. Kids and marriage had certainly come up, but I wasn't ready.

I went back into the clubhouse, sat down, and stared into the back of my locker. This was going to change my life forever. And unlike with Matthew, this would mean full-time dad status. I was happy we were going to have a child, but it was a shock to my system, especially a few hours before the World Series started. I was going to have to put my personal life to the back of my mind and concentrate on the game. I thought about it during the game. How could I not? But I wasn't digging in the box against El Duque—Orlando Hernandez—thinking, *Oh my god, I've got a kid coming. This is crazy.* You can't lose focus playing third base either, or you will get your teeth knocked out. When I let my mind wander, it was during lulls in the game and between innings.

El Duque was perfect through three and two-thirds innings, and Doggie was pitching great. The game was still scoreless when I came up in the bottom of the fourth.

Duque, with his patented high leg kick, was just in his second year in the league after defecting from Cuba. We'd faced him earlier in the year in interleague play and somehow lit him up for four homers, but this was October. It was cold, and he was bringing it.

All right, stay short, stay compact, and let's try to get something started. He took a page out of the Mets' book and threw me a fastball in. I mean, I turned on it. I got out in front of it and kept it fair down the right field line for a homer to put us up 1–0. I hadn't gone deep since our sweep of the Mets a month earlier. It was my first home run in a World Series game.

The 1–0 lead wouldn't last, though. The Yankees scored four off Doggie in the eighth. That buried us because they had a really good bullpen with the big boy—Mariano Rivera—now at the end closing games. We didn't score another run that game, and we had a tough time all series. The Yankees swept us—two games in Atlanta, two games in New York.

In '99 it was glaringly obvious the Yankees were a better ball club than we were, just as I thought we were the better team in '96. A lot of those Yankee teams in the late '90s and early 2000s were better than everybody. A team of National League All-Stars probably couldn't have beaten them.

The end of the World Series meant no more daily diversions from my divorce proceedings. Karin wanted everything, and she was threatening to come after my future earnings. Was she entitled to something? No doubt. But we'd been haggling for more than a year and I was sick of it.

Finally one day, I sat down with my attorney, Jeffrey Bogart, and asked him how to put an end to it.

"Well, there's one way to make it go away right now," he said.

"Give her everything?" I said.

"Yep."

"How much do I have?" I said.

"Everything you have liquid, all your assets, is probably seven million dollars," he said.

"Give it to her," I said. "I want fifty thousand dollars. I can put forty thousand down on a new house and still have ten thousand to put some furniture in it. Give her everything else."

I had a new contract on the horizon, and we suspected she wanted to come after that, too. I didn't want to go into those negotiations, much less another season, with a divorce hanging over my head. We finalized it in January 2000, and I felt as if the weight of the world was off my shoulders.

A couple of days before the end of spring training, Sharon and I got married in my parents' front yard in Pierson. Going through an entire pregnancy with Sharon was really cool. I didn't get to experience that with Matthew. Our son Larry Wayne Jones III—we call him Trey—

was born on June 30, 2000. I flew home for the delivery, from where else—New York.

I probably could have had my own reality TV show in '99. But even with all the drama of ongoing divorce proceedings, a new relationship, and getting to know Matthew, I had a career year and won the National League MVP. Don Baylor is the main reason why.

Under his tutelage, I put up a combination of numbers nobody had before. I hit over .300, knocked in 100-plus runs, scored 100-plus runs, walked 100-plus times, hit 40-plus homers, hit 40-plus doubles, and stole 25 bags.

Winning an MVP propels you into the upper echelon of players in the league. I never thought of myself as an MVP, even after I won it. Baggy—Jeff Bagwell? Perennial MVP candidate. Barry Bonds, Matt Williams, Caminiti, Piazza. Those guys were the upper echelon.

No doubt the Mets series pushed me over the edge in a lot of voters' minds. I was shocked I got so many first place votes—twenty-nine of the thirty-two—but hitting four home runs in a tight race against a team from New York put me on the front pages of a lot of newspapers. Everybody was watching that race.

A lot of people thought the love/hate relationship between the Mets fans and me was my primary motivation. I got my inspiration long before 1999, with everything I grew up hearing about Mickey and New York. So it was fitting that to accept my MVP, I was invited to the Baseball Writers' Association dinner in New York.

Hank Aaron flew up to present it to me. If you're an Atlanta Brave and you don't bow down at the feet of Hank Aaron, you don't have a pulse. I cherish every moment I get to spend with him.

I also got to hobnob with some of the best players in the game, including some of the Yankees we had just faced, like David Cone, Derek Jeter, and Mariano Rivera.

When it came to the fans of New York, my relationships weren't quite as civilized. At that point, it wasn't really a love/hate relationship; it was more hate/hate. In '99, I was a villain in the city of New York.

I hated going there. My first eight years in the big leagues, I didn't leave my room at the Grand Hyatt until it was time to leave for the ballpark. New York is one of the reasons I went under an alias, because I used to get crank calls in my hotel room. It was intimidating being out in public around that many people, especially as a Brave. Everybody knew us. When we walked out of the hotel, we were hounded. So I chose to stay in.

Eventually, I learned how to sneak out of the Grand Hyatt without being followed. I threw out decoys. I'd walk into the second-floor lobby and wait until I saw the autograph hounds coming. Then I'd shoot back down the escalators and out the front door to a car I'd arranged to have waiting. Before long, they started using walkie-talkies, which made it tougher. If I went out the main lobby, they'd tell the guys upstairs to come down. It was crazy.

I had people chase me for blocks. Even if I had stopped and signed in front of the hotel, they'd lie and say, "You didn't get me." But I knew who they were. I'd fuzz up every once in a while. There's no way you can get to everybody. But it's New York. There are guys there who'd run over their mom in a bus to get to you if they could make money off your autograph.

I wanted to beat the Mets more than any other team on the planet, and it had nothing to do with their players or manager. It was their fans. When you walked out on deck in Shea Stadium in Flushing, New York, in an opposing team's jersey, you were going to have your ancestry questioned as well as your mother and father's honor. I hated making a right-hand turn from first base and giving them any kind of satisfaction. I hated striking out and having that long walk back to the third base dugout. It motivated me to play at my best whenever we were there.

Whatever news my relationship with the fans of New York made in 1999 was nothing compared to the shitstorm Rocker kicked up that offseason.

He and I both got caught up in the emotion of that last regular season series in New York, but he took it to a different level. I had to pull him by the collar coming off the field after the last game. He was screaming at people over our dugout: "I just struck out your best hitter!"

John was being John. But a month after the season was over, after he'd had a chance to cool down, he trashed the city of New York in a *Sports Illustrated* article, taking shots at every minority group in the book. He became public enemy number one.

I have no doubt that the reporter who wrote the *Sports Illustrated* story exploited Rock. And in some ways, Rock exploited the situation, too. He got to villain status because he wouldn't shut up on a car ride with a reporter, and maybe that's a stereotype Rock likes—I don't know.

I'll say this about Rock: He was a good teammate. He said very little in the clubhouse, and he was always jacked up to pitch. I don't know if some of that was artificially enhanced—he admitted to taking steroids a few years back—but he was ready to go every time he was called upon, and that's all you can ask for from a closer.

Once everything broke in *Sports Illustrated*, though, he stopped talking to the media. He left his teammates to talk on his behalf, and none of us wanted that responsibility. He should have explained himself to the reporters and taken the heat.

But he didn't do much of anything to defuse the situation and it was still volatile in June of 2000 when we went to Shea Stadium for the first time since the NLCS. Normally, we walked past Mets fans when we got off the bus at Shea and walked thirty yards to the tunnel. This time, we walked through sixty or seventy of New York's finest in full body armor—all because people wanted to hurt Rocker.

We took batting practice with police snipers on the roof. We had bomb-sniffing dogs running through our clubhouse. We were on a first-name basis with some German shepherds. It was unbelievable.

Rocker wouldn't back down from Mets fans either. He taunted them. He goaded them. It was ridiculous. The media didn't see half of it. There's a reason John got traded in 2001. He was good at his job and pitching in his prime. The brass, his teammates, and his coaches were sick of the extracurricular stuff.

John was still under contract to go on a morning radio show in Atlanta after he got traded to Cleveland. He had the audacity to call me white trash on the air one morning.

Isn't that the pot calling the kettle black? I wanted to fight the guy.

I knew our clubhouse guys had Rocker's cell

phone number. So when I got to the ballpark, I closed the doors in Chris Van Zant and Ben Acree's office and called Rocker. We screamed at each other for about fifteen minutes. We got a bunch of stuff off our chests, and toward the end, it actually became almost civil.

I talked to Rocker for the first time since that phone call at a Braves alumni weekend in 2014. He was on my softball team, and we signed autographs together. He came up and shook my hand. It was all I needed.

John took all the pressure off me in New York. Compared to John Rocker, I was Opie Taylor.

My relationship with the fans of New York changed after 9/11. I didn't spend all day in my hotel room. I would walk down Forty-Second Street to Portabella men's clothing store and interact with people along the way.

"Hey, Larry," they'd say. "Take it easy on my Mets tonight."

Or "Hey, Chippuh, take it easy on my Yanks tonight."

If I took just five or ten seconds to acknowledge them, I got a smile instead of venom.

The owner of Portabella, Joel Oks, used to invite guys to his store for lunch. He'd order out and have my favorite Chinese food, Shrimp Grand Marnier, waiting on me. I'd buy some suits or sign autographs for a while.

Joel is a Yankee fan and a fun-loving guy. He used to moon our team bus every time we left the Grand Hyatt. He came to our games sometimes and yelled at me in the on-deck circle.

"How's your whole?" he'd say.

I'd turn around.

"Family," he'd say. You had to laugh.

Over time I think the fans of New York and I gained a mutual respect. That respect was at the root of Sharon's and my decision to name our second son, born in 2004, Shea. People assumed, "Oh, you owned the Mets at Shea Stadium; that's why you named your kid Shea." But that wasn't the full story.

Yes, I hit a lot of meaningful home runs in that ballpark and I had almost 50 homers overall against the Mets. I tied one of my boyhood idols, Mike Schmidt, for the second-most homers against the Mets behind my old mentor Willie Stargell, who had 60. I enjoyed playing on that stage. Other than Atlanta, there's nowhere else I wanted to play more than New York. I didn't mean it to be a slap in the face to the fans of New York. I wanted them to take it as a sign of respect.

And I always loved the name Shea, as in Shea Hillenbrand, the former infielder for the Red Sox and Diamondbacks. Whether we had a boy or a girl, the name was going to be Shea.

When our son Shea was young and he saw Shea Stadium on TV, he'd say, "Is that my stadium?"

"Yep," we'd say. "That's it."

We got two of the old seats from Shea bolted to his bedroom wall.

I wanted him to see Shea before the Mets demolished it to build Citi Field, so I took him to our last series there in September 2008 when he was four. Sharon, the boys, and I got there early one afternoon. As we got out of the car and walked past about fifty people on our way into the tunnel, some Mets fan yelled out, "Which one is Shea?"

Shea raised his hand, like "Right here!" He loved it.

I used to hate Derek Jeter. *Hate* him. He was my archnemesis. He was the good-looking captain of the Yankees. He'd won all those championships. He'd beat me out of two World Series, not to mention the 2000 All-Star MVP after I'd hit a homer in my home ballpark. Then we played together in the 2006 World Baseball Classic (WBC).

I didn't know what to expect from him when I got to Phoenix for our first workout with Team USA. I was going to keep to myself and do my own thing. But Jeter walked right up to me in the clubhouse. We chatted for a minute, then he said, "Hey, after we're done working out, take a shower, get dressed, you're coming with me."

He took me out to dinner in Phoenix, and we

went out afterward for a couple of drinks. From then on, we were attached at the hip. We hit in the same group during BP. We warmed up together before games. We talked throughout the games. I ate it up. I soaked up everything I could learn from him.

And it wasn't just Jeter; it was other guys as well. That first US WBC team was an intergalactic all-star team. We had Roger Clemens, Jake Peavy, and Dontrelle Willis in the rotation and some really good relievers like Joe Nathan, Brad Lidge, and Chad Cordero. We had my old childhood nemesis Jason Varitek catching. Ken Griffey Jr., Johnny Damon, Vernon Wells, Michael Young, Frenchy—my Braves teammate Jeff Francoeur—were in the outfield. We had Derrek Lee and Mark Teixeira, Chase Utley and Alex Rodriguez on the infield.

Our manager, Buck Martinez, sat A-Rod and me down and told us we would split time at third base. When one of us was playing third, the other would DH.

"Buck, I don't care how much you play me or where you hit me," I said. "The only thing I want to do is hit a home run with 'USA' across my chest."

One of my dreams was to hit a home run for the United States in an international game. I'd never gotten to play for an Olympic team. It didn't take long to get my wish.

Our first game was against Mexico, and I was facing one of my current Braves teammates, Oscar Villarreal, who had come on in relief.

I'd kidded him in batting practice, "If I face you, just give me a fastball middle away and I'll hit a ground ball to short and we'll make each other look good."

He threw me a sinker middle away and I hit it out of the ballpark to left center field. I wasn't trying to hit a homer. I was just trying to go up the middle with the pitch. He didn't lay it in there; it was a painted pitch, but I felt so bad. All I could think making the turn around first was *Man, he is going to be pissed at me when we get back to spring training.* I wouldn't look at him.

We won the game 2–0, but Mexico ended up knocking us out of the WBC in the second round. Oscar, who was one of my favorite Braves teammates, got the last laugh.

That '06 WBC experience was some of the most fun I'd ever had playing baseball. It was pretty damn cool catching a ball from Derek Jeter, throwing it around the infield and flipping it to Roger Clemens. It was cool to hit a home run and have Ken Griffey standing at home plate waiting on me.

I'd never even spoken to Roger Clemens before. He had an aura about him and didn't seem all that sociable. Of course, when I was young, I was intimidated. I wasn't going to go up and say, "Hey, Rocket! How you doin'?" He would have squashed me like a bug.

But once you share a clubhouse and a dugout, it's different. Jeter and Clemens rented a house in Anaheim during the WBC, and we spent a lot of time over there. Derek and I probably went out to dinner ten times. I asked him about playing for the Yankees, and he asked me about how things were done with the Braves.

I think he and I realized we were connected. He was the face of the Yankees and I was the face of the Braves, and we had had so many great battles throughout the years. We respected each other's game and wanted to learn from each other.

From then on, whenever I went to New York to play interleague games against the Yankees, he'd send a note over to our clubhouse: "After the game, you're coming with me." We would go out for dinner or a drink.

Derek could walk right through the door of a club that cost a hundred bucks to get into; there was no waiting in line. The guy's meal ticket was signed the second he walked into a restaurant. He always had everything set up beforehand. If we were eating dinner, there was a table in the back. If we showed up at a club, we were ushered right up to VIP.

Most people knew Jete was there, but they'd

take one look at me and say, "Wait, what? Chipper Jones? You're hanging out with Jeter?"

The first time he invited me into his home, I walked up to the base of his apartment building and looked up. It was a cloudy, rainy night in New York and I couldn't see the top of his building. My ears popped going up the elevator. He lived in the penthouse, of course, and it was lavish. Looking out his big glass windows, I couldn't even see the city for the clouds, we were up so high. I was in awe.

He had dinner, which was prepared by a personal chef, waiting on us. Chicken parmesan—it was phenomenal. He went all out to impress me, and he certainly did.

The next day, he drove us to the ballpark. Walking into Yankee Stadium from the players' lot was weird. Yankee fans yelled, "Hey, Jeter! . . . Wait, that's Chipper Jones. What's going on?" It was cool to walk in his shoes for a moment. I've made the same walk into Yankee Stadium that Jeter has.

It would have been different if we played in the same division and faced each other eighteen times a year. I never would have had that relationship with somebody like a Piazza or Ventura, a Chase Utley or Ryan Howard. They were rivals. You hated them. But this was a unique opportunity. For three hours we'd do whatever we had to do to help our team win a ball game. Once that game was over, we hung out as friends.

It was a little different when Jeter came to Atlanta. I was married, and I had to go home from the ballpark to the wife and kids. But Sharon and I met Derek and Jorge Posada out in Atlanta a time or two. We always took the opportunity to hang out and reconnect.

I saw an interview Derek did when the Yankees came to town in 2012. He was asked about me as I was approaching retirement. He said, "He just looks like a ballplayer, you know? His actions, his mannerisms, everything he does."

I felt the same way about him. He was a consummate professional, and he deserved everything he got. If there was one guy I would have wanted in my foxhole day in and day out, it was Derek Jeter. If he and I had played side by side for twenty years, we'd have done a lot of winning. I can promise you that.

CHAPTER 20
A One-Team Guy

Staying with one organization from draft day to the day I retired was as much a part of my dream as making the big leagues. I wanted to be a face-of-the-franchise guy. A Cal, a George Brett, a Tony Gwynn. There's something that makes those guys different. They're down-to-earth, grounded, and humble. They're loyal. You can't imagine Derek Jeter with a Cincinnati Reds jersey on, and I couldn't imagine dressing up in colors other than red, white, and blue.

I'm a Brave. I'm from the South. Atlanta is slow-paced, just the way I like it. I was willing to do whatever I could to stay there. Fortunately, I was playing for a team willing to do what it took to keep me. We had the perfect marriage—this one I got right.

I had a great rapport with Bobby Cox and our general manager, John Schuerholz, and I needed it when it came time to negotiate my big contract. My trust in my agent, Steve Hammond, was rapidly deteriorating. I got the impression that Steve cared more about taking me to free agency than working out a deal with the Braves.

I started to lean on B.B., my best friend from

Pierson. B.B. had just graduated from law school and wanted to become an agent. He approached me about it at a time when Hammond's group, Leader Enterprises, was going through a terrible tragedy, and Hammond was going out on his own. Leader was run by Robert Fraley and Van Ardan. Both of them were killed in a plane crash with PGA golfer Payne Stewart in October '99.

B.B. was already helping me navigate my divorce and he signed on to pick up some of my marketing. He and Steve were both registered to represent me heading into the last year of my contract with the Braves. B.B. came to see me in Atlanta over the All-Star break in 2000 and we sat down at my kitchen table to talk it out.

Every baseball player lives for that one payday—the opportunity to set himself and his family up for life. I was coming up on my twenty-eighth birthday. I was in my baseball prime. I wanted fair market value, but I had no desire to go onto the free agent market to get it. I wanted it from the Braves.

The Braves had made me an offer during spring training of five years, $60 million. It's hard to say $12 million a year was lowballing me, but for the going rate, it was a conservative offer. Steve and I rejected it immediately. But the Braves hadn't come back with anything else, and I was starting to get antsy.

B.B. asked me flat out what I wanted. I

told him I wanted to stay in Atlanta. So he put together some numbers he thought would make that possible.

I knew I had leverage coming off an MVP season. I felt that I was one of the top four or five position players in the game. I had hit third and played third for the best team in the National League for the past five years. I had played in three World Series. I had demonstrated I was capable of playing 155 to 160 games a year and with regularity I could hit .300, drive in 100, score 100, walk 100, and have a .400 on-base percentage. Those numbers warranted elite pay, and I wanted to be the highest-paid player in terms of average annual value.

At the time, my old nemesis Kevin Brown had that distinction, making $15 million a year. But he was a pitcher, starting thirty-five, thirty-six games a year. I was helping the Braves win every night, so matching Kevin Brown at $15 million a year seemed plenty fair to me.

B.B. pointed out that Manny Ramirez, Ken Griffey Jr., A-Rod, and Jeter would blow that figure out of the water when they became free agents over the winter. That didn't bother me. The Braves probably weren't going to pay me that kind of money anyway, and I didn't want to bend them over a barrel.

B.B. and I settled on that $15 million figure. I went to Steve Hammond and said, "If the Braves offer six years for ninety million, take the deal."

Then I went directly to Schuerholz and told him that I wanted to be the highest-paid player in the game. B.B. prepared a memo, which he gave Schuerholz, asking for six years, $90 million.

At the time, the Braves had never given a player longer than a five-year deal, which Schuerholz made a point of telling me. But the ball was rolling. We were negotiating. Schuerholz would come down to the clubhouse and we'd meet in the conference room next to Bobby's office. The back-and-forth went on for about a week.

Ultimately, Schuerholz came back to me and said, "Look, we're going to give you your fifteen million a year. You have earned the right to be one of the highest-paid players in the game. There are certain responsibilities we expect you to fulfill for this amount of money, but we're going to give you what you want."

The deal guaranteed me $90 million with the potential to make another $30 million over two option years, bringing the total package to eight years, $120 million. John and I shook hands on it.

Then I turned my attention to Hammond. I needed to find out if he was doing what I asked him to do, so I asked Schuerholz to call him and offer the deal we had just agreed on.

"He said he was going to sit on it," Schuerholz said, pulling me aside at my locker about fifteen minutes later.

Three days went by and I didn't hear from Steve. Every day John asked me if I'd heard anything and I hadn't. By the third day, I couldn't take it anymore. I called Hammond on my way to the ballpark.

"Steve," I said. "Have you heard from the Braves?"

"Yeah," he said. "A couple days ago."

"And?" I said.

"They offered you six years at ninety million dollars, fifteen per, with two option years for fifteen per, so all told, eight years, one hundred twenty million."

"What did you say?" I said.

"Chip, man, I think it came too easy," he said. "I think we can get a little more."

It was exactly what I was afraid of.

"Steve," I said. "I told you if we got a guaranteed six-year deal for fifteen per to take it. We're done. You're not my agent anymore."

I hung up.

An agent's job is to get you as much money as possible. I get that. He or she has also got a family to support. But if you're my agent, you work for me. Steve got clouded into thinking that I was working for him. When I trusted my general manager more than my agent, I knew I had a problem.

B.B. had been there for me from day one. I've always thought he was one of the smartest guys

I've ever met. I couldn't think of a better person to represent me. B.B. helped me iron out the final details of the deal and we signed in August of 2000.

Until Derek Jeter signed a ten-year deal worth $18.9 million per year six months later, I was the highest-paid position player in the game, and I was proud of that. I didn't need any more. I think those negotiations set the tone for my relationship with the Braves from that point forward. Not only did I never go to free agency, I never got to my free agent year without an extension in hand. We established that there would be give and take on both sides, and there was.

For as long as I could remember, I'd wanted to have my own hunting property. My new contract allowed me to do it.

I grew up a mile from our hunting club in Pierson, a seven-thousand-acre lakeside property. It's where I learned how to drive my dad's truck. It's where Dad and I spent every weekend during hunting season, becoming best buds.

When I was twelve or thirteen, I told Dad, "One day when I'm old enough and if I can afford it, we'll have our own hunting club."

Dad and I had hunted at a place called the Perlitz Ranch in South Texas early on in my career. From then on, I had South Texas in the back of my mind. When I got close to signing in 2000, I sent Dad and B.B. to look at some property. The broker mentioned a place across the street from the Perlitz Ranch that was privately listed.

Dad and B.B. showed me footage they took with a Handycam, and we all agreed: This was the place. It had a horse barn and an indoor arena for Mom; Dad would have a four-thousand-acre cattle and deer ranch to run however he wanted, and I had somewhere to get away.

I did not lay eyes on the ranch until the day after the 2000 season ended. Mom and Dad were already living there. We'd been swept by the Cardinals in the Division Series, and as soon as Game 3 was over, I was gone. My buddy Marty Malloy, who had been a teammate for a couple of months in 1998, and I drove seventeen hours nonstop from Atlanta to South Texas in a monsoon. We got there about four o'clock the next afternoon.

We put our camo on and went straight to the deer stand for the last hour or two of daylight. We saw only one deer, but it was a giant. I was hooked. We named the ranch the Double Dime, since Dad and I had both worn number 10.

Five years later I bought the six-thousand-acre ranch adjacent to it to the north. We needed a bigger place to run our own hunting camp.

It was without a doubt my favorite place on

the planet. My boys loved it, too, Shea and my youngest, Tristan, especially. They were just like I was with my dad: Whatever Dad and I were doing—whether it was hunting, fishing, baseball, football, or hoops—they wanted to be doing it, too.

When the 2000 season ended, I was in a defensive funk. I'd made 23 errors at third base, the most since my rookie year.

The trouble started in spring training when I was diagnosed with loose bodies in my elbow. It was extremely painful to throw over the top, so I threw from the side or even underneath. I got into some bad habits.

We talked about the possibility of surgery, but I didn't want to miss any time or jeopardize the rest of that year. I decided to just play through the pain and hope the loose bodies worked themselves into a spot that didn't hurt as much. Luckily, that's what happened, but the bad habits stuck around.

On the last day of the season, I made an error against the Rockies that cost us home-field advantage in the playoffs.

We were ahead 5–3 with two outs in the ninth inning when Jeff Cirillo hit a ground ball that I let skip off my glove. I took my eye off it, and a run scored. Todd Helton followed with a three-run homer to open the floodgates. The Rockies scored seven runs after my error and won 10–5.

Getting on the bus after the game, I felt terrible. Instead of sleeping in our own beds that night and starting the postseason at home, we had to jump on a bus and a plane and go to a hostile environment in St. Louis. I heard the whispers from some of my teammates about us losing the day off at home. My true friends came up and said, "Hey, no big deal. We'll get it done in the playoffs no matter where we play."

We committed three more errors in the first game in St. Louis and never really got any traction in the series. We lost three straight to make our quickest exit from the playoffs since our run of division titles started nine years before. That just goes to show you how fast the ball can get to rolling downhill.

My defense improved quite a bit the following year; I made sure of it. But after the 2001 season, Schuerholz and our team president, Stan Kasten, approached me about changing positions. They wanted to sign Vinny Castilla to play third, and to move me to left field. They said moving to the outfield might take some stress off me defensively and allow me to concentrate on my offense.

I never really wanted to switch positions, but I was willing to do whatever they thought was best for the club. My main concern was winning ball games, and I thought we'd be a better team with Vinny coming in. I'd played with Vinny in instructional ball and against him in Colorado. I knew he was a solid third baseman, who could hit the long ball and drive in some runs. Plus, it was a lot cheaper to sign Castilla than a top-notch free agent left fielder.

I knew I could put up the offensive numbers that a corner outfielder should, so I thought, *Let's try it and see what happens.* I'd played some left field in spring training of '94 and a little bit in '95. I could show my versatility instead of being arrogant and refusing to move.

Schuerholz came to me again that winter. The Braves were on the cusp of making a blockbuster deal with the Dodgers, and he wanted to know if I thought Gary Sheffield would fit in our clubhouse. It was a reinforcement that he knew I could separate my ego from the needs of the team.

I told John that Sheff could be surly toward the media, but he always treated me with respect. Sheff and I were both Florida boys and had lockered next to each other at a couple of All-Star games because we both wore number 10. Whenever we played against each other, he always had a bright smile for me when he got to third base. I could give him a little hip bump and say, "What's up, bro? How's the family?"

Even before I got to know him, I thought the world of Sheff as a player. He had the quickest hands I've ever seen. I've always said Barry Bonds is the best player I saw don a uniform. But when it came to bat speed and hands, Sheffield had him beat. Maddux, Glavine, and Smoltz will tell you they feared him. He could hit a ball that looked like it was destined for the left fielder's glove and it would still carry five rows deep. He hit one-irons—screaming low liners—out of the park. Mere mortals who hit the same ball were out.

He also hit wicked line drives. Whenever Sheffield was up, the infield dirt was not deep enough for me at third base. I played on the left field grass. I'd look over and the third base coach would be right there next to me. He wasn't going to stand in that coach's box either and risk getting drilled.

We traded for Sheffield heading into the 2002 season, and I like to think my conversation with Schuerholz helped us pull the trigger. On the day of the trade, Sheffield called me right away. When I saw his name pop up on my caller ID, I didn't bother with hello.

"You ain't getting number ten, bruh," I said.

He started laughing.

"I don't want number ten," he said. "That's your number. I'll make do just fine."

I knew at that point we were going to be best buds.

Then he said, "You got a little puppy at home?"

"Yeah," I said. "Why?"

"I'm going to be your little puppy in spring training," he said. "I'll be following you around, nipping at your heels, doing whatever you do."

He wasn't kidding. Sheff was a puppy dog pretty much the whole year, from spring training on. We hit together in the cages. We hit in the same group on the field. We took fly balls together in the outfield.

As a rule, Sheff was a pretty intense guy. He could have come to the clubhouse, played the game, and left without cracking a smile. But to see Gary let his hair down and joke with the fellas told me more about Gary than anything I'd heard in the media.

From the day he got to Atlanta to the day he left two years later, he was one of the guys. He never caused waves. He played hard. He was one of my top five teammates of all time. Not only did I learn a ton from him, but it was also fun hitting either in front of or behind him in the lineup.

We'd be standing on deck before a big inning, and he'd lock eyes with me and say, "It's up to us. Let's go. Let's do it."

There was a day game at our place against the Rockies in August 2002 when it came down to the two of us. We were trailing by a run in the bottom of the ninth. Jose Jimenez, who had thrown a no-hitter as a starter for the Cardinals, was closing for the Rockies. Sheffield was leading off the inning and I was hitting second, so we walked out on deck together.

I had done my homework. As a closer, Jimenez threw a fastball and a split. The fastball he threw was one of the hardest sinkers in the game, probably 94 or 95 mph, and the bottom dropped out of his split. But I had picked something up in my pregame video session. Jimenez was tipping.

"OK, watch this guy warm up," I told Sheff. "When he sets high, up around the letters, he's throwing a fastball. When he sets low, down near his belt, he's throwing a split."

We watched four or five pitches. Sure enough, every pitch he set high, he threw a fastball. Every pitch he set around his belt, he threw a split.

"Are you kidding me?" Sheff said.

"Book it," I said. "It's up to us. Let's go."

"I got him," he said, as he turned toward the plate.

Sheffield worked the count to 2-1, and after watching Jimenez set high, he teed off on a sinker. He launched one of his one-irons into the left center field seats to tie the game. He crossed home plate, smiling from ear to ear.

OK, cool, I thought. *Now it's time to win it.*

Jimenez set low on a 1-1 pitch and hung a split. Sheff hadn't even gotten all his high fives in the dugout when I sent one to the right field seats for a walk-off.

I rounded third base and the first guy ready to

greet me in a scrum at home plate was Sheff with a big ol' smile on his face. He was pointing at me, saying, "This one's because of you."

Those are the moments that are etched in your mind forever.

I wasn't the greatest left fielder in the world, but I got a chance to play in one of the best outfields in the majors with Andruw Jones in center and Sheff in right, and we also made one of the most formidable three-four-and-five hitter combinations in the game at that time.

I was hitting fourth between the two. It was the only time in my career I didn't hit third. I wasn't very comfortable batting cleanup, and I said so publicly from time to time, but that was me letting my ego get in the way a little bit. I didn't understand it then, but I was hitting fourth so Bobby could split up the two right-handers. If Sheffield had been a switch-hitter and I was right-handed, I'd have been hitting third.

You can't argue with how well it worked, especially in 2003. We had a monster year offensively as a team, and the three of us in the outfield drove in 100 runs each.

Playing the outfield also gave me an even greater appreciation for Andruw Jones. Say what you want about Willie Mays, Mickey Mantle, and Joe DiMaggio, you can't convince me there was or ever will be a better defensive center fielder than Andruw Jones. That guy played as shallow as anybody and caught more balls than I've ever seen. And the years when he hit .300 with 30, 40, 50 homers, drove in 100 runs, and played Gold Glove defense, he dominated the center field position.

I think Andruw is a Hall of Famer. If he had just held on for another four or five years, he would have been a first-ballot guy. Voters might question why he was out of the big leagues at thirty-six, but during the time Andruw was playing, there was not a better center fielder. That includes Junior. Ken Griffey Jr. was a better all-around player than Andruw, but Junior was not a better center fielder than Andruw. Andruw was a man among boys out there.

Andruw could cover it all, and he got the best jumps. I was ten feet away when he made the best catch I ever saw him make. We were in Montreal in May 2002 and Glavine was up 2–0 in the ninth inning, going for a shutout. We were one out away, but the Expos had runners on first and second.

Wil Cordero split Andruw and me perfectly in left center field. Vladimir Guerrero was rounding third when Andruw laid out, at full extension, to backhand the ball six inches off the ground at the last possible second. I have no idea how he caught it, but Glavine got his twenty-second career shutout.

I'd been hauling the mail to get there, so all I could say between breaths was "Oh . . . my . . . god." Walking back to the dugout, I put my arm around Andruw's neck and said, "Bro, that's the greatest catch I've ever seen."

He had that little shit-eating grin on his face.

Outfield is a much different animal than third base. There's too much time to think. I wasn't into the game out there. You've got people constantly talking to you from the stands. "Nice swing last at-bat" or "Way to miss the cutoff, man" or the old standby, "Hey, how was Hooters last night?"

I'd find myself whistling, looking in the stands, checking out fights at Shea Stadium—stuff I never would have paid attention to at third base because the next ball hit could have been down my throat.

I never really felt at home in left field, and I knew I wasn't as good a player out there, but Vinny helped the team defensively the two years he played third for us. Then, in 2004, the brass came to me and said Mark DeRosa had earned an opportunity at third base after all his years in the organization. I totally agreed.

But DeRo struggled the first half of the season, both offensively and defensively. We were scuffling as a club. And I couldn't stay healthy.

I'd heard a pop in my hamstring chasing down

a Luis Castillo liner in the gap against the Marlins in April. It sounded like the pop I heard when I tore my ACL; I thought I was done for the year. I went on the disabled list for the first time in eight years. Luckily, I only missed sixteen games, but my hamstrings were giving me fits.

I was still on the DL in early May when we went to Colorado and DeRo made four errors in a game. On the bus afterward, I turned around and halfway smiled at DeRo, as if to say, "Hey, man, we all have games like this."

"It's not fuckin' funny," he said.

I should have just left him alone.

But the more I thought about it, the more I wanted to talk to Bobby about moving back to third. I would have given my left arm for it to be anybody but DeRo that I'd be bumping off third base. He was one of my best friends in baseball. But more than two months into the season, I was hitting .210 and destined to end up back on the DL. The only way I could nurse my hamstring back to health and stay in the lineup every day was to get back on the infield where I wouldn't be running all out three or four times a game. The most logical place was third base.

That's hard to explain to a guy like DeRo, who had busted his hump for so long for the opportunity to play every day. But he wasn't our number three hitter, and to a certain extent I had to pull rank. In early June, I went in to see Bobby.

He agreed that we needed to do what we could to keep me in the lineup every day. So for about a week, I took my fly balls in the outfield during BP, then came in and took ground balls at third. DeRo looked at me one day and said, "Are you taking my job?"

"Dude," I said. "I can't stay healthy out there."

After DHing in a couple of American League parks during interleague play, I moved back to third base for a home series against Kansas City. Joe Randa hit a bullet to my glove side for my first ground ball. I gloved it and threw him out. I just needed that first rocket hit at me before I knew everything would be OK.

DeRo and I didn't talk for a while. His feelings were hurt and I got it. There was nobody who felt worse than I did. I think over time he realized it was a decision I didn't want to make but had to make and he gradually came back around. My batting average was beyond trying to get back to respectable—I hit a career-low .248 for the season—but I hit my 30 homers and drove in 96 runs without ever going back on the DL.

Ultimately, I think the move to left field made me realize how much I loved playing third base. I gained an appreciation for how difficult playing the hot corner really is. Once I moved back, I never really had the defensive problems I had early on in my career.

• • •

My relationship with the front office was so strong by then, I felt comfortable raising my concerns, and I had had a big one early on in 2003. I thought I might be traded.

Ted Turner, our colorful larger-than-life owner that everybody loved, had all but given up his stake in the Braves. Time Warner, the company that had merged with Turner Broadcasting, had been bought out by AOL. Everybody knew our payroll was going to drop significantly, and soon. That got me spitballing one night. Come September, I was going to reach 10-and-5 status, which meant I would have been in the league for at least ten years and with the same team for at least five years. At that point, I would be able to veto any trades. I started to wonder if the Braves might try to trade me before I got that right.

I'd seen what happened to David Justice and Marquis Grissom, two guys nobody thought would ever get traded, when the Braves had to cut payroll in 1997. I had a house and a family in Atlanta.

I wanted to go over scenarios with Stan Kasten. Not only was he our team president, he was also president of the Hawks and Thrashers, our NBA and NHL teams in Atlanta, which were also owned by AOL Time Warner. Kasten was the closest guy I knew to the money. I had a great rapport with Stan, much as I did with Schuerholz, so I went in to talk to him.

"I want to see what y'all are thinking," I said. "I'm going to be a ten-and-five guy here pretty soon. I hope this doesn't happen, but let's just say we fall out of contention by the end of July or August. Could I be traded before you guys no longer have leverage on me?"

He started laughing.

"There is not a scenario on the planet in which you would get traded," he said.

I took a deep breath and smiled. I never had to have that conversation again. The next offseason, when trade rumors cropped up again, I already knew what I needed to know.

Later in my career I was willing to make concessions for the financial well-being of the club. That was a price I was willing to pay, not only to maintain a good relationship with the team but to help us stay competitive. If we needed to free up payroll to re-sign one of our starting pitchers, I volunteered to restructure my contract.

As the big dog on the payroll totem pole and a leader of the ball club, I felt responsible. The last thing I wanted was the Braves to feel like they were spending so much money on me they couldn't make a blockbuster trade or a free agent acquisition.

When we traded for Tim Hudson coming into the 2005 season, Time Warner had cut $20 million from the payroll. We'd watched Sheff, Maddux, Glavine, and Kevin Millwood walk in recent years. Hudson was going to be a free agent at the end of the season. He was a top-of-the-rotation guy and an All-Star. I wanted him to be in my foxhole for a while. So when the Braves negotiated with him in spring training of 2005, I offered to restructure my contract.

Schuerholz told me the Braves didn't need my money to sign Hudson, but it would help with something else down the road. They wanted to re-sign our shortstop Rafael Furcal. So at the end of the season, I reworked my contract to leave $15 million on the table.

Ultimately, negotiations with Furcal fell through and he signed with the Dodgers, but the Braves were able to trade for Edgar Renteria and re-sign some arbitration-eligible guys. And we had Huddy locked down for at least four more years.

I knew I was going to be fine. I'd made my money. I wanted guys who could help us compete.

CHAPTER 21

Tools and Tricks of the Trade

My name was never linked with steroids, and that's one of the things I'm most proud of when it comes to my baseball career. But we all played in the steroid era, so we all had to answer for it. I did, even to my dad.

"If you did steroids," he said to me one day, "I would be the most disappointed in you I could ever be."

He's such a baseball purist. For him to even think I could have taken a shortcut got to me. Just his mentioning it made me tear up. This was coming from a guy who knew better than anybody the amount of work I put in. But that just goes to show you how rampant the general public thinks steroid use was.

"Well, it seems like everybody . . ." he said.

"Dad, everybody is not doing it," I said. "Some of the best players are taking them, but there are a lot of players who are doing it the right way. I wouldn't be able to look you in the eye if I had done steroids. So no, I never did them. You don't have to worry."

Yes, I was tempted. It was hard to watch guys go deep 45, 50 times a year while I was hitting my measly 25 to 30. I couldn't compete with them.

But Karin was right. I'd have bawled as a grown man if I ever had to sit across the table from my dad and mom and say, "I cheated." I'd already put them through enough when it came to my personal life. To have undercut all the work they put in for my professional life would have been too much to bear. It would have cheapened everything Dad and I did from the time I was seven years old.

Of course, once I assured Dad I hadn't done steroids, his next question was "Well, who is?"

In all the time I was with the Braves, I suspected only a handful of guys were taking steroids. I never actually saw anybody get shot up or take a pill. I saw people rubbed down with creams, but I don't think it was steroids. Early in my career, I saw people taking amphetamines. Having a greenie back in the day was like drinking a cup of coffee or popping a piece of Bazooka bubble gum in your mouth. That was just the way it was.

Players respected Bobby Cox and the rest of the people in our clubhouse enough not to deface it by bringing in steroids. Fear of being caught probably played a role, too. And the Braves didn't allow personal trainers or other hangers-on who could administer them around the clubhouse anyway.

You just knew some people were doing it,

though. You weren't stupid. Their 'roid rage was quite obvious, as were their bodies with their shirts off.

The first person I really suspected was Rocker. I only say that openly now because he admitted to it. I know there were others, but I would never call anybody out. Beyond that, I didn't pay a lot of attention. Maybe I was a little naive. But Jose Canseco's estimate that 75 to 80 percent of major league players were doing steroids was completely ridiculous.

What gets to me is the fact that guys who most people suspect of doing them—Barry Bonds, Mark McGwire, Roger Clemens, and A-Rod—didn't need to do them. They were going to be Hall of Famers regardless.

Somebody outside the organization offered me andro once. It was before androstenedione was found in McGwire's locker and everybody found out what it was. I was told it was a precursor to steroids. I knew there was gray area there, and it wasn't worth it.

I always tried to keep it vanilla. Give me my multivitamins and fish oils. I drank a lot of whey protein shakes, especially before the 1999 season. Frank Fultz used to make them for me before we worked out to help me put on the weight—but no steroids.

I'm proud of my .303 batting average. I'm proud of 468 homers. I'm proud of 2,726 hits. I'm proud of 1,623 RBIs. That was all legit.

If I had been on steroids, 500 homers would not have been a problem because I wouldn't have missed two and a half years with injuries. I'd have been able to bounce back quicker. You would have seen more than one 40–home run season out of me, too. But you wouldn't see me looking you in the eye as much.

An issue like steroids is black and white, but baseball has a lot more gray area when it comes to its unwritten rules. That's part of what makes it so fun.

A lot gets made over pitchers using "foreign substances" to doctor balls. If a ball is doing something it shouldn't be, then there's a problem. Otherwise, I really don't care. You've still got to throw it over that plate.

Only once or twice in my career have I wondered what the heck a pitch was—when it had two-seam spin but also cut—and I immediately asked the umpire to check the ball. But I've never said to an umpire, "Hey, go check him," as in the pitcher. Just check the ball and leave it at that.

We always thought Dennis Cook raised the seams. Every time he came in for the Mets, he would rub up the ball. It almost looked like he was trying to cut the seams with his fingernail, but I think he was trying to compress the white cowhide underneath to make the seams stand out.

That would give him a better grip and a better bite on breaking balls.

One of our coaches, Pat Corrales, used to scream every time Cook came in the game. "Check the baseballs! He's raising the seams! Check his finger when he's rubbing up that ball!"

The umpire finally went out to the mound and checked the ball one time. He didn't find anything. Who cares? I'm thinking, *Pat, shut up, sit your ass down, and let me try to get a hit off this dude. I don't want him pissed off. I want him nice and relaxed.*

Some sinkerball guys loved to throw scuffed baseballs. Doggie was a prime example. He didn't scuff them himself, but every time a ball hit the clay, he wanted it back. He used to get on me as a rookie not to throw those balls out. Fulton County Stadium was like a parking lot. That clay scuffed up ground balls pretty good.

If there was a short-hop line drive hit to me and we made the play, I got the ball back to Doggie and he'd take a little stroll around the mound. He was checking it out to see where the scuff was. If there was a scuff on either side of one of the horseshoes in the stitching, he'd use it. And Doggie could pitch with the same ball an entire inning if he got three ground balls.

Not that I could really say what the scuff did for him. Personally, I think it's overblown. Guys like Maddux and Hershiser could sink a ball a foot, and they could do it with a brand-new baseball right out of the box. It's something about finger placement, pressure, and their arm movement. And it's God-given.

When John Burkett pitched for us, he used more pine tar than a hitter. He struck out the first guy in a game one time, and when I got the ball back, I literally threw it into the ground. The ball was so caked in pine tar it stuck to my hand. *Good gracious, Burky.*

Hitters use a pine tar rag to dab the bat handle so it doesn't slip out of their hands. Once in a while, ball boys put a new batch of pine tar on the rag, which makes it all liquid and nasty. You have to pat it down with rosin to get it tacky again. But Burky would lather up his glove with a new batch of pine tar while it was still gooey. The balls he caught back from the catcher turned brown they had so much pine tar on them.

Nobody ever checked him, at least while he was with the Braves. I played against Burky after he left Atlanta, and I knew what he was doing. But he's such a good dude I wasn't going to say anything. He'd throw me that 68 mph eephus pitch, smirking the whole time.

I was slow to accuse somebody of cheating and I didn't appreciate it when somebody accused me of it either, like Jamie Moyer did in Colorado the last year of my career.

I have a lot of respect for Jamie. He's a guy

like Glavine, who will beat you with sheer will-power, and I dig that. But he stood on the mound that May and accused me of stealing signs when it was completely unfounded.

I had just doubled in a run to pull us within four runs of the Rockies, down 6–2 in the fifth inning. I was taking my lead off second base and talking to Troy Tulowitzki, the Rockies shortstop. When I turned back to look at Jamie, he had stepped off the rubber and was yelling at me, "I see you! I know what you're doing!"

I looked at Tulo and said, "Is he talking to me?"

It finally dawned on me he was accusing me of relaying signs to Brian McCann at home plate. I'd been talking to Tulo. I wasn't even paying attention to the signs.

I started screaming back at Jamie. McCann hit a liner in the gap, and Moyer and I were still screaming at each other as I crossed home plate. We knocked Moyer out of the game in the sixth inning, and I was still fired up. I came up twice with the bases loaded after he left and got two-run singles both times. I ended up with five RBIs that game, and we pounded them 13–9. It was one of the more gratifying comeback wins in my career.

I never gave signs, and I never wanted them. Moyer had questioned my integrity. I talked to Tulo the next day, and he just rolled his eyes. "Don't worry about it," he said. "If anybody asks me, I've got your back."

Tulo said Moyer was paranoid to begin with, that you needed a rocket science degree to decode his signs. Tulo said he didn't even know what Moyer was throwing half the time.

I know this: If *we* were convinced somebody was stealing signs, we would have sent a message. We'd have flipped him or hit him—something. Nobody knocked me on my rear end or threw anything under my chin the rest of that game, which told me Jamie was the only one in that dugout who thought I was relaying signs.

I always thought if the runner could pick up the catcher's signs, it was on the pitcher and the catcher anyway. Moyer could have taken a page from Doggie's book. Maddux policed sign stealers without saying a word to anybody.

His test was simple enough. He would come set with a changeup grip. As he went into his motion, he'd look back to see if the runner at second base moved. Normally, when you're getting your lead off second, you're either in constant motion or you make an abrupt movement. Constant movement means there's nothing going on. But if a runner is still while the pitcher comes set and then moves after he sees a sign or a grip in the pitcher's glove, something is up. The runner might tap his helmet on one side or the other. He might step forward or back. He might stand straight up, then come back down. There are a bunch of ways to give signals from second base.

If Doggie thought the runner was giving signals to the hitter, he would change his grip, say from a fastball grip to a changeup, mid-delivery.

Most pitchers wouldn't dare try that because it would cross up their catcher. But Eddie Perez was such a good catcher, it didn't matter what Doggie threw. Eddie could think fastball was coming and still catch a changeup. The runner didn't stand a chance.

I paid as much attention to who was umpiring games as I did who was pitching. My first couple of years in the league, I kept notebooks on both pitchers and umpires—which ones you could talk to, which ones you couldn't, which ones were hitters' umpires, which ones meant you better leave the dugout swinging.

I also got scouting reports from David Justice.

"You got Joe West behind the plate," he'd say. "He's going to 'rookie' you. He'll call a pitch three or four inches off the outside corner a strike, then watch your reaction. If you show him up, he'll call balls even farther off the plate strikes. He'll push you until you say something. Then he'll throw you out of the game. Just take it. Don't say a word, walk back to the dugout and the next time you come up, the strike zone will get a little better for you. Don't give him any ammo, he won't burn you. Eventually, you'll earn his respect and get the benefit of the doubt."

He was right. Joe West, Paul Runge—all those guys were exactly the same way.

Ol' Balkin' Bob Davidson was the first umpire to throw me out. He was one of those guys who had to get his five minutes of fame. Even if he wasn't behind the plate, he was going to make the telecast at some point. How do you get noticed umpiring at first base? Call a balk. Bob was a pretty nice guy but not a real good umpire, and if he was having a bad day, he was going to be the center of attention at some point.

We were in extra innings against the Dodgers in Los Angeles in August 1996. It was a day game after a night game on the second-to-last day of a nineteen-day road trip while our stadium was being used for the Olympics. We were tied up in the top of the thirteenth inning, and Scott Radinsky struck me out on a pitch that was borderline at best.

I was already at my wit's end with Bob's strike zone. I didn't say anything at the plate, but when I got back to the dugout, I was throwing stuff and screaming. The dugouts in Dodger Stadium were fifty yards from home plate, so there was no way he could hear me. But I was looking at Bob and he knew I was saying something to him, so he rang me up.

Mike Mordecai came in after I got ejected, and up in the visiting clubhouse, I told the guys, "Mark this down, Mordy is going to win this game for us. And Balkin' Bob is going to hear me laughing all the way in here." The game dragged on for five more innings, but sure enough, Mordy got a base hit to win it in the eighteenth inning.

Umpires have to fill out a report saying why an ejection was warranted. Bob couldn't have known what I said that day, so I never got fined. Now, if you get up in an umpire's face and call him something colorful, you're going to get written up and fined.

I was playing shortstop in a game in Colorado early in my career, and I tagged out Ellis Burks at second on a stolen base attempt. I swipe-tagged him and just barely got him, but I got him. Jerry Meals called him safe, and I couldn't believe it. I was 0-fer that day and we were getting hammered, so at first I kept my mouth shut. But during a pitching change, TP—who was playing third that day—came over to me and said, "Jerry Meals said you missed the tag." I lost it.

I walked up to him and said, "Jerry, you're saying you called him safe because I missed the tag?"

"Yeah, Chipper," he said. "You missed the tag."

"Jerry, you're a blind motherfucker," I said.

I got fined for that one.

Billy Hohn was probably the worst of the worst because he would bait you. He threw three of us out within about twenty seconds one time in Fenway Park. Eric O'Flaherty, our lefty reliever, had struck out J. D. Drew on a fastball right down the middle. Hohn called it a ball. J.D. hit the next pitch off the wall to give the Red Sox a one-run lead. When Bobby came out to get O'Flaherty, O'Flaherty asked Hohn how he could miss that call.

"What'd you say?" Hohn said. "What'd you say? Say it again."

Then he threw O'Flaherty out. I snapped.

"That's bullshit," I said. "You were baiting him. You wanted to throw him out."

Then I couldn't help myself. I said, "Nice porn 'stache." Then he threw me out. Bobby came to my defense, and he got rung up, too. It was one of seven times I got ejected in my career. That was a drop in the bucket compared to Bobby, though. He set the major league record with 158 ejections!

Bobby was all business when he went out to argue. I can only imagine what went through umpires' minds when they saw him coming. They had to be thinking, "Oh, here we go again." But every once in a while, it was downright funny—maybe not to the umpire but to everybody else.

Everybody but Cox and Smoltzie had to laugh at an argument Cox got into one time in Cincinnati in 1998, and I had a front-row seat at third base.

Bret Boone, the second baseman for the Reds and a future teammate with Atlanta, slid into third base, and I missed the tag coming in; but he slid off the bag, and I held the tag on him. He was out. Smoltzie was backing up third and saw the whole thing. I saw it. Boonie saw it, but apparently Hunter Wendelstedt didn't see it. He blew the call.

Hunter was a second-generation umpire. His dad, Harry Wendelstedt, was one of the most respected umpires in the game. Everybody loved Harry. He wasn't confrontational. He wasn't cocky. Hunter didn't exactly live up to his father's legacy that day.

Smoltzie came charging in and started going at it with Hunter. Somehow they got tangled up and Hunter must have stepped on Smoltz's foot because Smoltzie couldn't move. And they bumped. Hunter immediately overreacted and threw Smoltz out of the game. Smoltzie went apeshit.

It was only the fourth inning, and we were going to have to go five, six innings with our bullpen, so Bobby came out and started going apeshit, too. He took his hat off and went nose to nose with Hunter.

Hunter gave some cockamamie explanation as to why he threw Smoltzie out of the game. Bobby looked him dead in the eye and said, "Hunter, you wouldn't have made a pimple on your daddy's ass."

So then, Bobby was gone. I was laughing so

hard I almost got tossed, too. Before Bobby went back to the dugout, he told Smoltzie to get back up on the mound. He told him it was Hunter's fault they bumped and he was not being thrown out of this game.

Bobby was still barking at Hunter, "It's the fourth fucking inning. You're going to ruin our bullpen for the next week." Smoltzie was standing on the mound with his arms folded like "I'm not going. You can't throw me out of this game." Finally, Bobby said, "C'mon, Smoltzie." And they tucked their tails and walked back to the dugout.

I talk a lot about umpires I didn't see eye to eye with, but there were quite a few who were very good at their craft and took a lot of pride in their job. My favorite umpire was Randy Marsh.

Not only was Randy a good ball/strike umpire and a good base umpire, you could share a laugh with him. He wasn't afraid to tell you what he thought, which I respected, and if you had a beef, you could talk to him about it. He wasn't going to take something you said personally or fly off the handle.

When Randy Marsh umpired third base, I knew he and I were going to talk all night. Maddux would be carving hitters up, and Marsh would say, "Man, that guy is unbelievable." I'd strike out on a check swing and when I went back out in the field the next inning, he'd say, "Looking fastball right there, huh?"

"Shut up, Randy," I'd say.

When Bruce Froemming was behind the plate, you had to dip your toe in the water to see how warm it was. If you walked up and said, "What's up, Bruce?" and he said, "Get in the box, Jonesy," you had a tough Bruce Froemming that day.

But if you said, "What's up, Bruce?" and he said, "Hey, Jonesy, what's going on?" you knew you got the good Bruce.

I could turn around at home plate and say, "Gosh dang it, Bruce, that ball is five inches outside."

"Nah, Jonesy," he'd say. "That ball is right on the corner. I've been giving this pitch all day."

"Bruce, just because you've been giving it all day doesn't mean it's a strike," I'd say. "I know you got dinner plans. I know you got a plane flight out of here."

When he got tired of the banter, he'd just say, "Ah, Jonesy, get back in the box."

I loved Tim McClelland. A lot of people hated how deliberate he was with his calls. But the hitter and the catcher knew what it was right away because he would say "yip" before he stood up and gave the strike call.

Tim was quiet, a little standoffish, but he was a hitter's umpire. He made pitchers throw the ball over the plate, which is one reason we got along. And if the game was dragging, I could always count on Tim saying something funny to kill time. That's what you look for as players. Let us know you're human, have some personality, have some feelings. Cut us down, cut the other team down, cut the fans down, whatever is going to make you laugh. I enjoyed interacting with those guys; it took the monotony out of the game.

Hitting is so psychological. If you feel good physically, your bat and batting gloves feel good, and you're confident walking up to the plate, you'll be successful more times than not. If you're not sure—*This bat doesn't feel right; my shoes are tied too tight; this helmet is a little loose*—you're not going to get a hit. Lucky for me, from that time I picked up one of Ron Gant's Rawlings MS20s in Double-A, I never worried about my bat.

I was still swinging the same 35-inch, 34-ounce model the last day I played in the big leagues. Left-handed, anyway.

I used a different model when I swung right-handed. My swings were different, so I wanted a different bat. My left-handed swing was long and flowing, with a lot of moving parts. I wanted a heavier bat with more weight in the end. My right-handed swing was short and compact, so I wanted the bat a little lighter. It actually took me longer to find a bat I was comfortable with from my right side. I started with Louisville and then I went to Glomar. In '99, when I won the MVP award, I swung a 35-inch, 33-ounce Glomar right-handed. It was a hard, durable bat, and I got good results out of it, at least until I got a bad batch.

Generally, I did not break bats. They might flake and I'd get rid of them, but I broke maybe ten or twelve in a year. I broke five of those Glomars in a week. The bat was disintegrating in my hand even on balls I squared up. That can't happen. So I never picked them up again.

I went to another Rawlings model right-handed that was 35 inches, 33 ounces and painted black. That made it easier to get to the right bat in a hurry, without having to thumb through gamers, backups, and BP bats.

I tried Mizuno bats off and on throughout my career, but when it was all said and done, I couldn't find anything that made me feel as good as the Rawlings ash.

For everything other than bats, I used Mizuno. I liked their shoes. I wasn't going to wear any other glove. They had their US headquarters in Atlanta. It just made sense. I could go through one company and get everything I needed head to toe: wristbands, batting gloves, gloves, shoes.

As part of my contract with Mizuno, I was obligated to make one trip to their headquarters in Japan, so I went in January 2003. I did a few appearances and signed some autographs, but mainly I think Mizuno wanted me to come so I would get comfortable with one of their bats. They took me to Tokyo to meet their master craftsman.

He took measurements from one of my Rawlings bats, and in a matter of fifteen minutes made the identical bat, spec for spec, out of a tubular piece of wood, right there in front of me. The guy was a stinking artist with the lathe. He rounded off the knob and the end, then sanded it from handle to barrel. It was one of the cooler things I had ever seen.

He handed me the bat right off the lathe and sent me to a batting cage right there at the factory. B.B., who was on the trip with me, threw batting practice, and I swung with the bat for about fifteen minutes. It felt pretty good, and I left Japan planning to give it a shot. Mizuno shipped a batch to Florida for me to use in spring training.

I didn't make it through batting practice before something felt off. Balls I thought were gone would hit off the bottom of the wall. Or I would backspin a ball that should one-hop the wall, and it would trickle to the wall instead.

I'm not sure if it was the durability of the wood or the balance of the bat, but it just felt different. My Rawlings model was a little top-heavy, and since I had a tendency to pull off balls, I wanted more weight in the very end of the bat. Mizuno bats could be 35 inches and 34 ounces, too, but if they were weighted more evenly, they weren't going to feel the same as mine. The Rawlings MS20 was the perfect bat for me.

Smoltzie loved my bats. He used them in BP every once in a while but never in a game. He was a big dude, and I told him he was strong enough to use one in a game; I just had no idea he would take me up on it at the worst possible time. I was fifteen games into an eighteen-game hitting streak—the third-longest of my career—when I looked up to see Smoltzie walking to the plate with my bat.

He didn't even ask. I was in the dugout, fuming.

Right on cue, Smoltzie got a jam sandwich. He swung at a pitch inside and shattered the bat. Everybody on the bench started laughing. I did not. I was sitting there holding pieces of the bat that the bat boy brought me, when Smoltz got back to the dugout.

"What the hell are you doing?" I said. "Go get my BP bat. Grab a backup. Don't use my gamer. I'm on a fifteen-game hitting streak right now, and this is *the* bat, and you break it?"

He apologized. Eventually, I could laugh about it. It helped that Smoltz got fined twenty dollars in kangaroo court for it, and I got another handful of games on the streak with another bat.

• • •

Hank Aaron asked to hold my bat one day in spring training, sitting on the bench behind the batting cage.

"Man, this is a big old bat," he said. "It's like something some of the boys back in my day would use. Yeah, I could have hit a few homers with this bat."

Hank Aaron is a baseball god, especially in the Braves organization. When I first got to know him, it was for a picture here or there. We exchanged pleasantries, and that was basically it. But as I got a little older and more comfortable, I started approaching him. And I loved hearing old war stories or asking him questions.

I'd heard a trivia question that Hank took Don Drysdale deep seventeen times in his career—*seventeen times!* Don Drysdale was one of the most intimidating pitchers of his era. He was not afraid to throw one up under your chin or knock you on your rear end. And he had devastating stuff to go with it.

The most homers I hit off one pitcher in my career was seven, off Steve Trachsel. Granted, pitchers probably faced guys a lot more often before expansion, but seventeen homers blew my mind. So I asked him about it.

He flashed a sheepish grin.

"You know as well as I do that you see some pitchers well or you're on the same page as they are," he said. "You're right whenever you face him and you have good at-bats against him."

For just a minute, Hank Aaron made me feel like we had something in common. Sharing a moment with him was really cool.

My version of having big numbers against a dominant pitcher of my era was hitting six homers off Randy Johnson. That's a stat I look at now and think, *How in the hell did I do that?*

I caught Randy in some instances where I was swinging the bat well. It wasn't that I enjoyed facing him by any stretch of the imagination. I had my one and only sombrero—a four-strikeout game—in one of Randy's starts late in his career in San Francisco. He struck me out three times that day and a reliever got me once. Randy was forty-five at the time, so yeah, he was still getting it done.

CHAPTER 22
Teaching Points

The last year we had Maddux, Glavine, and Smoltz all together was 2002. The way baseball payrolls and free agency work, keeping players the caliber of the Big Three on one team is nearly impossible. Smoltz stayed six more years, but even he finished his career with the Cardinals.

We had to watch Maddux and Glavine win their 300th games elsewhere—Maddux with the Cubs in 2004 and Glavine with the Mets, of all teams, in 2007. I would love to have played in their 300th wins, but I'm proud of the fact that I was behind them for a bunch along the way.

I wanted no part of facing Glavine with the Mets. It was awkward. I think everybody knew Glav wanted to stay with the Braves, but he and the brass painted each other into a corner, and after the Mets made him a bigger offer, he made the decision to go. It was the wrong one, and he knew it, but Glav being a man of his word went along with the deal. It was like an alternate universe seeing him in a Mets uniform.

I knew exactly what I was up against. Most hitters would tell you at six thirty in the evening that the thought of facing Tom Glavine didn't strike fear in their hearts, but more times than not, you walked away at eleven o'clock with an 0-for-4 and a loss.

When I saw a pitcher with a big ego and a big fastball, I was licking my chops. But I struggled with guys like Glav, who knew they didn't have a fastball they could blow by you. They got their jollies by off-speeding you early in the count and then breaking your bat on an 88 mph fastball late. I could almost hear Glav giggling inside his head when he threw a sequence like changeup, backdoor breaking ball, changeup, changeup, then 88 mph chain saw in on the hands. You hit a ground ball to short, and pieces of the bat went farther than the ball.

Against Randy Johnson or Pedro Martinez, hitters feared embarrassment. With Glavine, you knew you were going to put the ball in play. You just hoped he'd make a mistake, and you could hit it hard. Problem was, Tommy never made those mistakes. I took Tommy deep in Shea Stadium once, and there was nobody more shocked than I was.

I only hit .188 off him, but I could get under his skin every once in a while. I knew I was doing well if he gave me a "Swing the bat, you pussy."

If you got any kind of reaction out of Glav between the lines, you'd done something. I had to get the cheapest base hit of my life to get him to smile. He threw me a changeup one time in Atlanta that I literally cued off the end of the bat. The first baseman was playing me off the line, and the ball hit six inches inside the first base bag and spewed over toward the tarp—one of the worst possible hits you can ever get.

Glavine covered first, thinking there might be a play, and as I was crossing the bag, he said, "You gotta be shittin' me."

"Bruh, I'm sorry," I said, laughing. "I was trying to hit it a lot harder than that. But sometimes you got to hit it the way they throw it—softly."

That got a little wry smile.

Facing Glavine or Maddux never made for a normal game, especially when Smoltzie was pitching for us. Smoltzie made the most unbelievable play of his life right in front of me at third base, all because he was facing his old pal Glav.

I played in on the grass a lot, and if there was a swinging bunt, I had it. A pitcher's first reaction is to go after the ball, but he is supposed to pull up when he hears me call him off. Well, Glavine hit a swinging bunt, and I was yelling, "I got it, I got it, I got it," and Smoltzie kept going. He wanted to have something to rag Glav about after the game.

Running toward the third base dugout, Smoltzie barehanded the ball right in front of me, threw back across his body, and got Glavine by a step. Then he walked back by me and said, "Did you have that?"

"In my back pocket, bro," I said. "I could have fielded it with my glove and thrown him out, and you're trying to be Brooks Robinson over here."

He got a step past me, stopped, and turned around.

"Yeah, but it was a great play, wasn't it?" he said.

The last year or two before Glavine and Maddux left, I got more comfortable with the idea of being one of the leaders of the club. The MVP year and a couple of good seasons gave me credibility I didn't have in 1997 when David Justice said the clubhouse would be mine.

Without Maddux and Glavine, Smoltz and I became the elder statesmen, at least in terms of longevity. We led in tandem, once we figured out how that would work.

The first time Smoltzie said something about the offense in a meeting, I could see the hackles on the backs of position players' necks rising. I'm sure I did the same thing to our pitchers when I talked about that facet of the game.

I called a meeting once in 2006. Todd Pratt was our backup catcher and a mentor to our young stud Brian McCann. I didn't like the way Pratt was calling games for our young pitchers. In our heyday, we pitched away and we played away.

Todd Pratt liked to get people out inside because as a hitter, that's the pitch he had trouble with.

"Every time we have a scouting meeting, what is Leo Mazzone's first word?" I said when everybody got quiet. "*Away.* Locate your fastball away, away, away. Our defense is geared toward pitching away. So when we decide to pitch people inside and we don't execute the pitch, guess what happens? Doubles. Triples. Big innings."

I hadn't named any names, but Todd knew. He came up to me after the meeting and said, "Was that directed at me?"

"To a certain extent, yeah," I said. "There's a reason Andruw Jones is playing in right center with a right-handed hitter up. If you're crossing up the defense by calling pitches in and we've got young kids who can't execute that pitch ninety-five percent of the time, that's a problem."

"I hadn't really thought about that," he said.

But the way I made my point probably fuzzed up some pitchers. I halfway wanted it to, but it became pretty obvious to Smoltz and me that our dynamic wasn't going to work. From then on, Smoltzie would handle pitching in meetings, and I'd talk about hitting.

There's a divide between pitchers and hitters in every clubhouse because pitchers don't play every day. Everyday players would argue they are the tougher and better athletes. Obviously I'm biased, but I'm inclined to agree. I respected the job pitchers had, though. As long as you went to the post and gave me everything you had every fifth day, I treated you like another position player. But as hitters and pitchers, we had our differences. That went for Smoltz and me, too.

We got into it through the media once when Smoltz insinuated in a postgame interview after a loss to the Tigers that I should be playing through a groin injury. Our offense was really struggling at the time, and he said, "I certainly appreciate the effort of the guys who are on the field busting it, because I'm on the mound busting it just as hard as I can. We all could wish we were feeling better. But that's just the way it is."

He didn't call me out by name but it was pretty obvious he was talking about me to everybody, including the radio guys I listened to on the ride home that night. One of them said, "Is it just me or was that a backhanded slap at Chipper?"

I stewed over it all night. I was ready to fight him. I rushed back in the lineup the next day and hit a homer off Justin Verlander. I'd gone to my knees in pain the swing before, but I managed to get out in front of a heater and hit it out of the park. We still lost 2–1, and I shot back at Smoltz through the media after the game.

"I'll play the rest of the games this year and do what I can," I said. "Somebody I know better not miss a start, though."

We both got called into Bobby's office. We

screamed at each other for five or ten minutes, and that was basically it. We cleared the air, but being called out by one of my brothers jaded me a little bit. Let's just say it did not escape my attention that Smoltz went on the disabled list with shoulder problems two weeks later.

Constructive criticism was always easier to take coming hitter to hitter. I always loved talking hitting with my teammates, especially young hitters late in my career. My dad always made it seem so easy to get his point across, but it wasn't. I learned the hard way with my buddy Adam LaRoche.

Rochy played first base for us in the mid-2000s and became one of my best friends in baseball. Adam struggled with ADHD and had trouble focusing. I didn't realize that his rookie year— he hadn't been diagnosed yet—when we sat down in Arizona to watch film of Brandon Webb. Webb had a dirty sinker, and I was trying to get Rochy mentally prepared for it.

"This guy has got the best sinker you're ever going to see," I said. "Make it start above the belt. If it starts below the belt, spit on it."

That's baseball-speak for take the pitch. Basically, anything that started below the belt was going to be a ball. For one of Webb's sinkers to be a strike, and worth swinging at, it had to start chest high.

Rochy got the perfect opportunity to put our game plan to use right away. He came up with the bases loaded and one out in the first inning. I was on second base willing him to throw up a good at-bat. *OK, you've got Brandon Webb, Cy Young winner, on the ropes. This is where you find out what you're all about. Let's go get it.*

First pitch from Webb was a sinker in the dirt. Rochy swung at it and missed. Second pitch, another sinker in the dirt. Rochy swung at it and missed. Third pitch, same thing. Sinker in the dirt, Rochy struck out. I was standing at second base screaming at him.

"We just went over all this!" I said. "You didn't make one ball start above the belt!"

Adam had a hose of an arm, and when we were on the field warming up in the bottom of the inning, he threw me a ball at third base that had hair on it. I'd pissed him off. I thought, *Good.* But I knew I had to bite the bullet, be the leader, and make it right. So after the inning was over, I put my arm around his neck and took him down into the tunnel.

"I apologize," I said. "I was trying to give you the advice you needed to be successful, and then you didn't use it. But I promise you that reaction will never happen again. Now, put that last at-bat behind you and go out and do your thing."

Rochy's next time up, he had two outs and a man on first. He got a sinker up in the zone and whaled on it. I didn't even have to watch it to know it was gone. I put my head in my hands and smiled while he ran the bases.

Everybody on the bench was like "You need to do that more often!"

I sent the message, got him focused, and it worked, but the way I went about it was wrong. I, of all people, know you're not going to execute in every at-bat, especially against the best in baseball. But you better be prepared for the one mistake you might get during the course of the game. Ultimately, Rochy was, and he won the game for us.

I knew better when Matt Diaz came to me two years later looking for help. Matt was a good pinch hitter for us and when he made spot starts in left field against lefties, he always did well. But when he first got to Atlanta in 2006, he was still trying to find his confidence.

One day I found him sitting in my favorite spot in the players' lounge, where I liked to play solitaire. I made a crack about him being in my chair. It didn't get much of a smile, so I said, "Y'allright?"

"Other than the fact that I've forgotten how to hit," he said. "I'm good."

Matt had bounced up and down between Triple-A and the majors with Kansas City and

Tampa the past couple of years. He was worried he was going to do more of the same with the Braves.

I told him we were having a powwow in the batting cage the next day in Philadelphia. I'd been rounding guys up to talk hitting before games like my dad and I always did. My only thing was the hitter had to come to me first, and Matt did.

He didn't show up the first day in Philly. He told me later he didn't want to take swings away from me. After I convinced him he wouldn't, he was there the next day.

Matt had an unorthodox swing with a lot of lower body movement that wasn't conducive to having a good base. He had trouble keeping his back foot on the ground.

"If you look at all the great hitters, their base is virtually the same at contact point," I told him. "You could draw a straight line, from their knee all the way up the side of their pants through the middle of their head. It's like they have a rod going through them that allows them to hit off of a stiff front side."

All he had to do, I told him, was keep his back knee bent through the entire swing. It clicked.

He started backing balls up and hitting balls out of the ballpark to right field. That night in Philly, he tripled on a ball to right center. He started a couple of nights later in Florida, against Dontrelle Willis, and got five hits.

When we took the field after his fifth hit, I turned around to left field and flashed him five fingers. "Wow," I mouthed. He gave me a little smile and a shrug.

To this day, Matt tells people I saved his career. I wouldn't go that far, but it's nice to know he got something out of our conversation. I was just doing for him what Dad always did for me—getting in the cage and talking hitting until something clicked.

Even when I was a veteran giving advice to the younger guys, my dad was still my hitting coach. He always was.

He is the reason why for the first fifteen years I was in the big leagues, I never went more than thirteen at-bats without a base hit. If I had a great game, I'd call Dad on the way home. If things were steady as she goes, we wouldn't talk much. But if I was in the middle of a 2-for-30 slump, we talked every day.

Nobody knew my swing inside and out like he did. He built it. He and I used to watch VHS tapes of my at-bats, whether it was Babe Ruth League, high school, or American Legion. I was a visual learner, and I needed that immediate feedback, especially from the left side, so my mom videotaped every game.

Once I got to the big leagues, Dad saw every one of my ten thousand or so plate appearances. By the time I called him after a game, not only had he seen my at-bats, but he'd also watched replays of them and already had some suggestions. He could see what I was doing wrong better than anybody. And when it wasn't enough for him to talk me through it, he got on a plane and came to Atlanta.

I called him one time when we were in Milwaukee, and I was scuffling.

"What are you seeing?" I said as soon as he answered the phone, not bothering with a "Hey, it's me."

"You're drifting," he said. "Bad."

One of the keys to hitting is keeping your head still. If you're drifting forward, 95 mph seems like 100. Dad taught me to hit against a stiff front leg. When I drifted, I landed hard on my front side, with a bent front leg. It caused my head to move six to eight inches forward and there was no way I could center a good fastball.

Dad gave me a couple of things to think about over the phone and told me he'd meet me in Atlanta after we finished out our road trip in St. Louis. In the meantime, I decided to ask Bobby for a cage day.

Bobby was old-school. Unless you had an appendage hanging by a piece of meat, you were playing. And that's fine. I loved it. But he must have seen the conviction in my eyes, not to mention the fact that I already had my hands taped up, my batting gloves on, and my bat with me.

"I need two hours in the cage to iron this shit out," I said. "I'm not going to be much good to you in a game today because my hands are going to be jacked up. I'll be ready to go tomorrow, and Dad is meeting me in Atlanta when we get back home."

"Great idea," he said. "Go get it done."

That's why everybody loved playing for Bobby. He let you be a grown man and do what was best for you.

Our first game back in Atlanta, I doubled, tripled, and homered. I homered in three straight games against the Padres, off Adam Eaton, Kevin Jarvis, and Jake Peavy. It was crazy.

From then on—this was August 2003—Bobby actually came up to me sometimes when I was struggling at the plate and suggested cage days. And it got to be almost comical how hot I got every time Dad came to town. The Braves should have put him on the payroll.

Of course Dad and I were both self-conscious about stepping on anybody's toes. I never brought him down into the cage unless I had run it past our hitting coach first, whether it was Clarence Jones, Terry Pendleton, Don

Baylor, Merv Rettenmund, or Greg Walker. Every one of them welcomed him down.

For me, having Dad at games meant more than just having his coaching; it took me back to being a little kid again.

Whenever my parents showed up, they invigorated me. I wanted to impress them. I didn't get to play in front of them very often, especially late in my career when they lived in Texas. Sometimes one series a year in Houston was all I got.

People wondered why I always played well in Houston. My parents were a big reason why. I could be 0-for-14 and biting everybody's head off in the clubhouse, and we'd get to Houston and I'd have a 10-hit series just because my dad was there.

CHAPTER 23
The End of an Era

The attitude of every player in our clubhouse during our string of fourteen straight division titles was "We're not losing this streak on my watch." Nobody felt stronger about it than I did.

We had some teams in the early 2000s that probably shouldn't have kept it going, but we did out of sheer will, fortitude, and loyalty to our manager. The first year I looked at the roster and didn't see any way was 2004. We had a lot of turnover and a lot of young kids cutting their teeth in the big leagues.

I had a terrible first half. That was the year I hit .248 and moved from left field back to third base. But pitchers like Russ Ortiz and John Thomson picked up the slack, and we still had the mental edge. We had a lot of teams beat before we ever took the field because we were the Atlanta Braves. We won ninety-six games and won the NL East by double-digit figures for the third straight year.

Then in 2005 came the influx of "Baby Braves." At one time or another, we had eighteen rookies on the squad, guys like Brian McCann,

Jeff Francoeur, Kyle Davies, and Kelly Johnson, and we didn't miss a beat.

A bunch of them had grown up in Atlanta, which made it an even bigger deal. Francoeur was a two-sport stud at Parkview High School in the Atlanta suburbs. He broke into the big leagues by hitting a three-run bomb in his debut. He got off to such a hot start he made the cover of *Sports Illustrated* his second month in the big leagues.

I'll admit I was jealous of Francoeur when he first got called up. I'd catch myself mumbling, "He hasn't earned it yet." Eventually, it dawned on me. My veteran teammates probably felt the same way about me when I was a rookie. And here I was calling Frenchy the Golden Child and saying, "This is going to be your team," just like David Justice had said to me.

The difference between Jeff and me was that he was a lot more grounded than I was at that age. Yeah, he was cocky, brash, and vocal, but Jeff was in a better place with his spirituality than I'd been. Ultimately that helped him deal with the attention he got better than I did.

Brian McCann (BMac) was another Atlanta kid. He didn't make quite the splash his buddy Frenchy did when he got called up that year, but he wasn't far behind. When it was all said and done, he was probably more of a bona fide major league star than Jeff was. We knew Brian was going to be special when he caught a complete game for Smoltzie his second day in the big leagues. Then four months later, he hit a three-run homer off Roger Clemens in the Division Series against the Astros.

"Do you realize what you've just done?" I said, walking up to him in the dugout after his homer. "You just threw Roger Clemens in the fucking drink!"

He'd been trying to play it all cool, but after I said that, he started dying laughing. That's taking my home run off Clemens in Toronto to a whole different level.

Unfortunately, McCann's homer was probably our last highlight in that series. We didn't win another game. We had had the upper hand on the Astros for years, dominating them in three playoff series starting in the late '90s. But the tide started to turn in 2004, when Carlos Beltran had a monster Division Series and they knocked us out of the playoffs in five games. Then in 2005 we lost the Division Series to them in an epic eighteen-inning marathon in Game 4.

We were up 6–1 with six outs to go at Minute Maid Park. Andy Pettitte, who was scheduled to pitch Game 5 at Turner Field for the Astros, had already left to fly back to Atlanta.

Kyle Farnsworth was on in relief for us, and I would have taken him against any of the Astros hitters, but for whatever reason, he didn't get it done. Farnsworth gave up a grand slam to Lance Berkman in the eighth. Then Brad Ausmus tied it up with a solo shot off Farnsworth in the ninth.

We managed to stop the bleeding and were getting a little momentum back in extra innings when we saw Clemens warming up in the bullpen to come into the game in the sixteenth inning. I didn't say it out loud but I was thinking, *Welp, we're not scoring the next time through the lineup.*

By the seventeenth, we were basically out of pitchers. We had to put in a rookie reliever, Joey Devine, and give him an "OK, kid, go get 'em." It was almost unfair. He'd just been drafted out of college in June and pitched all of seven games in the big leagues. Devine got through the seventeenth, but in the eighteenth, Chris Burke homered him to end our season on a walk-off.

It was shocking for all of us. But you play one team in that many meaningful games, over that many years, eventually they're going to get you.

I was sitting at my locker in my underwear, exhausted. After an eighteen-inning game, with that kind of emotion, I was done. I had my head in my hands when I felt a tap on my shoulder. I turned around and it was Farnsworth. He was sobbing. He stuck his hand out and said, "I am so sorry."

Now, this was one of the scariest dudes you'll ever meet in your life. He once took down Paul

Wilson, the former first pick of the draft by the Mets, in a brawl and then nailed him with a couple of haymakers.

I shook Farnsworth's hand and said, "Dude, it's baseball."

My dad always said there would be days when you gave everything you had and it wouldn't be enough. The loss fell on the offense, too. But Farnsworth was inconsolable. So was Joey Devine. Baseball can be devastating but that's what makes it so great. If you play the game long enough, you'll see some crazy things. And we had to admit we snatched victory from the jaws of defeat a few times that 2005 season.

We'd been the cardiac kids plenty of times during our fourteen-year run. We gained our reputation on plays like Sid Bream's slide, by winning close well-pitched games, and by being in the World Series over and over in the '90s. The road to the World Series championship had to come through Atlanta. And when people beat us, it was special for them. I'm proud I was a part of that.

Our streak ended the following year, even with the infusion of young talent we'd had on that 2005 team. It just goes to show how hard it is to win as consistently as we did for as long as we did.

Bobby Cox called a few of us into his office one morning in spring training in 2008. It was me, Francoeur, McCann, and Tim Hudson. I was thinking, *Oh god, what did I do? Who did I piss off?* I always got nervous when I got called into the principal's office. Bobby was the last guy I wanted mad at me.

"I just wanted you guys to hear this from me before you hear it from anybody else," he said. "I quit yesterday."

Everybody's jaws dropped.

"Yep," he said. "I drove halfway to Georgia, and Schuerholz called me and talked me back down. I can't work with Frank Wren. Can't do it."

Schuerholz had stepped down to become team president over the winter trying to lighten his load, and Frank was in his first few months as our general manager.

"You can't quit, Skipper," Frenchy said, voicing what all of us were thinking.

Frenchy was about to cry. I was just taking it all in. I knew there was tension. Whenever Bobby was standing there and Frank walked up, Bobby would immediately leave.

Frank was a micromanager. He wanted to put his two cents in about pitching, hitting, defense, baserunning, everything, instead of letting the coaches do their jobs. He was the opposite of Schuerholz, who hired personnel, made some suggestions, and let the men in uniform do the coaching.

The Braves had been a well-oiled machine from top to bottom for the entire run of division titles. We brought back pretty much the same coaches every year. We had great leadership in the clubhouse. Everybody knew their place. But by 2008, there was unrest in the organization that eventually led to Wren's firing and a complete rebuild.

We appreciated the fact that Bobby let us in on his thinking that day. He didn't have to tell us. But thank goodness Schuerholz talked him off the ledge. That's who John was; he was the liaison, the mediator, the calming influence. He was the Tom Glavine of the brass.

John put a Band-Aid on the situation for a while, but Bobby was in the beginning of the end of his career as manager of the Braves. And Bobby is a lifer. He'll be buried in that Braves uniform. I think if Frank hadn't been there, Bobby would have managed a lot longer than he did. But he gave us a wake-up call that morning that times were changing in our organization, from the front office to the clubhouse.

Smoltzie made five starts that season, had shoulder surgery, and then he was gone, too; 2008 was his last season with the Braves. All of a sudden, I was the one in Smoltzie's locker, by the door to the showers. Now I was overseeing everything that happened in the locker room. I was calling team meetings. Smoltzie and

Glav had deflected so much attention off me throughout the years. The media could go to Smoltz or Glavine, and now that fell squarely on me.

My first inclination was to lead by example, but you had to be able to relate to people, to know which guys needed a pat on the back and which ones needed a foot stuck in their ass. When a young guy like Freddie Freeman or Jason Heyward approached me in the clubhouse, I needed to come out of my shell.

The way Sheff used to put it was that there were times I didn't want a whole lot of company. My teammates kidded me that I was an asshole sometimes. Sometimes I just wanted to be left alone. None of them knew what was going on in my personal life and they couldn't help me with it anyway; so I kept it to myself.

My second marriage was going downhill, and it had been for a while. Here I was, a guy who wanted to be liked by everybody, and I couldn't even get along with my spouses. When it came down to it, I had to ask myself, *Do they love me for me?*

By my late thirties, baseball was my haven again. I took my mind off what was going on at home by enjoying my time with the young guys on the team. They made me feel young again. And they wanted me to let my hair down a little. One way I could do that was with my uni.

I'd always liked my uniform tight. You could take it all the way from my head to my toes. I liked my jersey tight—I wore my mock turtlenecks tight—my batting gloves and my pants, too. I liked neoprene sleeves snug on my knees for extra support. I even liked my shoes tight. I was almost thirty before I figured out that squeezing three pairs of socks into a size 12 shoe was causing me foot problems. What I really needed was a size 14.

I felt most comfortable when everything was held together pretty good. But by the late 2000s, the young guys were wearing baggy pants with the big cuffs that looked like a boot-cut pair of Levi's. They were wearing T-shirts if they wore a shirt underneath their jersey at all while I was still mock-T'd up to the chin. They were like "Bro, you got to loosen the collar."

One afternoon I went up to McCann and said, "Mac, give me your pants, let me wear them today." He thought it was the coolest thing in the world. I went out and got three hits that night, so I wore baggy pants from that day on. The mock turtle was something I couldn't get away from, though.

I listened to the radio driving into the ballpark every day. I heard the talk about me being old. *He can't do this, that, and the other anymore.* There's no doubt I'd struggled with a lot of injuries in my early- to midthirties. But I knew I could still hit. At age thirty-six in 2008, I managed to shut everybody up for a while because even when I wasn't feeling good physically, I could tailor my approach at the plate and still do some pretty cool things. It helped that I got off to a hot start.

For the first twelve weeks of the season, everything I hit fell. It was crazy. I'd break bats, and balls would fall in front of the center fielder. I'd hit a topper off the plate, and the pitcher would break his neck trying to field it. I'd roll over one for eighteen hops—the first and second basemen would both dive for it— and it would glance off one of their gloves. I'd hit a weak pop-up into right field, and the second baseman would think the right fielder had it, and the right fielder would think the second baseman had it, and it'd fall in. I'd leg out an infield base hit; the ball would beat me by six inches, and I'd get the call. Everything went my way.

Three months into the season, I was milking a .400 average. I was actually getting questions about Ted Williams. Reporters were coming up to me every day asking, "You think you can hit .400?"

Really? It wasn't like I was hitting .480 and had something to play with. I was hitting more like .404, so coming down from the clouds was just a matter of time. I made it halfway through June before I dipped below .400.

There were a bunch of times during those first twelve weeks when I didn't feel very good at the plate, but I didn't take many 0-fers. That's how you hit .400 over an extended period. But never for one minute did I think I was going to hit .400 for an entire season, so I didn't worry about it. My mom was the only one in my family who really talked about it as a possibility. There's a reason why she is my biggest fan.

I don't know how people hit .400. George Brett was hitting .400 in September in 1980 in the American League, getting five at-bats every game. As a National Leaguer, I only got three or four sometimes. Brett finishing at .390 in the American League, Ted Williams hitting .399 (technically .3996) going into a doubleheader on the last day of the 1941 season and ending up at .406—that's top dog. That's king of the holy shit.

I think Mom was trying to motivate me, and she was always good at that. If I shot for .400, then maybe my first batting title could be a by-product.

At the break, I was hitting .376. I had 18 homers with 51 RBIs, so I was well within a 30-homer type of season. Then all of a sudden my power disappeared. My shoulder was hurting and I couldn't get my arms extended. It didn't hurt until the follow-through—and right-handed once I extended out—but when things hurt past contact with the ball, it affects the way you swing. So I just said, "I'll be a slap hitter." I hit only 4 homers in the second half, but I hit a lot of singles.

I'd missed out on a chance at the batting title the previous year, finishing second behind Matt Holliday. But it was hard for me to get pissed off when I hit .337 for the season. That's getting a hit one-third of the time for an entire year. And Holliday was a damn good hitter. Couple that with the fact that he was playing his home games in Colorado; I felt lucky I was even in the hunt on the last day.

If you're going to win a batting title, chances are you're going to have to beat a Hall of Famer to do it, and in 2008, that was Albert Pujols. He hit .357. I ended up at .364.

I don't know if I would have won the batting title if I hadn't had a sore shoulder. I was relegated to pinch hitting the last two weeks of the season because it was stinking killing me. If I'd been out there getting four, five at-bats a day, grinding on that shoulder, the numbers probably would have suffered.

Hitting .364 also meant I came one hit shy of Mickey Mantle's record for the highest batting average in a season by a switch-hitter, so I was told. He hit .365 in 1957. Breaking that record never even crossed my mind. You know what was cool? The fact that I was even in the same freakin' zip code as Mantle.

The milestone that was on my mind much of that 2008 season was 400 homers. Once I hit my 399th homer on June 3, a ton of my friends and family came into town to watch me gun for my 400th. We had five more games on that home stand before heading to Chicago. As much as I wanted to do it in front of all my friends and family, chances were I wasn't going to. Sometimes I would go ten days to two weeks without hitting a homer. Lucky for me, I got a favorable matchup two days later.

The Marlins were in town and we were facing Ricky Nolasco, a right-hander. I was 6-for-10 against him at the time and had homered twice against him the last time we faced him down in Miami.

I knew how he was going to approach me. The two homers I'd hit in April were on two fastballs—one to the opposite field and one to right field. I knew if I saw a fastball, it was going to be either up and in or six inches off the plate. I had a feeling Nolasco would show me the fastball, but try to get me out with off-speed stuff. So in hitter's counts—2-0, 3-1, 3-2—I was going to get his get-me-over breaking ball.

Sure enough, I got to 2-0, and he threw me a little get-me-over slider. I was waiting on it.

Hitting my 400th was special. It put me in a different class of power hitters, not that I considered myself a power hitter. But 400 sounds a lot cooler than 300. And I was proud that the homer I hit to get there epitomized what I tried to do to pitchers throughout my career: Make the adjustment before the pitcher does.

What also made hitting my 400th special was being able to do it at home in front of Braves fans and in front of my family. I could flash the "I love you" symbol to Sharon and the kids right there in the stadium. I used to buy them a luxury box at Turner Field every year so they could come and seclude themselves, get food and drinks whenever they wanted, and be comfortable.

My box was on the club level, right over the top of our dugout, so whenever I hit a home run and Sharon and the boys were at the game, I would flash them the "I love you" sign language symbol. If I homered on the road, I flashed it to the TV cameras by the dugout to let Sharon and the boys know I was thinking of them.

One night I looked up and all the fans standing over the top of our dugout at Turner Field were doing it back to me. Later in my career, it became more of an "I love you" to the fans than anything else.

A little more than two years to the day after hitting my 400th homer, I woke up in Minneapolis before an interleague series against the Twins in June 2010 with an overwhelming thought: *I don't want to do this anymore.*

I sucked at the time. I couldn't throw the ball up and hit it. I was thirty-eight years old and hitting .228 three months into the season. I was not having any fun. I missed my family.

My dad always said, "One day you'll wake up and you'll know when it's time to retire."

I called my parents in Texas, choked up.

"I need you to come to Atlanta," I said. "I think I'm going to quit."

My dad didn't try to talk me out of it over the phone. He told me I would have their blessing whatever I decided to do. He just said he learned from his father never to make a decision when things were going really bad or really good. He told me to give it a couple of days and see how I felt.

Bobby Cox said the same thing when I went to his office that afternoon. He sat me for the last two games in Minnesota to give me a chance to think. A long talk with a therapist probably would have helped me at that point. Instead, I got some therapy from Frank Wren, John Schuerholz, and Bobby, when they sat me down for a meeting back in Atlanta. I got a few things off my chest and decided to keep playing, at least through the end of the year.

All of a sudden, out of nowhere, I started

hitting. I went on an 11-game hitting streak and raised my average 30 points in two weeks. I stopped thinking about retiring.

The question still lingered whether I planned to play beyond the end of the year. Honestly, I didn't know, I told the media. I wasn't going to make a decision until after the season. Then I blew out my knee again.

My surgically repaired ACL had lasted me sixteen years. But seven pounds of pressure is all it takes to blow one, and I had a lot more than that on my left knee when I went to make a jump throw one night that August in Houston.

Hunter Pence hit a ground ball up the third base line, and I extended into foul territory to make the catch when I heard the dreaded pop. As I took off on my left leg, I blew out the ligament, including eleven millimeters of trans-planted patellar tendon. I managed to make the throw on pure adrenaline, but when I landed, I knew I was in trouble.

The pain wasn't as excruciating as the first time. It felt more like the ligament stretched than tore, like maybe I partially tore it. An MRI back in Atlanta the next day said as much. The ligament wasn't completely torn, but it was torn enough that I needed surgery.

In that instant I knew retirement was out the window. No way did I want to go out like that. I couldn't retire limping off the field. All the negative thoughts I'd had in Minnesota had subsided. I was playing well. I was enjoying myself, enjoying the team. I'd gotten my urge to play back, and I wasn't ready to go yet.

Four days later I had the operation. At that point, ACL tears required only six months to recover, so my target date to return was Valentine's Day. That's about when we reported to spring training anyway.

But missing the rest of that 2010 season meant I'd be sitting on the bench for Bobby's swan song.

Bobby and I had been through so much together over the years. I was sick that I couldn't be a part of the end of his last season. Our 2010 club was not the most talented but the guys played their rear ends off all year, especially the last month when they pushed as hard as they could to get Bobby into the playoffs.

We didn't say it out loud, but that team had a destiny feel to it, like the baseball gods were going to shine on Bobby one last time before he retired.

We clinched a postseason berth on the last day of the season by beating the Phillies 8–7 to win the NL wild card. That got us back in the playoffs for the first time since the "Baby Braves" team in 2005. We had a pretty good showing in the Division Series, but we lost three one-run games to a good Giants team that went on to win the World Series.

I would have given anything to have played in that Division Series. Omar Infante had to move from second to third in my place, and my buddy Brooks Conrad made three errors at second base in a one-run loss in Game 3. Baseball can be so cruel sometimes. I told him after the game, "Brooksy, I'll take you in my foxhole any day, bro." But I couldn't help but feel like somewhere along the line I would have gotten a big hit or made a diving play.

Reality set in quickly after we lost the clincher 3–2 at Turner Field. Bobby's managerial career was over after twenty-five years with the Braves. When he walked into the clubhouse, we were all seated at our lockers waiting to hear what he had to say. You could have heard a pin drop.

Bobby had always been sure of himself when he talked to the team. That night he couldn't get ten words out before he choked up.

It was one of those times you wanted to stand up and give the man a hug. But Bobby wasn't a touchy-feely kind of guy. So as he turned to go to his press conference we all got up from our lockers and gave him a standing ovation. There wasn't a dry eye in the room.

After a loss ends your season, when the team is good enough to make a run deep into the playoffs, most guys are in shock. We used to stay in the clubhouse until well after midnight drinking beers, telling funny stories about the season, and consoling each other until the shock wore off. After the last game against San Francisco, Bobby came back in the clubhouse and actually sat down with the guys.

Bobby never crossed that line with players. He always kept it professional, knowing at some point he might have to stick a foot in somebody's rear end. Some of my most vivid memories of Bobby after games were of him being pissed off after a loss. We would hear him yelling, "FUCK," every fifteen to thirty seconds behind his office door while we sat in front of our lockers cringing.

There was one time in San Francisco when we let Barry Bonds walk us off on extra-inning homers twice in three games. Bobby slammed the metal swinging doors in the visiting clubhouse at AT&T Park so hard he scared the crap out of me.

But on that last night in 2010 we got to see his sentimental side. Two dozen guys sat around and drank Bud Lights with Bobby Cox, one of the greatest managers of all time, and for the first time in the twenty years since he'd drafted me, I saw him let his guard down. He laughed right along with us as we swapped war stories well into the night.

Seeing Bobby's career come to a close forced me to take stock of my own, to figure out what I still wanted to accomplish. My goals were pretty much the same every year: hit .300, drive in 100, score 100, and be one-ninth of the equation for a world championship team. But by 2011, some of my numbers were adding up. It was hard to ignore one milestone in particular: I was coming up on Mickey Mantle's career RBI total.

Among the many things Willie Stargell preached was that your batting average, on-base percentage, and slugging percentage would all fluctuate through the years but your RBI total just kept building.

I needed one RBI in a game against the Padres that April to get to 1,510 and pass Mantle. I got it in the first inning by hitting a ground ball to shortstop to drive in Martin Prado from third base with less than two outs.

I tripled in my next at-bat to drive in two more runs. At thirty-nine years old, it was the last triple of my career. But I was happy I passed Mantle the at-bat before, playing "ABC" baseball.

Willie always said, if you need to hit a ground ball to shortstop or second base to get that guy in from third base with less than two outs, that's exactly what you do. Who's the weakest fielder on the field? The pitcher. Get it past him, and it's an easy RBI.

That RBI epitomized the kind of hitter I wanted to be—knowing what the situation dictated and having the bat control to get it done. You don't have to get a hit to be productive, but you do have to put the ball in play.

I like to think that kind of RBI is why Bobby—and by 2011, Fredi Gonzalez—hit me third; because they trusted me to make the right decisions with the bat at crunch time. Those situations dictate the outcome of a game.

That RBI made for a pretty nice phone call home that night, too. My dad's voice was cracking.

"You just passed Mickey Mantle on the all-time RBI list," he said. "That boggles my mind. And you don't even realize what you've done."

In all honesty I probably didn't. I never thought I'd have even a remote chance to pass Mickey Mantle in any category, and it felt weird to say that I had. But that was just the first of a litany of full-circle moments Dad and I had in store before I hung it up.

CHAPTER 24
Walking Off

Usually in spring training, you feel nothing but gung ho about the start of the season. In 2012, I was just hoping the aches and pains that had bugged me in recent years wouldn't come back.

Slowly but surely, they cropped back up, until all I could think was *I've been doing this for too long, and I'm tired of hurting.*

I was about to turn forty. I'd had six knee operations. I survived the 2011 season on a daily dose of five milligrams of Percocet and a Red Bull.

I was tired of waking up wondering if both feet were going to hit the ground at the same time. I was tired of taking ten minutes to walk to the bathroom. My knees were hurting. My back was killing me. Playing pro baseball for twenty-three years had taken its toll on me. When you can't play catch or throw the football with your kids because of what you've put your body through, enough's enough.

I knew I could strap it up for one more season. I'd give it everything I had, but after that, I was done. Mentally, physically, I was done.

There was no struggling with the decision this time. My parents flew to Orlando so we could talk it over before I called a press conference to announce I would retire at the end of the season. I was pretty dead set on it, but I knew the time was right when my dad looked me in the eye and said, "You're my son. I want you to play forever, but I see what it's done to your body and how at peace you are with this decision. I'm comfortable with it."

I also know how gut-wrenching it was for Tom Glavine, John Smoltz, and Greg Maddux to say goodbye to the Braves organization. I learned a lot from those instances, and I never wanted the Braves to have to come to me and say, "We can no longer afford to keep you."

I had an option left on my contract for 2013. I could have played one more year for $10 million, which was a rebate compared to the $14 million I was making in 2012. But I didn't want the Braves to resent still having me around.

There was no clearer sign that I'd been walking that fine line already than when I walked into the Braves' offices at Disney in mid-March and told Wren and Schuerholz, "This is it." There was no "Are you sure? Are you really thinking this through?" They were both like "Hey, whatever we need to do to make this as easy as possible on you, we'll do it."

And Schuerholz said "we'll do this, this, and

this to honor you," as though he had already lined it up. The writing was on the wall.

I wanted to announce the decision right away because I didn't want to have to answer questions about when I was going to retire all season long everywhere we went. I didn't want my teammates to have to answer them either. Everybody would know that my last regular season game was going to be October 3 against the Pirates. Anything past that would be gravy.

As if I didn't have enough reinforcement that I'd made the right decision, between talking to John and Frank and announcing my retirement at a press conference, I went out and tore my meniscus warming up for batting practice.

I'd had surgery for a meniscus tear in my right knee the July before and was still having problems with it. Then I slipped running on wet grass in the outfield and tore my left meniscus, too. I didn't tell the media that day. They didn't need any more evidence I was falling apart.

We lost the first four games of the season while I recovered from arthroscopic surgery. I was back in the lineup by the second series of the season, sixteen days out of surgery. We were in Houston, which meant I'd be playing in front of my parents. The Braves wanted me to go to the minors for a rehab stint, but I knew that wouldn't help as much as a few minutes in the cage with my dad.

I got a base hit in my first at-bat. I homered in my second.

As I rounded the bases, my locker mate and buddy Eric Hinske yelled at me from the dugout, "It's not that easy!" It was fun seeing the looks on some of my teammates' faces when I came back to the dugout. Michael Bourn was slack-jawed watching me walk by.

"Man, you've swung the bat twice in six weeks," he said. "And you're 2-for-2 with a jack."

We won our first game of the year, and as I was shaking hands with my teammates walking off the field, I thought, *I still mean something. I can still help this team win.*

Watching highlights that night, I saw that cameras had panned to my parents in the front row at Minute Maid Park after I hit my home run. My dad jumped up out of his chair fist-pumping and you could read his lips: "He did it!" Both my parents were going nuts. Showing that much emotion was so unlike them. I could already tell 2012 was going to be different.

In my first home game of the year, wearing number 42 on Jackie Robinson Day, I hit a three-run homer.

I homered on my fortieth birthday in Los Angeles. I'd always gotten pumped up to play on my birthday, but it was so cool to homer where I dreamed of playing as a kid. I also got the game-winning hit in the series finale there, to help us take two out of three. The season was two weeks old and already starting to have a storybook feel.

In the beginning of May, I hit a walk-off homer in the eleventh inning to beat Philly after we'd been down six runs to Roy Halladay. BMac hit a grand slam to tie it up, and it was a seesaw battle from there. Ultimately, I made the swing that sent everybody home.

Walk-off homers are the pinnacle of what we do. There's no thrill like hitting one. I figured that would probably be my last walk-off, so I cherished it. And it was a phenomenal moment. I watched replays of it over and over, and I wasn't looking at the pitch or the swing. I watched people's reactions, the fans' and my teammates'. I tried to savor what it felt like to round third and see everybody standing at home plate going nuts because your team worked its tail off for three hours and you got to be the guy who provided elation at the end.

I've got to admit, I was pretty fired up that night against Philly, and not just because of the big comeback.

We were up 8–6, when Carlos Ruiz hit a three-run homer off O'Flaherty in the seventh inning and absolutely pimped it. He flung his bat and took four or five steps out of the box before he started running—just blatant disrespect. *This guy has got like forty-two homers in the big leagues and he's walking them off like he's Barry Bonds or something.*

I came in after the inning irate. I told everybody in the dugout, "God help them if I hit a home run tonight."

When I hit the walk-off, I started to run. Then I stopped myself. I walked, and I did not stop walking until the ball hit the stands. Then I flipped my bat ten or twelve feet in the air.

I thoroughly expected to get drilled the next day, but it never happened. I guess I made my point. I tried to play the game the right way, but when somebody showed us up, I took it upon myself to stand up for my teammates. Sometimes I stooped a little bit, but I couldn't help myself that night.

B. J. Upton hit a one-hop bullet off my ankle in Tampa in the middle of May that gave me the mother of all bruises. Well, *bruise* doesn't really do it justice. I had to have it lanced, and when that didn't relieve enough pressure, Dr. Royster—my knee doctor—had to drain it surgically. By the time the medical staff was done with it, my leg was black and blue from the middle of my calf to my foot.

I wound up on the disabled list and stayed at home to get treatment while the team went on the road. At least it meant I could spend some quality time with my sons—or so I thought.

But the way it played out, I came face-to-face with the realization that I was headed for another divorce. Sharon and I were going to split in the midst of my last season. But by 2012, I knew I could handle it.

The Braves paid me a lot of money, and I had a job to do. It paled in comparison to the importance of what was going on off the field, but I couldn't control that.

It scared me to think I would have less time with my kids. I was already basically a part-time dad with my baseball schedule. But then I thought about what my buddy Cledus T. Judd, a country singer and entertainer, told me one time: "I knew my parents when they were married and I knew them when they were divorced. And they were ten times happier when they were divorced, which made me ten times happier."

CHAPTER 25
Fireworks

I used to have this recurring dream where I showed up to the ballpark five minutes before game time and I couldn't find my shoes or my batting gloves. Or I got halfway down the tunnel and realized I left my wrist bands and didn't have my bats.

I usually had the dream the night before a day game because I was always terrified of oversleeping. I was late a couple of times, getting to the ballpark maybe an hour before first pitch, but never five minutes before a game.

I could go from my car to ready to play in about fifteen minutes if I had to. In my younger days, I could fall out of bed and be ready to go. But by 2012, I needed a couple of hours.

After nineteen years in the big leagues, my daily routine had become second nature. I took comfort in the repetition. As baseball players, it's as if we're in our own little world, our own little cycle of the day. For a night game, we would go out, stretch, take batting practice, and get our ground balls. Normally that left you sweating bullets, so you'd want to come back into the clubhouse, get out of your wet clothes, take a shower, freshen up a little bit, and get something to drink.

That's when I could usually be found with a can of Skoal Mint tucked into the leg of my sliding shorts and a *USA Today* crossword in hand.

Then about an hour and a half before first pitch, I started getting into game mode. I got taped if I needed it, took a couple of pills if I needed them, and started little by little to get dressed. It usually took me a while because I always wore three pairs of socks and four pairs of sliding shorts—I hated getting strawberries. I usually went to the video room to watch my at-bats from the night before or the opposing starter's previous two starts. Then I might watch my last ten at-bats against him.

After that, I grabbed a snack, put my pants on, played some cards, or watched a little TV, just to unwind and take my mind off the game. Then at six fifteen, the fun started. That's when everybody was at their lockers getting ready. We were talking smack and laughing.

That to me was the best time of the day. It was the calm before the storm. *OK, I've done everything to get myself mentally prepared. Before I get brain fried, just forget about the game for thirty minutes.* That's when 'Ske (Eric Hinske), David Ross, Pete Moylan, Huddy, BMac, Freddie, Uggs, JHey (Jason Heyward), Kris Medlen—we all came together in one spot and made each other laugh for half an hour.

I cherished that time with my teammates especially my last couple of years. By six thirty, I'd be screaming at Craig Kimbrel or Tyler Pastornicky to get Red Bulls for me and anybody else who wanted one. I picked a different rookie every year.

When I was a rookie, I had to carry bats. And I got absolutely lambasted on the backs of buses. These days you can't say anything to anybody. The extent of my hazing with the rookies was "Look, if my Red Bull is not on my seat or in my hand by six thirty, me and 'Ske, BMac, and Huddy are going to drill you."

At 6:29, Kimbrel would be on his phone, and I knew he wasn't going to have my Red Bull in time. I'd wait for the clubhouse clock to click to 6:30, then yell, "KIMBREL!" at the top of my lungs. "Get your ass up and get us our Red Bulls!" He'd be up and gone.

As if my knees didn't make me feel old enough, I had young teammates like Kimbrel, who grew up in Alabama, telling me how he cheered for my old Braves teammates and me during the '90s.

A lot of kids from Atlanta and Georgia who grew up pulling for the Braves are making a huge impact in the big leagues now, and it always makes me feel good when people insinuate that my time with the Braves and our team's success played a part in it.

I was proud to watch McCann become a seven-time All-Star, to watch Francoeur burst onto the scene as he did, and to watch Kimbrel become one of the best closers in the game. And those are just Braves guys. A ton of other guys from Georgia and the Southeast made their mark with other teams, like Adam Wainwright and Buster Posey, just to name a couple.

In 2012, knowing it was my last season, I tried to soak up what was going on around me. Driving to the ballpark, especially for day games, I got there about ten thirty or eleven o'clock, just as fans were arriving. I'd see them walking down the side of the road and tailgating; number 10 jerseys were everywhere. It made me really proud.

Whenever I heard a TV reporter ask a little kid who his or her favorite Brave was, if they didn't say me, I stuck out my lower lip. You'd think guys would tune that out, but I didn't. I wanted to be every little kid's favorite player.

To this day, I can be out in public in Atlanta and Ozzy Osbourne's "Crazy Train" will come on and everybody will stop to look at me. They associate it with me walking to the plate. I just wave and give them a little "Hey!" I love it. That was absolutely the perfect walk-up song for me.

I'd heard Larry Walker walk up to it in Montreal in 1993. Nobody was in the stands, so Ozzy echoed through Olympic Stadium. I thought it was the coolest thing ever. We didn't do walk-up songs at Fulton County Stadium, but when we started them at Turner Field in 1997, I used "Crazy Train" from day one.

You pick a song because it jacks you up. When it jacks the entire crowd up, it's even better. It's like "Hells Bells" for Trevor Hoffman. Watching seventy thousand people coming to their feet at Qualcomm Stadium when he came in from the bullpen to AC/DC during the 1998 NLCS was spine-tingling. Or "Enter Sandman" for Mariano Rivera. "Welcome to the Jungle" for Kimbrel.

In 2012 the Braves put out a commemorative program for my last season. Ozzy was quoted in it thanking me for using "Crazy Train" as my walk-up music. That's Ozzy Osbourne, man, the king of darkness. I always loved digging in against the Mets and hearing Piazza say, "I hate this fuckin' song." He didn't hate the song. He hated the spectacle of what might happen when I got into the box.

All the ovations and gifts I got from teams around the league were awesome, but given what was going on at home, I didn't enjoy the first couple of months of the season because I didn't have anybody to share it with. Then I met Taylor, and she made the last couple of months of 2012 one of the best times of my life.

I met her at a place called Dive Bar in the Buckhead area of Atlanta. It was a Monday night.

I didn't like to go out on Fridays or Saturdays when clubs were slammed. Mondays were like her weekend, too. She was off work from her job as a cocktail waitress at another bar.

I was standing there with my buddy Tom Green, who used to play baseball at Georgia Tech and in the minor leagues with the Pirates. When I saw her walk through the front door, I thought, *Wow.* I tapped Tom on the shoulder and said, "That's the baddest chick in here tonight. I've got to talk to her at some point."

Fifteen minutes later, she walked up to me and said, "My friend is a big Braves fan and she is not leaving here unless she gets a picture with you."

"Seriously? You're walking up to me, asking me to take a picture with your friend?" I joked. "What about you?"

She gave it a shrug and a little "eh."

"Well," I said. "You tell your friend that I want a picture with her friend."

She brought her buddy over and we took pictures. A little while later I approached her again. She had some dude following her around and you could tell she was perturbed by it.

"Hey, I know you don't like this guy," I said. "If you need to have a boyfriend tonight, I'm your guy."

We talked on the phone and texted for the next two weeks. I went to see her at work a couple of times, and in early July, I invited her to a game.

July 3, 2012, might have been the best day of my life, from the time I woke up to a text message that Taylor could come to the game until the time I went to bed. I had invited Taylor the night before, but she was two hours away in Blue Ridge, Georgia, on vacation with her family and wasn't sure she could come.

"I came to see you at your job," I'd said. "I really want you to come see me at mine."

Given that the Cubs were in town and it was the Fourth of July, there would be a packed house. My buddy Matt Duff and his wife, Jessie, were in town. I knew we were going to have a fun night, and I would finally have a chance to get to know Taylor.

I found out before the game I'd made the All-Star team. I was up for the final NL roster spot through fan voting, but Frank Wren pulled me aside during batting practice and told me La Russa went ahead and named me to the team. Matt Kemp was hurt, which opened up a roster spot. That meant I got to play my final All-Star game at Kauffman Stadium in Kansas City, the only stadium in the majors I'd never played in, and I could have all my boys come with me.

To top it off, I went 5-for-5 that night against the Cubs. It was only the third five-hit game of my career and my first at home. The fact that

Taylor was there was no coincidence, if you ask me.

We were facing a pitcher I had had no success against: Chris Volstad. He's a big six-foot-eight guy with really good angle and good sink. But that night, I was flipping stuff down the left field line for doubles. I was turning on fastballs in the hole. Then I was getting ahead in the count against some of their relievers and sitting on fastballs. I didn't hit any homers, but I hit rockets everywhere.

We were ahead after my fifth hit, and when I rounded first base, I had a premonition Fredi Gonzalez was going to pinch run for me. It was the bottom of the eighth and Fredi was the kind of manager who would make sure I got a moment, especially with two months left in my career. No sooner had I turned around than Juan Francisco was standing right in front of me. *Damn, that was quick.* The second I shook his hand and stepped into foul territory, Turner Field went nuts.

During the course of my career, I had reached 1,500 hits, 2,000 hits, 2,500 hits, 400 home runs, and after achieving each of those milestones, I got great receptions from the crowd, but none were bigger than the one I got for the 5-for-5 game in 2012. That curtain call was my first rousing ovation of the year and the one that set the tone for all the spine-tingling moments the rest of the way.

To get five hits and make a couple of diving plays was as close to playing a perfect game as I was ever going to get. The magnitude of the game wasn't as big as my two-homer game against the Rockies in 1995, but I did it at age forty.

Taylor was only twenty-three. A lot of people—namely B.B. and my divorce attorney—were telling me I should lie low in my personal life. But as far as I was concerned, my marriage was over. I had filed for divorce. I was ready to be happy.

Taylor had been through a lot for someone her age. Her father died of cancer shortly after she was born, so she never knew him. She was a single mom. She had her son, Bryson, when she was twenty and had to mature really quickly. And I had a lot more in common with her than with either of my ex-wives.

Taylor loved to hunt. She enjoyed spending time with my parents. And she had a heart of gold. She was just as beautiful on the inside as she was out.

CHAPTER 26
Curtain Calls

My last All-Star game was the first time I could bring all four of my boys when they were old enough to enjoy the experience on the field.

Bryce Harper almost beheaded Shea, who was seven at the time. Shea and Tristan were in uniform with me out on the field shagging flies during BP. Balls were whizzing by them. They must have thrown a hundred balls up in the stands to fans. They had a blast.

It was as much an experience for them as it was for me, being on the field with some of the best in the game. Watching guys hit balls 450 feet during the home run derby was awe-inspiring for all of us.

Tony La Russa treated me like the captain of the National League team. I had grown to respect him and like him an awful lot through the years, and I'll never forget what he did for me that All-Star game.

He gave me the floor to talk to the team before the game. I didn't know what I was going to say, so I just spoke from the heart.

"Guys, it's an honor to stand here in front of

you," I said. "It's been a dream of mine to play this wonderful game since I was four years old, and to sit here in a clubhouse full of this many guys that are the elite of the elite—it's an honor for me to share a dugout, a clubhouse, a field with you guys.

"I want to impress upon you guys to soak up each and every opportunity that you have," I went on to say. "You never know when that opportunity is going to come and go."

And I added a little rah-rah at the end, quoting Lou Brown from *Major League.*

"We've won two. Win three? That's a winning streak," I said. "And I am not going out losing my last one. Are you with me?"

The guys were up to the task because we won 8–0. La Russa pinch hit me in the sixth inning. I'd never played in front of Royals fans before, but they sure knew how to make a guy feel good with a stirring ovation. I got a little misty, which made trying to pick up 97 mph from Chris Sale all the more difficult.

I hit a little six-hopper through the right side, which tested my forty-year-old legs and had me laughing the whole way to first. I wouldn't say Ian Kinsler made a tremendous effort to get to it at second base, but I was credited with a single in my last All-Star at-bat, and I was happy to take it.

Walking off the field after the game, La Russa came up and hugged me, and Pap—Jonathan

Papelbon, the closer for the Phillies—grabbed me by the collar and said, "This win was for you."

That All-Star game was really the first time I got to know Pap. When you see him on TV, he comes across as arrogant and sometimes aloof. But getting to know somebody across the field is not a fair judgment. I enjoyed his company at the All-Star game. When I faced him a couple of months later against the Phillies, it was a little bittersweet.

Just a little.

Some days I went to the park knowing I was going to hit a homer. Other days I knew I wouldn't sniff one. Driving to the park the day the Braves were giving away bobblehead dolls in my honor that August, I knew I was going to hit a home run.

Something felt different. I could almost sense the planets aligning for our series finale against the Padres. I knew we were going to have a packed house. And we were facing Jason Marquis, a former teammate and a pitcher I hit really well.

I respected Jason's abilities. He's had a long, great career, and he and I are good friends. But there are times when you're on top of your game, and you know the pitcher's got nothing he can get you out with. And Jason didn't have anything for me that night.

In the first inning, I knew he was not going to let me beat him, so I'd see a bunch of breaking balls. He threw me six sliders in a row. You throw anybody six straight sliders, and he's either going to walk or make the adjustment on you. Jason made a mistake on a 3-2 slider, and I hit it out of the ballpark for a two-run homer.

Even then, I knew I was going to hit another one. Coming into the season, I had 39 multi-homer games for my career. All season I'd been thinking, *Surely you can get one more.* I didn't know if I had it in me anymore to juice two balls in a game—it's not easy—but I realized then, this was my shot.

I had Jason covered. Now he was scared to throw me a breaking ball for a strike. He couldn't throw his changeup for a strike. And I was thinking right along with him.

When he got to 3-1 on me in the fifth inning, I thought, *Man, he hasn't thrown me many fastballs all night. This is a good spot to try and sneak one in.* The next pitch was a fastball out over the plate where I could get extended on it, and I hit it out to center field. The second I touched it off, Jason bent over and put his hands on his knees. He knew it.

There were fifteen or twenty times during the course of my career when I walked to the plate knowing I was going to hit a home run. The last time was against Papelbon.

• • •

I was not the most gifted athlete physically, especially when you look around at some of the guys in the NFL and NBA. But I prided myself on having heart and working at the game. I'm a big believer that preparation pays off, especially from the seventh inning on. I was always thinking three, four, five hitters ahead. If you got surprised by a situation, nine times out of ten you were going to fail.

We were down 7–3 to the Phillies going into the ninth inning on September 2. I knew I would bat seventh in the inning. I also knew if I came up, I would have a chance to win the game, and I'd be facing Papelbon.

Running off the field after the top of the ninth, I told the guys, "Just give me a chance. Get me up there this inning."

Sitting in the dugout, I started thinking back: *OK, the last time I faced Pap he came at me with heaters.* I'd struck out and popped up in my only two at-bats against Papelbon when he was with the Red Sox.

His fastball was his best pitch. It was a little uphill and got on you quicker than you would think. If he stayed up around the belt, he was hard to hit. But if he threw his fastball down in the zone, it was easier to get the bat to it.

I'd had some long talks with Papelbon sitting around the picnic table in the players' lounge at the All-Star game. He was a funny guy. He was engaging. He was cocky. I liked him. And I knew, when I walked up there in the ninth inning, he was coming after me.

He does not respect that I can turn around his fastball. Hell, I'm forty years old. There's no way I can turn around ninety-five miles an hour, right? He's going to try to blow me away.

By the time I came to the plate, we'd cut the Phillies lead to 7–5. Kevin Frandsen misplayed a ball that Prado hit to third base, and we had runners at second and third. First base was open, but Charlie Manuel, the Phillies manager, said in the paper the next day, "We didn't pay Papelbon to come here and pitch around people. He's supposed to be the best in the game, go out and earn it."

Hell, yeah.

Pap had a little slider, but he didn't throw it much to lefties; something breaking down and in is my nitro zone as a lefty. Besides, he wouldn't want to risk throwing something in the dirt. He was going to be aggressive. *There are two outs. It's his strength against my strength. Let's go.*

First pitch, he threw me a heater away for a ball. *I knew it.* Pap has an ego just as we all do. I'm sure one day he wanted to tell his kids, "I blew Chipper Jones away with heaters," just like I wanted to tell my kids, "I took Pap deep with a walk-off homer to win a ball game."

The next pitch, he threw one by me. I took a big rip and fouled it off. Take that swing three times in a row and I'm struck out. There was no way I could come out of my shoes and square this dude up. He was throwing too hard.

All right, I thought, stepping out. *If he throws me that pitch again, I'm going to take him deep. Just don't miss it. Shorten up. Get your foot down. Nice, simple, easy swing. Get the bat barrel out. Let him provide all the power.*

And he threw the next pitch right . . . down . . . Broadway.

When you square up 95 to 100 mph, and you hit it just right, you don't even feel it. There's a sweet spot inside the sweet spot, a two- to three-inch area that is unmistakable. When you hit it there, it's like warm butter on a hot muffin. You don't get the vibration you normally get swinging with wood. And the ball just jumps.

I knew it was gone, and so did the crowd. It sent chills down my spine.

For six innings, Cole Hamels had shoved it up our rear end. We were down five runs going into the ninth inning, and we scored six. We punctuated the comeback with a home run off one of the best closers in the game. Winning that way against the Phillies made it even sweeter. The Phillies and the Mets were our biggest rivals in the NL East throughout most of my career. And we walked off twice on the Phillies in one season.

When I got to the scrum at home plate, my teammates punched me in the ribs. They kicked me in the nuts, trying to knee me. They rubbed dirt all over me and threw cups of water down my back—Prado was the king of that. That's why you always throw your helmet off before you get to home plate, or else your teammates beat you to death. If you take the helmet off, they leave your head alone.

Normally after a walk-off celebration, your teammates go back to the clubhouse and start taking showers. That night a bunch of guys stayed at the mouth of the tunnel while I did my TV interview on the field. When I got to the dugout, Uggla gave me a big ol' bear hug. I hadn't known Paul Maholm, one of our pitchers, very long at all, but he came up and said, "I just had to tell you, man, that was frickin' awesome."

As I walked up the tunnel to the clubhouse, I saw Rob Smith, our video guy, and got a huge hug. Schuerholz shook my hand and said, "Unbelievable." Then when I walked into the clubhouse, my teammates gave me a standing O.

I don't get real sentimental but that meant a lot to me. That home run was my send-off. It was my Derek Jeter walk-off. It was the last home run I ever hit in the big leagues.

I would have loved to hit another four or five, but that was a good one to end on. I always wanted my legacy to be that I was clutch. When people talk about my career, I want them to say there was nobody they wanted up with two outs in the ninth and the game on the line more than me.

I hadn't hit a walk-off homer in six years, and I got two in 2012. They were surreal. I've killed some monster deer and hit some awesome golf shots, but nothing compares to bringing forty thousand people out of their seats with one swing of your bat. I wish everybody could experience that because it's the most incredible feeling ever. I get chill bumps just thinking about it. I hit nine walk-off homers in my career. I remember every single one.

The last week of the season was a blur.

More than fifty thousand fans showed up at Turner Field for a ceremony the Braves held in my honor before our final home series against the Mets. I could look up from my seat on the infield and see fans flashing number 10 posters all over the stadium. I was sitting on a stage with Hank Aaron and Bobby Cox, John Schuerholz, Paul Snyder, and Tony DeMacio, the scout who signed me. I had my boys and my parents up there with me.

I was emotionally exhausted before the first pitch was even thrown. I went 0-for-4 that night, and as I told Josh Thole, the Mets catcher, walking up to the plate, "How am I supposed to hit with all this going on?"

I'll always cherish the way the fans of Atlanta, the Braves organization, and my teammates honored me. Every one of my teammates wore a mock turtleneck that night, or nerdleneck as they liked to call it. And they let me run out to third base by myself to start the game, unbeknownst to me.

I was easy pickings for that move because the last few years of my career, I always ran out onto the field first. It was a sign of respect my younger teammates gave me. The starting pitcher didn't take the field until I was ready, and he let me lead us out. I was in my own little world at that point anyway. I didn't like a lot of shenanigans and chitchat once the game was about to start.

So after Tim Hudson said, "Let's go," off I went. I always ran behind the mound and touched third base, then got deep behind third to stretch out my arm during warm-ups. I was almost to the outfield grass before I turned around and realized I was the only player out there.

There was nothing to do then but smile sheepishly, acknowledge the crowd, and tip my hat to my teammates. It was a great moment, and I cherished it.

Fredi Gonzalez tried to give me another moment in the series finale, but I didn't need it. We were up 6–1 in the seventh inning when I drew a walk. Fredi whistled at me as if he was going to send in a pinch runner. I waved him off.

There was no way I wanted to come off that field with only a few innings left in my career.

I had gotten more than enough ovations. What I wanted was to finish the game with my teammates. I wanted to do my corny handshake with Freddie Freeman. I wanted to congratulate David Ross on his three-run homer. I wanted to pat Craig Kimbrel on the back for yet another save.

The handshake line that Sunday afternoon was the last one I got at Turner Field. I was too lost in the moment to realize it might be the last time I walked off that field a winner. I was busy working my way into the seats behind home plate, burying my face in my mom's shoulder and then my dad's, too choked up to say a word.

I'd always prided myself on never being the last out of a game. The last game of my career was no different.

The wild card game against the Cardinals had been disastrous from the fourth inning on, starting with my throwing error that cost us three runs and a lead. Everybody will remember the infield fly call that went against us in the eighth inning on an Andrelton Simmons pop-up that fell in shallow left field. Sam Holbrook signaled that it was an infield fly and Andrelton was out, even though the play was fifty feet into the outfield and the shortstop wasn't camped under the ball. Instead of protecting our baserunners as the rule was intended, it cost us a chance to send McCann to the plate with the bases loaded.

People can say what they want to say about the infield fly, but the most important play in that game was my error. If I had turned the double play, it would have been a completely different game, infield fly or not.

I put all that to the back of my mind in the bottom of the ninth. We were down to our final out, but we still had a chance, down 6–3, when I came to the plate against Cardinals closer Jason Motte. No way was I going to be the last out.

With two outs and nobody on, my job was to help get the tying run to the plate. I had to find a way to get on base.

Barring an unbelievable comeback, I knew this would be the last at-bat I ever had. My heart was beating a thousand miles per second. Walking up to the plate, I reminded myself to enjoy the moment, to embrace it, but also to approach it like I did all the other ones.

I looked over to the visitors' dugout, and all the Cardinals were standing on the top step clapping. Yadier Molina, their catcher, went and stood out in front of home plate, giving our crowd a chance to cheer for me one more time. I tipped my cap to the fans. Then I put my helmet back on and told Yadi, "Let's go, baby."

Normally at that point, to use a *For Love of*

the Game reference, you clear the mechanism, and everything else goes away. I step in the box and lock in. It's tunnel vision, just me and the pitcher. But tuning everything out for that at-bat was impossible. Thoughts were rushing through my head. *This is it? How is it going to end? What's going to happen?*

As south as the game had gone, I wanted to end it on as good a note as I could. I was mentally prepared for the at-bat, like always. And honestly, I felt like I was going to take the guy deep.

Motte had really good stuff, but guys who throw 95 to 100 mph were right up my alley. The problem was not only did I get 97 mph when I got to two strikes, but it cut.

My bat exploded into pieces on contact, and I thought, *Oh no.* I hit a slow roller up the middle, and second baseman Daniel Descalso made a great jump throw. I almost stopped running, thinking I was out, but the throw pulled Allen Craig off the bag, and I just beat him to it.

Cool, I thought, *full circle.* I got a base hit in my first at-bat in the big leagues and now in my last.

Freddie Freeman doubled behind me, so we did our jobs. We brought the tying run to the plate. That was it, though. Uggs grounded out and the game was over.

I think my teammates expected to walk into the clubhouse afterward and see me bawling my

433

eyes out, but I didn't. I sat in my locker for ten minutes after the game and just stared, thinking, *It's finally over.*

I was tired. I was mentally and physically beat-up. I had had so many emotional moments up until that point that I was out of emotion. I knew it wouldn't be the last time I donned an Atlanta Braves uniform. I'd be back to coach in some capacity when I got the itch again.

The one guy who did choke me up was TP. I had just come out of the shower when Terry Pendleton walked up, still in uniform from coaching first base, with tears in his eyes.

He and I hadn't cried together since I blew out my knee in 1994. He was there when I thought my career was over. So he understood why I wasn't devastated when it actually was.

A couple of days after we lost to the Cardinals, I got in my truck and drove to Kansas to hunt. I had fifteen hours alone with my thoughts. I turned the phone off, turned the radio off, and meditated.

I let my mind go to "what if." I wondered how far we would have gone in the playoffs if I had made a good throw to second and we turned that double play. I wondered what it would have been like to finish my career the same way it started, with a World Series championship.

But I could dwell on that for only so long.

At forty years old, I'd seen plenty of failure in my life. I was living through my second divorce, and I knew I would be OK. I had come up short of a World Series title in all but one of my twelve trips to the postseason as a Brave. I knew there was something far worse than failure, and that's not getting the chance in the first place.

I bawled like a thirteen-year-old in Babe Ruth League when I struck out with the bases loaded because I never took the bat off my shoulder. I carried the weight of a World Series loss on my shoulders for weeks in the winter of 1996 because I had to make an about-face in the on-deck circle at Yankee Stadium and leave the tying run on second base.

In my last game as an Atlanta Brave, I stood at third base with my forty-year-old surgically repaired knees flexed and my glove up. I was ready for Holliday to hit me a rocket. Say what you want, I was still the guy who wanted it that way.

EPILOGUE

I had a lump in my throat all day long on July 27, 2014. Bobby Cox was being inducted into the Baseball Hall of Fame that afternoon, as were my old teammates and friends Greg Maddux and Tom Glavine. I knew I couldn't watch the ceremony live on TV, so I was looking forward to nine o'clock when the kids went to bed and I could stay up and watch it on the DVR.

Taylor was in and out of the living room, but I was locked in, sitting on my couch in Atlanta. Tommy was Tommy, very well spoken, eloquent, pretty much what I expected. Doggie was a little awkward and funny—so typical—and it was hard to keep a straight face watching his speech.

Bobby was the hardest one to watch, from a sentimental standpoint. I've always thought of Bobby as the ultimate father figure. He had my back in the darkest days of my personal life. He stood up for me when I got into it with umpires. He acted as mediator between my Braves brothers and me from time to time. He scolded me when I needed discipline. And on the day he went into the Hall of Fame, he thought enough of me to mention me in his speech.

He had just thanked John Schuerholz for

bringing in the players to win fourteen straight division titles when he singled me out.

"Because of free agency and monetary restraints on some clubs, it's difficult for a player to stay with one organization his entire career," he said. "But Chipper Jones did it. Chipper, you'll be standing here soon, and thank you for everything you've done for the Braves' organization."

I couldn't believe it. But that's who Bobby was. Bobby gave his players all the credit. And that's why we all loved him so much.

All I ever wanted to do as a baseball player was to make my mark, and one of the greatest managers of all time was standing on a stage in Cooperstown, New York, telling everybody that I had his respect.

Bobby took a chance on me, drafting me number one in 1990 when I was a skinny, cocky young punk from Pierson. He stuck his neck out for me by penciling me in to hit third from day one of my rookie year. I've been trying to prove him right and make him proud ever since.

I will guarantee this: If the day ever comes for me in Cooperstown, Bobby's name will be among the first three I mention, along with my mom and dad.

As for my own chances for the Hall of Fame, I came up just short of 3,000 hits and 500 homers, which are the magic numbers to gain entry, so long as you aren't suspected of using steroids. I never played the game to reach a number, and I didn't need to hit those marks to know what kind of player I was.

But I'd be lying if I said there weren't moments when I think of what could have been. If I had sucked it up and played another couple of years, or if my knees hadn't cost me almost two full years in the big leagues, I might have been the last National Leaguer to ever get *both* 3,000 hits and 500 homers.

Craig Biggio was the last National Leaguer to get 3,000 hits, in 2007. Before that, it was Tony Gwynn in 1999. If you throw 500 home runs on top of those 3,000 hits, you're in a completely different stratosphere. Only five players have ever gotten 3,000 hits and 500 homers—Hank Aaron, Willie Mays, Eddie Murray, Rafael Palmeiro, and Alex Rodriguez—and only Aaron and Mays played almost exclusively in the National League.

It's tough for National League players to get as many plate appearances as American League players. For nineteen years I had the pitcher hitting three spots in front of me at least three times a game. When you have a designated hitter who's going to hit 50 to 100 points higher than any pitcher, you get a lot more at-bats during the course of a season.

At the end of the day, I just knew that if I

helped us win on a nightly basis, the numbers would be there. I did all I could do with the amount of healthy time I had in the big leagues, and I'm proud my accomplishments were never linked to steroids. You can't get 2,700-plus hits and hit 400-plus homers and walk away feeling bad because all we did when I played for Atlanta was win. And I was a big contributor to that for the better part of two decades. That's all I ever wanted.

I got two phone calls in 2013 from GMs trying to talk me out of retirement. Ruben Amaro gave me his best salesman's pitch to sign with the Phillies, and Stan Kasten rolled out the red carpet trying to convince me to play for the Dodgers. I couldn't fathom either one.

"Ruben, I love and respect you," I said. "But if I put on a Phillies uniform, they would burn my house down here in Atlanta."

Stan, who was the president and a part owner of the Dodgers by then, knew I was a big Magic Johnson fan. Stan had introduced me to Magic during the 2013 Division Series in Atlanta and now he was offering to fly me out to Los Angeles so Magic, who was also part of the Dodgers ownership group, could show me around town.

"Stan, that's dirty," I said, laughing.

He was offering me a dream assignment: play when I felt physically up to it, mentor the young guys on the team, and hit in the middle of the lineup I grew up imitating. But I told Stan I'd made promises to my boys that I couldn't break. They deserved my time now. In retirement, I could give it to them.

Matthew was a sophomore in high school when he asked me to help him with his swing during a spring break visit to Atlanta from Michigan, where he lived with his mom. I took him to hit in the cages out at Brian McCann's dad's place in Alpharetta.

Matthew had a tendency to lock his arm out and sweep through the zone. He needed to release his hands at the bottom of the swing. The only way I knew how to explain it to him was the same way my dad had explained it to me.

"Hips and hands," I said, watching him go into his toe tap. Boom. He hit a line drive into the back of the cage. "Hips and hands."

Halfway through the second bucket of balls, Matthew took off his batting glove to look at his hand.

"You've got a blister already?" I said.

"Yeah," he said.

"Well, you're at a crossroads, buddy," I said. "You can quit or we can tape it up."

He looked at me and said, "I guess we'll be taping it up?"

"Damn skippy we're taping it up," I said.

We taped it up and he hit three more buckets. I

was testing Matthew that day, and he showed me something. He had heart.

Growing up the son of a professional baseball player isn't easy. When my three younger boys were little, Sharon told me they referred to me as "Chipper" when they saw me on TV, even though I was "Dad" at home. I'm sure it was a little confusing.

I haven't been the greatest father in the world, but my boys know I love them unconditionally. I sensed some resentment after my divorce with Sharon, but I don't think it's anything that can't be overcome in time.

Taylor and I drove down from my lake house in Blue Ridge, Georgia, to Atlanta for my kids' soccer game one Saturday morning a couple of years after I retired. We were up at 7:00 A.M., it was 30 degrees, and the kids played to a 0–0 tie, but we had a blast. We took the boys out for brunch afterward.

We got two miles up the road after dropping them off, and Sharon called to say, "The boys want to spend the weekend with you up in Blue Ridge."

I slammed on the brakes and made a U-ey in the middle of the road like something out of a cop show. It was one of the greatest things that ever happened to me. I'd been shooting for something like that since Sharon and I divorced.

By the time I hung up the phone, Taylor already knew.

"The boys want to come hang out this weekend," she said.

I saw she had a tear in her eye. She knew how important this was to me.

After two failed marriages, I'd been insecure at first about Taylor's true feelings for me. *Is she in love with me or is she in love with the guy who plays baseball?* But moments like that put the question to rest. Taylor earned my trust, and for her I did something I never thought I'd do. I got married again.

I'd been out of baseball for two years when Schuerholz started asking me if I'd be interested in coming back to the Braves in some capacity. I told him I wanted to get back into it in some small way, but I didn't want the grind of having to travel somewhere every three or four days.

He came back with the idea of being a special assistant to the GM. That meant I could spend a couple of weeks every spring training, hanging out in the batting cage, talking hitting. I could come down to the ballpark every once in a while just as a third set of eyes. I could break down some film and get in the heads of some of these young hitters and help them with their mental approaches. I could have a bit of a voice evaluating players, but not too much. It was perfect.

I missed being around the clubhouse. Ever since I'd retired, walking back in there felt strange. That had been my home for nineteen years and it wasn't anymore. I didn't feel like I belonged. The job Schuerholz offered gave me an excuse to go back in, hang around the cages, interact with the guys, and impart some knowledge.

I stay in my civvies when I'm at the ballpark. I don't want to draw too much attention to myself. But I'll put the uni on in spring training. I didn't look as good in the uniform as I used to my first spring training back. I had a little bit of the "dunlap" disease—my belly done lapped over my belt.

It felt weird getting dressed without the neoprene sleeves on my knees or the four pairs of sliders. But it was nice to hop up the dugout steps and have fans give me a little cheer as I headed out to play catch.

My favorite part of the day was talking hitting by the cage. There was one day the guys needed somebody to fill out a hitting group during batting practice, so I said, "I'll jump in there."

I was hitting left-handed, with Alan Butts, our bullpen catcher, throwing right-handed. It always took me a long time to get the feel of my mechanics back left-handed after an offseason. So after four years without swinging, I had the serious duck-hook line-drive swing working.

But a day or so later, Buttsy was throwing

443

down in the indoor cages beyond the center field fence. The players had finished their work for the day, and he said, "Jump in there, Chip."

I didn't have spikes on, and I grabbed a bat that was just lying around. I've always felt like I could jump out of bed and hit from my right side, so this time I decided to bat right-handed against him. I just wanted to see how I matched up against Buttsy's fastball.

I took a few swings before I saw backspin and a familiar flight of the ball. I didn't need an outfield fence or even a saran over some fern to know it. I could still hit the ball out of the ballpark.

CHIPPER JONES'S CAREER STATISTICS

- Number one overall pick in the 1990 draft by the Atlanta Braves
- Career batting average of .303 and 468 home runs made Jones the only switch-hitter in Major League history to post a .300 or better career batting average and hit at least 300 home runs
- Batted .303 left-handed and .304 right-handed for his career, to become only the second switch-hitter with at least 5,000 plate appear-ances to bat .300 or better from both sides of the plate, joining Frankie Frisch
- Ranks second in all-time batting average among switch-hitters to Frisch (.316), third in home runs to Mickey Mantle (536) and Eddie Murray (504), and second in RBIs behind Murray (1,917) with 1,623
- His 1,623 RBIs are the third-most by a player who spent a majority of his career at third base, following Hall of Famers George Brett (1,596) and Mike Schmidt (1,595)
- Won the 1999 National League MVP award and finished in the top ten in National League MVP voting six times
- Batted .309 with 49 home runs and 159 RBIs in 245 career games against the Mets
- Won 2008 National League batting title with a .364 average
- Inducted into Braves Hall of Fame and his uniform number 10 retired in June 2013

Jones's Complete Record

Year	Club	AVG	G	AB	R	H	2B	3B	HR	RBI	SH	SF	HP	BB	SO	SB-CS	OBP	SLG	E
1990	GCL Braves	.229	44	140	20	32	1	1	1	18	2	2	6	14	26	5-3	.321	.271	18
1991	Macon	.326	136	473	104	154	24	11	15	98	1	10	3	69	70	40-9	.407	.518	56
1992	Durham	.277	70	264	43	73	22	1	4	31	1	3	2	31	34	10-8	.353	.413	14
	Greenville	.346	67	266	43	92	17	11	9	42	4	4	0	11	32	14-1	.367	.594	18
1993	Richmond	.325	139	536	97	174	31	12	13	89	3	6	1	57	70	23-8	.387	.600	43
	Atlanta	.667	8	3	2	2	1	0	0	0	0	0	0	1	1	0-0	.750	1.000	0
1994	Atlanta					Injured—Did not play													
1995	Atlanta	.265	140	524	87	139	22	3	23	86	1	4	0	73	99	8-4	.353	.450	26
1996	Atlanta	.309	157	598	114	185	32	5	30	110	1	7	0	87	88	14-1	.393	.530	17
1997	Atlanta	.295	157	597	100	176	41	3	21	111	0	6	0	76	88	20-5	.371	.479	15
1998	Atlanta	.313	160	601	123	188	29	5	34	107	1	8	1	96	93	16-6	.404	.547	12
1999	Atlanta	.319	157	567	116	181	41	1	45	110	0	6	2	126	94	25-3	.441	.633	17
2000	Atlanta	.311	156	579	118	180	38	1	36	111	0	10	2	95	64	14-7	.404	.566	25
2001	Atlanta	.330	159	572	113	189	33	5	38	102	0	5	2	98	82	9-10	.427	.605	18
2002	Atlanta	.327	158	548	90	179	35	1	26	100	0	5	2	107	89	8-2	.435	.536	7
2003	Atlanta	.305	153	555	103	169	33	2	27	106	0	6	1	94	83	2-2	.402	.517	7

Year	Team																		
2004	Atlanta	.248	137	472	69	117	20	1	30	96	0	7	4	84	96	2-0	.362	.486	6
	Rome#	.000	1	4	0	0	0	0	0	0	0	0	0	0	0	0-0	.000	.000	0
2005	Atlanta	.296	109	358	66	106	30	0	21	72	0	2	0	72	56	5-1	.412	.556	5
	Rome#	.500	3	6	1	3	0	0	0	2	0	0	0	3	1	0-0	.667	.500	1
2006	Atlanta	.324	110	411	87	133	28	3	26	86	0	4	1	61	73	6-1	.409	.596	18
	Mississippi#	.167	2	6	1	1	0	0	0	0	0	0	0	0	2	0-0	.167	.167	1
2007	Atlanta	.337	134	513	108	173	42	4	29	102	0	5	0	82	75	5-1	.425	.604	9
2008	Atlanta	.364	128	439	82	160	24	1	22	75	0	4	1	90	61	4-0	.470	.574	13
2009	Atlanta	.264	143	488	80	129	23	2	18	71	0	6	1	101	89	4-1	.388	.430	22
2010	Atlanta	.265	95	317	47	84	21	0	10	46	0	3	0	61	47	5-0	.381	.426	10
2011	Atlanta	.276	126	465	56	125	33	1	18	70	0	6	0	51	80	2-2	.344	.470	6
	Rome#	.333	2	3	0	1	0	0	0	1	0	1	0	2	1	0-0	.500	.333	0
2012	Atlanta	.287	112	387	58	111	23	0	14	62	0	3	1	57	51	1-0	.377	.455	11
	Rome#	.250	2	4	0	1	0	0	0	1	0	0	0	2	1	0-0	.500	.250	1
Minor	Totals	.312	466	1,702	309	531	95	36	42	282	11	26	12	189	236	92-30	.379	.484	152
Major	Totals	.303	2,499	8,984	1,619	2,726	549	38	468	1,623	3	97	18	1,512	1,409	150-46	.401	.529	243

Bold indicates led league; # indicates injury rehabilitation assignment.

*Sources: Atlanta Braves, ESPN

ACKNOWLEDGMENTS

From the time I was in Little League until the end of my Braves career, my grandmother Nana made me a scrapbook every year for Christmas. It might be two inches thick with articles and photographs she'd clipped out of local papers and magazines about my previous baseball season. At about nine o'clock, after the excitement of Christmas Day had died down, I would sit down with it. And I would stay up all night thumbing through it and reminiscing.

Looking back now, I realize I came full circle. I can't tell you how many times growing up in Pierson, Florida, my mom walked into the den and found me sitting on the floor, reading scrapbooks about my dad and my mom. I was an only child. If Dad wasn't home to play backyard baseball or I was bored, I would sit there for hours and read about my dad's career as a shortstop at Stetson University, my mom's career as a professional equestrian, and about how they met in college.

When it came time to organize my thoughts to write this book, my grandmother's scrapbooks were invaluable. They also give me a great starting point when it comes to who I want to thank for helping me capture the essence of my baseball career.

As far as I'm concerned, God never put two better people on the planet than Nana and Poppo. My grandparents lived on one corner of our ten-acre farm in Pierson, and we lived on the other. I'd go over to their house four or five times a week to eat lunch with them. Nana made me the best corned beef sandwich on rye with Gulden's mustard and American cheese. I can't tell you how many times throughout my adolescent and professional years my dad and I would be up at the baseball field taking hundreds of swings. At every one of those sessions, my grandfather was in the outfield picking up balls and throwing them back to the infield, so we could start hitting again sooner. And my grandma was sitting in the stands watching the whole thing. I was forty-three years old before I lost my first grandparent; I'm so lucky in that sense. Poppo died the day before Thanksgiving in 2015. Nana passed six months later on May 3. I miss them both so much.

Nana and Poppo were second only to my parents as far as helping me realize the dream I had from the time I was four years old, to play major league baseball. It's hard to find the words to explain what my parents, Larry and Lynne Jones, mean to me and how much I appreciate all they have done for me and continue to do for me on a daily basis. They are my rock, my foundation, and I thank God for blessing me with parents like them. They were the first people I wanted my coauthor, Carroll Rogers Walton, to visit to start the process of researching this book, and I want to thank them for the time and hospitality they gave her on multiple visits to the Double Dime ranch in southwest Texas.

B. B. Abbott is not only my agent, but my best friend, and has been from the time I was three years old when we moved half a mile up the road from the Abbotts in Pierson. B.B. has been the single most important friend throughout my life. He continues to be as integral a part now as he was when I was a kid. Between B.B. and my financial advisor, Chuck Foss, I get invaluable support for every big decision I make. I've leaned on B.B. for guidance in so many facets of my life; this book is just another example. Not only did he give Carroll extended time and help with research and fact-checking, he's the one who led me to the group of professionals at Dutton who helped shape this book.

At Dutton, I want to thank publisher Ben Sevier for his enthusiasm and leadership and editor Jessica Renheim for her tireless efforts with the manuscript. Thanks to my literary agent, Eric Lupfer at William Morris, for his encouragement, as well as Carroll's agent, Sarah Smith at the David Black Agency. We want to thank David

Larabell, formerly of the David Black Agency and now with CAA, and Michelle Hiskey, formerly of *The Atlanta Journal-Constitution*, for their work on the proposal. Thanks also to *Atlanta Journal-Constitution* photo editor Kent Johnson and Braves photographer Pouya Dianat for their help in providing photos.

Carroll and I would like to thank Carroll's husband, Gus Walton, for his patience with late-night phone calls and trips out of town, and their son, Wade, for waiting until his due date to arrive so Carroll could finish the manuscript on time. We also want to thank Wade's grandmothers Happy Rogers and Betty Rogers for babysitting during the editing process. Carroll wants to thank her father, Larry Rogers, as well, for encouraging her to become a writer and for his steadfast support throughout her career.

For their extended interviews with Carroll, I'd like to thank Stacy Jones, Pete Dunn, Rick Hall, Don Suriano, Charles Edwards, George Zuraw, B. J. Thompson, Paul Snyder, Bobby Cox, Tony DeMacio, Don Baylor, Frank Fultz, Jimy Williams, Brad Clontz, Matt Diaz, Adam LaRoche, Terry Pendleton, and Eddie Perez.

I was taught never to forget my roots. So many people in that little town of Pierson contributed to my development as a player and a person. I want to start by thanking coaches: Richard Hagstrom, Lamar Jones, Bernon Abbott,

Laurence Turner, and Dom Caputo. While they yielded to my father when it came to baseball fundamentals, they were sticklers for discipline and taught me many life lessons. Daryl Jones and Erik Hagstrom were two of my best friends. We played whatever sport was in season all day every day. Then there was the crew I ate lunch with at Carters Kitchen: Stacy Jones, Rusty Harper, Doug Peterson, Bobby Greenland, and Mac Yelvington. I always looked forward to catching up on the local news over a burger with the fellas.

Once I moved to Jacksonville, I met a ton of great people at the Bolles School, none more influential than my baseball coach Don Suriano, his wife, Linda, and my dorm advisor Charles Edwards. Had it not been for them I probably wouldn't have made it through Bolles. I want to recognize my football coach, the great Corky Rogers. That man can teach the Wing-T offense to a bunch of preschoolers and win a state championship with them three months later.

I want to thank B. J. Thompson and his parents—my "boarder family"—for illustrating what family values are all about, whether over a home-cooked meal or a weekend stay. I can't forget my Bolles roommates either. Ron Patrick, Bailey Luetgert, and I ate so many Domino's pizzas we deserve honorary stock in the company. I played football and baseball with both and treasured trying to get into and out of trouble with them. I was fortunate to ease into a really good crowd at Bolles, guys with big plans after high school. Ron graduated from Princeton. Bailey became an actor, better known now as Bailey Chase. Alan Verlander was athletic director at Jacksonville University and is now COO for JAXSport and the TaxSlayer Bowl. Travis Tygart is a lawyer and CEO of the U.S. Anti-Doping Agency and the man who took on Lance Armstrong. All Travis did in high school was play right field on our state championship team and head up our chapter of the Fellowship of Christian Athletes. Those guys remain near and dear to my heart, and I want to thank them for being great role models not only for me but for their own families and generations that follow.

When it comes to my Braves career, I owe a debt of gratitude that I cannot ever repay to Bobby Cox and Paul Snyder for taking a chance on this country boy in the 1990 draft and allowing me to live my dream. To John Schuerholz, I'm grateful for the incredible relationship we had that enabled me to wear one uniform my whole career. To my teammates, I love you guys. Time spent with you is what I miss the most in retirement. To Braves country, thank you, from the bottom of my heart, for standing by me through the ups and downs of my personal life and making my professional life such an amazing ride.

To my wife, Taylor, my Boo, thank you for allowing me the time it took to write this book, the countless marathon interview sessions over the phone, over lunch, dinner, and on into the night. I'm thankful every day that God brought you into my life when He did. Your love and friendship are what make me a better person. I will strive to continue to be the king of your castle for the rest of our days.

ABOUT THE AUTHORS

Larry Wayne "Chipper" Jones Jr. was a third baseman who spent his entire nineteen-year MLB career playing for the Atlanta Braves, and all twenty-three years as a professional baseball player in the Atlanta organization. An eight-time All-Star, he retired in 2012. Born and raised in Florida, he now lives in Atlanta, Georgia.

Carroll Rogers Walton covered the Braves for nearly twenty years as a sportswriter for both *The Atlanta Journal-Constitution* and the Macon, Georgia, *Telegraph*. She freelances from her hometown of Charlotte, North Carolina, where she lives with her husband and son.

Center Point Large Print
600 Brooks Road / PO Box 1
Thorndike, ME 04986-0001 USA

(207) 568-3717

US & Canada:
1 800 929-9108
www.centerpointlargeprint.com